The Bivouacs of the Dead

by

Steven R. Stotelmyer

Toomey Press
Baltimore, Maryland

For information about this and other titles, contact:
Toomey Press
P.O. Box 122
Linthicum, Maryland 21090
(410) 850-0831

Photograph Credits

B & L	Battles and Leaders of the Civil War
D.C.T.	Daniel Carroll Toomey
L.C.	Library of Congress
MCMOLLUS	Massachusetts Commandry Military Order of the Loyal Legion of the United States (USAMHI)
S.R.S.	Steven R. Stotelmyer

Library of Congress Card Number 92-061753

ISBN 0-9612670-2-X

To
A. Vernon Davis

The muffled drum's sad roll has beat
    The soldier's last tattoo;
No more on life's parade shall meet
    The brave and daring few.
On Fame's eternal camping ground
    Their silent tents are spread,
And Glory guards with solemn round
    The bivouac of the dead.

–Theodore O'Hare

Acknowledgments

Sometime in the summer of 1989 I became extremely interested in the fate of some Confederate soldiers that had been dumped down a well at Fox's Gap for burial after the Battle of South Mountain. My wife would tell you that my interest bordered on obsession. Perhaps she is right. I started talking to people and one thing led to another and the accidental outcome is this book. Many people helped me in my search and I will now try to thank them.

First I want to thank three local historians for their help and guidance in my quest. Mr. Tim Reese of Burketsvillle helped me get a start by suggesting what regimental histories to begin with. Tim also "turned me on" to the library at the United States Military History Institute at Carlisle Pennsylvania. Mr. John Michael Priest helped by sharing information on the Battle of South Mountain. John was instrumental in helping to find out the truth about Wise's well. It was John who told me about Sammuel Compton observing the burial detail throwing the bodies down the well. Rev. John Schildt was responsible for suggesting that I try researching the Middletown Valley Register, which proved to be a valuable source of information. Rev. Schildt also endured many phone calls and questions when I had no one else to ask. His suggestions always proved helpful.

Mr. John Frye at the Western Maryland Room of the Washington County Library was always ready to help with my research. He provided me my first look at Bowie's list, and I think he was as surprised as I was to find the 58 from the well listed in those pages.

Next, I need to thank two members of the staff at the Antietam National Battlefield, Ted Alexander and Paul Chiles. They made available the resources of the Antietam library and were always ready to listen to my questions and provide accurate historical answers. They are very familiar with the military aspects of the Maryland Campaign. They both shared my interest in seeing that the story behind the creation of the cemeteries be made available to the public.

I would like to thank Mr. Sam Pruit, trustee for the Washington Confederate Cemetery in Hagerstown, Maryland. Sam was very helpful in answering my questions concerning the creation of the cemetery.

I wish to thank Dr. Norman Nunnamaker at Gettysburg College. Norman provided me with access to the library at the college. When I need to find an old book I can always count on Norman.

Another local historian I wish to thank is Doug Bast of Boonsboro. Doug has opened the doors of his private museum to me on more than one occasion. Although we may disagree on the extent of Daniel Wise's participation with the soldiers in his well, we both realize what an important part of our heritage South Mountain is. Doug has contributed to our preservation efforts on the mountain on several occasions.

I want to thank George Brigham, fellow board member of the Central Maryland Heritage league, for his assistance. George has been able to provide me with books from his library. George has also been able to secure access to parts of the South Mountain battlefield not available to the average visitor.

I especially want to thank my friend John Means. John has always dutifully proofread my material and has provided many valuable suggestions concerning ways to improve my writing. John has also helped me with my photography. We have spent many hours walking the sites and taking pictures. Without John I would have never learned the wisdom of the maxim, "meter the monument."

I need to thank my family for their support. My wife has had to endure long and windy dissertations on the Battle of South Mountain and those men in the well. My children have had to endure countless trips to the cemeteries and the battlefields.

Lastly, I need to thank Mr. A. Vernon Davis, ye old editor of the *Cracker Barrel*. Vernon let me write a series of articles on the Legend of Wise's well for his magazine. It was the first writing I had attempted in a number of years. I made many mistakes, but Vernon didn't seem to mind them and it got me back in the habit of writing. Vernon had a rare sense of humor that used to amuse me to no end. He would refer to me as the "Wise" guy and moan that I was going to speak of "grave" matters. Vernon wanted me to write another series of articles on the Civil War cemeteries of our area. Those articles led to this book. However, I never got to publish those articles because Vernon died unexpectedly in April 1990. In the brief time that I came to know him, Vernon rekindled my interest in local history. So not only do I thank him for giving me the opportunity to write for the *Cracker Barrel*, but I also dedicate this book to his memory.

Steven R. Stotelmyer
Sharpsburg, MD
September, 1992

Contents

Introduction

Sharpsburg, Maryland, is a German farming village. Antietam Creek meanders through pastoral Western Maryland. As one roams the quiet fields near the village and the creek, it is hard to believe that the smoke of thousands of circling camps once "filled the air." In the Antietam Valley, on the 75th anniversary of the signing of the Constitution, more than 130,000 engaged in a battle to determine whether or not "the nation could long endure." The stakes were high. Foreign recognition of the South, and perhaps final independence for the Confederacy, hinged on the outcome. America's fate was in the balance.

September 17, 1862 brought America's bloodiest day. One soldier remembered, "The landscape turned red." The area north of Sharpsburg, bordered by the Poffenberger Ridge, the West and East Woods, and the Dunkard Church, became in the brief span of four hours, "America's bloodiest square mile."

Eminent historians have described the Maryland Campaign and the Battle of Antietam or Sharpsburg. Monographs have been written on the care of more than 18,000 wounded. But in every battle, in addition to the wounded and missing, there are those killed in action, those who have fought their last battle, those who enter THE BIVOUACS OF THE DEAD. They will hear the shout of command no more, nor the whistle of the bullet, nor the scream of shot and shell.

From North and South, East and West, they came to Sharpsburg in September of 1862. They were young men with hopes and dreams. Far from home and loved ones, at a place they probably never heard of, they "gave their last full measure of devotion." At Antietam, 2,108 Union and 1,546 Confederate soldiers answered "the last roll call." We must never forget they were flesh and blood personalities with parents, wives, children, neighbors and friends back home. Now the family circle was broken, and there was "the vacant chair."

History is people and places, and battles are a part of the story. But battles cost. The price is blood, suffering, and death. In a poignant, reverent manner, Steven R. Stotelmyer has researched and chronicled from letters, journals, period newspapers, and other sources, the previously untold story of the price of battle, and the sad task of caring for those who had entered THE BIVOUACS OF THE DEAD.

John W. Schildt
Chewsville, Maryland
1 March 1991

Prologue

Many people believe that cemeteries are only places for the dead; however, cemeteries have interest for the living also. Humans have customs concerning those who have left us. We try to rob the grave of some of its horror by decorations of flowers (symbols of life and rebirth). We place monuments over our departed so that they will always be remembered, and there are stories in those stones.

We especially have an affinity for veterans and for those who have paid the supreme sacrifice in time of war. We build monuments to call attention to the locality and the extent of their sacrifice.

At the Confederate cemetery in Hagerstown, Maryland, there is a place near the southern corner where nine dead Texans were laid to rest. I have come to call this spot the "Texas Corner." In the spring of 1989 a lone Texas flag marked their location. It wasn't much of a flag, as flags go, with a staff only about two feet high. It was the type of souvenir flag that one buys at a parade or a carnival. What was so interesting to me about the flag was that it was a Texas flag. As a native of Maryland, I did not have the first idea of where to purchase a souvenir Texas flag (other than Texas, of course).

On one of my visits to the Confederate cemetery that spring, I noticed that the flag had come partially undone from its staff. It was weatherworn and suffering from exposure. I thought it would be nice to take it home and fix it, and so I did. It was a Saturday morning visit.

Three days later, on Tuesday, I had an opportunity to return the repaired flag to its place. As I walked to the Texas Corner, I was dumbfounded to find a brand new Texas flag. In the scant three days since my visit, someone had observed that the flag was missing and had replaced it. I put the repaired flag beside the new one, and for a brief time, those nine Texans had two flags to mark their final resting place.

There are stories in the stones. The tragedy of the Confederate cemetery at Hagerstown is that there are no stones. There are almost 2,500 Americans buried there. What I find amazing is that someone felt the compulsion to provide some sort of marker in place of the missing stone.

There are those who feel that cemeteries are simply places for the dead. And then, there are those that know otherwise.

FOX'S GAP
SEPTEMBER 14, 1862

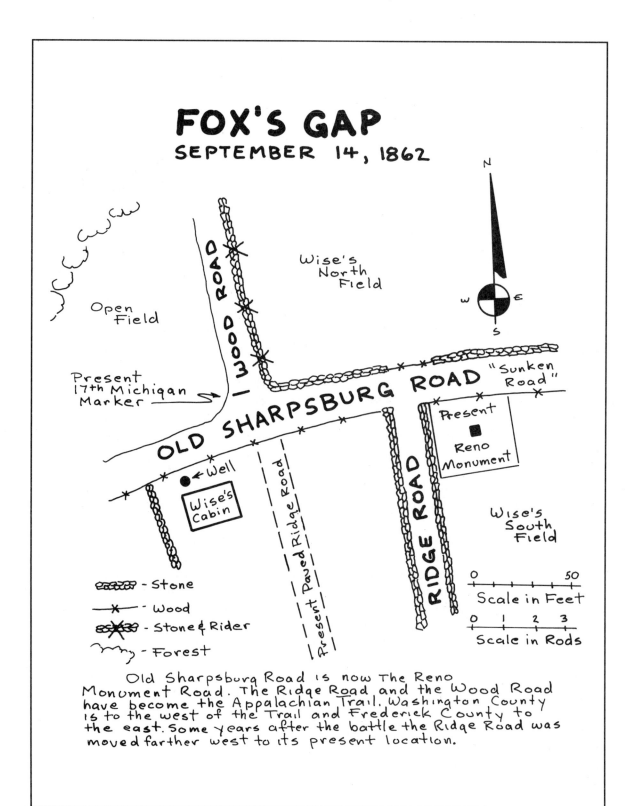

Open Field

Wise's North Field

N
W E
S

Present 17th Michigan Marker →

WOOD ROAD

OLD SHARPSBURG ROAD

"Sunken Road"

Present Reno Monument

Present Paved Ridge Road

RIDGE ROAD

Well →

Wise's Cabin

Wise's South Field

0   50
Scale in Feet

0   1   2   3
Scale in Rods

- Stone
- Wood
- Stone & Rider
- Forest

Old Sharpsburg Road is now The Reno Monument Road. The Ridge Road and the Wood Road have become the Appalachian Trail. Washington County is to the west of the Trail and Frederick County to the east. Some years after the battle the Ridge Road was moved farther west to its present location.

1

The Most Disagreeable Task

The treatment of soldiers killed and wounded in a Civil War battle depended on where the battle was fought and which side controlled the battlefield after the guns fell silent. This book will discuss the treatment of the dead resulting from two battles of the Maryland Campaign of 1862. The Battle of South Mountain occurred on Sunday, September 14, and the Battle of Antietam on Wednesday, September 17, 1862.

It is not enough to say that the civilian and military populations were caught by surprise by the large number of casualties they had to care for. No one expected that almost all the homes, barns, and churches between Frederick and Sharpsburg would become "hospitals" filled with wounded and dying soldiers. In the days and weeks following the fighting, one of every three soldiers hospitalized would die from their wounds. The numbers were just too great for the normal procedures associated with the care of the dead.

South Mountain

Fox's Gap was one of the areas where fighting occurred during the Battle of South Mountain. At the intersection of the Old Sharpsburg Road (a sunken wagon road) and a logging road that followed the ridge of the mountain stood a small cabin inhabited by a farmer, Daniel Wise, and his family. Daniel Wise was sixty-two years old in September 1862, and along with his son and daughter eked out a living as a farmer, day laborer, and local "Root Doctor." The family was forced to abandon their home as the fighting swayed back and forth across Wise's fields all that day. The next day, September 15, 1862, the Wise home was used as a field hospital, and the family did not return until after the wounded had been cared for. How could Daniel Wise have prepared for the carnage around his cabin? By the end of the month there were almost one hundred Union soldiers buried in one of his fields, more than fifty unknown Confederates to the east of his house, and more than twenty to the west. How could he have prepared for the fifty-eight bodies that would be thrown down his family's well? After the Battle of South Mountain the Wise family would coexist with large numbers of dead soldiers buried within the vicinity of their cabin.

The Wise Cabin on South Mountain showing the intersection of Old Sharpsburg Road and the logging road. The well was located just to the right of the cabin. (MCMOLLUS)

Sharpsburg

As farmer David Miller walked through his 30 acre corn field near Sharpsburg in early September, he probably anticipated the harvest of a good corn crop. How could he have known that four hours of battle in his cornfield on the morning of the 17th would result in thousands of killed, wounded, and missing men?(1) How could he have known that future generations would remember his cornfield as part of "America's bloodiest square mile."? Would he have believed that artillery and rifle fire would cut the corn "as closely as could have been done with a knife."? Would he have found it conceivable that in the following days there would be at least four thousand dead to bury? And like farmer Wise, he would also have to give up his house for a hospital.

How many of the local population surmised that the old sunken lane they used as a shortcut from the Hagerstown Pike to the Boonsboro Pike would be the scene of so much carnage that it would forever after be known simply as Bloody Lane?

The Burial Detail

At some point in his military service, the average soldier could expect to find himself on burial detail. It was not always the shirker, drunkard, or straggler assigned to this duty. The good soldier could end up on burial detail by being in the wrong place at the wrong time. These details were usually impromptu affairs and their creation usually depended on the type of battle that had transpired. Civil War burials often depended on the side which found itself in possession of the field after the battle.

The immediate medical concern of the detail was the elimination of certain diseases that could result from the decay process. Typhoid fever and cholera, two highly infectious and lethal diseases, can be spread by contact with a corpse. Flies also spread the diseases. After a battle it became important to inter the bodies as soon as possible. It always surprised burial details how quickly decomposing bodies became offensive to the human senses.

The emotional concern demanded a proper burial for a fallen comrade. Some regiments refused to let strangers bury their dead.

The Last Line

The Battle of South Mountain, as compared to Antietam, represents a relatively small engagement.(2) Burial details were composed of men from different regiments. The day after the battle was entirely devoted to burying the Union dead. By April of 1862, the War Department had instructed Union commanders to reserve plots of ground near every battlefield for the interment of the dead. All graves were to be marked and a register kept with the dead soldier's name and regiment; however, some Union soldiers were simply buried where they fell.(3) Since the government did not provide coffins, the bodies were wrapped in blankets and buried along with any possessions that had not been looted. Since they were buried by comrades, bodies usually were identified. A piece of scrap wood usually served as a headboard and was carved with the soldier's name and regiment.

James Wren was a member of the 48th Pennsylvania Regiment and had seen combat at Fox's Gap. He was present at Wise's cabin when some of the Union dead were buried, and noted in his diary: "...in a field to the left of this house was a long line of dead soldiers laying side by side with

Burial details at work during a truce. (B&L)

a little inscription on their breast giving their names and their company and the state they were from." Major Wren also noted that the details were, "engaged digging a long trench seven feet wide to bury them in, which makes the troops feel desperate towards the rebels. Many of them had brave comrades who stood in line with them and now they were taking their position in their last line."(4) Another soldier noted that corpses were buried with their feet facing towards Sharpsburg so that they could face the enemy.

Trench burial was the normal procedure for the burial detail. After a relatively small battle like Fox's Gap, the bodies would be brought to a central location. An abandoned bayonet, heated in a fire and bent into the shape of a hook, would allow the soldier to drag the corpse without touching it. Once the bodies were collected at the grave site, a shallow hole was dug, usually 18 to 24 inches deep, and the body rolled in and another hole dug beside it. The second hole provided the dirt to fill the first, and this procedure was repeated as needed.

There was no standardized system for identification of the dead. Most of the Union dead were identified by their comrades. There were no official "dog tags" issued by the respective governments. There were, however, enterprising individuals who cashed in on the soldier's fear of lost identity by selling wooden, ceramic, or tin identification tags. Some soldiers wore these, but this was the exception rather than the rule. Sometimes a note in a bottle was buried with the soldier along with any personal keepsakes that had not been stolen.

At Fox's Gap by the end of September 15, most of the Union dead were buried either individually by comrades or massed in trenches by burial details. The next day, Tuesday, September 16, 1862, the burial details were faced with the task of burying the dead Confederates. There was no precedent established for the burial of the enemy's dead.(5) There was a general agreement that an army passing over a battlefield was under no obligation to bury the enemy's dead. Indeed, many of the Confederates had begun their trek into Maryland by marching past the unburied bodies of Union soldiers on the battlefield of Second Manassas.

It was preferable, but not always possible, to arrange a temporary truce to allow the enemy to bury their own dead. Many of the men in both armies, however, thought it their moral duty to provide proper burial for the dead, and so the Union details set to work at Fox's Gap and elsewhere on South Mountain.

The Fallen Foe

Michael Deady was a member of the 23rd Ohio Infantry Regiment. He had fought at Fox's Gap and had been assigned to the burial detail. In his diary he remembered that on September 16, he had gone to Middletown to attain Confederate prisoners to bury their own dead, but the authorities would not release them. And so he came back, "and went at it. Buried 200 Rebs, they lay pretty thick…"

Confederate dead at the cross-roads on South Mountains. (B&L)

Another incident that occurred during the burial of the Confederates would turn into one of the most persistent legends of the Battle of South Mountain. Fifty-eight bodies were dumped into the well in front of Daniel Wise's cabin. In the years that followed, Daniel Wise was credited for this act. The legend recounted how he stopped the burial detail from dumping the bodies down his well, but realizing his well was ruined, contracted personally with General Burnside to continue the process for a dollar a body. This legend would persist, and local storytellers would swear that Wise was haunted by the ghost of those poor souls in his well. In reality, the Confederates were put in the well by members of a Union burial detail, and the circumstances of the incident provide a graphic example of the conditions at Fox's Gap two days after the battle. Sammuel Compton was a member of the 12th Ohio Regiment. He had fought at Fox's Gap and was present two days later to witness the burial details:

> "The morning of the 16th I strolled out to see them bury the Confederate dead. I saw but I never want to another sight. The squad I saw were armed with a pick and a canteen full of whiskey. The whiskey the most necessary of the two. The bodies had become so offensive that men could only endure it by being staggering drunk. To see men stagger up to corpses and strike four or five times before they could get a hold, a right hold being one above the belt. Then staggering as [the] very drunk will, they dragged the corpses to a 60 foot well and tumbled them in. What a selpucher and what a burial! You don't wonder I had no appetite for supper!"(6)

Some of the men assigned to burial detail used alcohol to make the work more bearable. After two days exposure, human bodies become quite offensive as gases are created by the decay process. These gases are noxious to the human sense of smell and they also have the effect of bloating the corpse and exerting pressure in the bowels, forcing the contents out. Many of the dead had suffered extreme forms of trauma. The Confederates had made use of stone walls for breastworks and had suffered an unusually high number of headwounds (one Union soldier joked that most of the dead "Johnnies" had a third eye). It comes as no surprise that some would seek the numbing effects of alcohol, and that they chose not to touch the corpses, but rather to drag them with picks to the well.

The bodies also started to discolor and this gave rise to another legend in the Union Army. It was believed that the dead Confederate soldier turned black quicker than his Union counterpart. Some regimental historians went to great lengths to explain this phenomenon. Consider the following description of the Confederate dead at Fox's Gap by a member of the 9th New Hampshire:

> "A singular alteration had already become noticeable in the countenances of the Confederate dead, distinguishing them at once from those of the Union troops; they were, without exception, rapidly turning black, so as to make them almost unrecognizable even to their own associates. This curious phenomenon has never been satisfactorily explained, though it continued to be observable throughout the war. Some surgeons conjectured that it might be due to the scarcity of salt in the Confederate army, others laid it to the habit said to be prevalent among them, of mixing gunpowder with their whiskey. Be the reason what it may, it was a sufficiently and painful sight to unaccustomed eyes."(7)

A dead body will decay at a rate which is not related to diet or political affiliation. If the Union men noticed that the Confederates turned black more quickly, it may have been because all they observed after the Union burials were dead Confederates.

The Souvenir Seekers

Identification of the Confederate dead was difficult because they were buried by strangers and, without exception, the bodies had been looted. One Union officer at Turner's Gap was horrified to find a couple of his men stealing a dead Confederate's wedding ring with a knife.(8) But it was not just the Union Army looting. Civilians also scoured the battlefield for souvenirs and keepsakes.

Doctor Thomas T. Ellis, a Union surgeon on duty at Fox's Gap, noted, "A number of farmers came on the field to witness the sight, of which they had so often heard but never seen. They collected as relics every thing portable: cartridge-boxes, bayonet scabbards, old muskets, and even cannon-balls were carried away by them."(9)

Frank P. Fiery's father was one of the farmers on the battlefield sightseeing that day. He remembered that his father "came upon the body of a magnificent specimen of manhood, which proved to be Colonel George S. James, of a South Carolina regiment. Before having him buried, my father cut several buttons from Colonel James uniform, and my sister had a jeweler arrange one of the large ones for a breastpin and two smaller ones for ear bobs."(10)

A soldier at Antietam observed that most of the bodies had photographs laying beside them. He conjectured that because the photographs were of little value, the looters simply dropped them where they had found them.

Mr. Deady

Not everyone involved in the burial of Confederates at Fox's Gap was a drunkard or a looting scalawag. In 1896 Michael Deady published a letter in a Confederate veteran's magazine:

> "After the Battle of South Mountain, Md. Sept. 1862, I was detailed to bury the dead. Among them I found a Confederate officer, on whose coat was pinned a paper with these words written in pencil: Capt. H.Y. Hyers, Mad River Lodge, North Carolina...' He must have placed the paper there himself so he might be known if he fell. He was buried as tenderly as could be under the circumstances. I cut on a board, letter for letter, what was on the paper and placed it at the head of the grave."(11)

Deady gave his address and offered to furnish any information to any relative of Captain Hyers. He must have received no response, for almost the same letter, word for word, appeared in the same magazine in 1923. Having a headboard over a grave was no guarantee of having ones identity preserved. Some headboards simply disappeared due to the weather. Others disappeared to the actions of the souvenir seeker or the farmer. A visitor to Fox's Gap in 1865 noted rows of headboards that had been knocked down by grazing cattle.(12)

In his diary Deady recalled there were seventy-five men on burial detail at Fox's Gap. As stated before they were a heterogeneous mixture of several men from the different Union regiments involved in the battle. In addition to the two hundred this detail buried on the 16th, it buried another two hundred fifty. On Thursday, September 18, 1862, Deady noted, "Same old work...awful smell to work by...today finished, today and glad of it..."(13)

On the same day another member of the 23rd Ohio on burial detail wrote: "Finished the burying of the dead at 4 P.M. and proceeded to Boonsboro and camped in a barn."(14) The burial details at Fox's Gap required four days to complete their work. They buried almost five hundred Union and Confederate dead. And when they finally rejoined their units it was at Antietam, where two days earlier the worst single-day's carnage in the history of North America had occurred.

Buried Shallow

The Battle of Antietam represents the other extreme of conditions for the burial of the dead. At Antietam, whole regiments were assigned the duty. The pattern was generally the same as at South Mountain. There was an undeclared truce the day after the battle, and although some of the dead were collected for burial, the main activity on the 18th was collecting and caring for the wounded. The Confederates withdrew on the night of the 18th, and on the next day, the burial details began work on the Union dead. On Saturday, September 20, most of the details had started on the Confederate dead, but did not finish until the 21st or 22nd.

Union burial detail at Antietam. Note soldiers carry picks and shovels while Rebel dead lay to the left. (LC)

Most of the dead at Antietam were buried in shallow trenches located near the place of battle. Lt. Col. David Hunter Strother was a topographical expert on the staff of General McClellan. On the day after the battle Hunter was in the area of the "East Woods" and observed:

"In every direction around men were digging graves and burying the dead. Ten or twelve bodies lay at the different pits and had already become offensive. In front of this wood was the bloody cornfield where lay two or three hundred festering bodies, nearly all of them rebels, the most hideous exhibition I had yet seen. Many were black as Negroes, heads and faces hideously swelled, covered with dust until they looked like clods."(15)

Unburied Reb lies near a buried Yank on the Miller Farm. (LC)

Strother observed one Union burial detail at work and with the trained eye of a map-maker noted, "Here was a long grave of ours made in a rain-washed gully, certain to be washed out the first time it rained hard." Strother walked over to one of the men toiling away at the task and told him of his observation. The tired soldier simply replied, "To be sure they will [wash out]," and went back to his work.(16)

In the area around Bloody Lane, the 5th Maryland Infantry was one regiment assigned burial detail and one of its members, J. Polk Racine of Elkton, Md., remembered:

> "Every man's pocket was turned inside out. Sometimes a piece of money, a pocket knife, or something else, would fall from the hands of the midnight robbers, in the dark, and we would find it where they had turned the pocket. But every one was robbed by the ghouls. Well, we had dead to bury, thousands of them… It was the most disagreeable days work of my life. First the grave had to be dug. You Elkton folks saw the workmen dig for the water-works pipe. Now then, add a few thousand additional workmen, and extend the ditch, or grave six miles, and make it two or three feet wider and deeper. Now look in every direction and see hundreds carrying the mangled bodies of those who had been shot…"(17)

Racine and three of his comrades employed two fence rails for transport of the dead. With the upper torso draped over one rail and the lower torso over another, they gathered the dead at a central locale.

The Lady Soldier

Miss Emma E. Edmonds, a nurse and occasional spy for the Union Army, passed over the battlefield of Antietam on the day after the battle. Her attention focused upon a young soldier wounded in the neck. The wound was still bleeding and the soldier was growing weak from loss of blood. Miss Edmonds began caring for the lad and asked him if there was anything she could do. The soldier replied:

> "Yes, yes; there is something to be done, and that quickly, for I am dying…I can trust you, and will tell you a secret. I am not what I seem, but am a female. I enlisted from the

The lady soldier of Antietam. From "Nurse and Spy in the Union Army."

purest motives and have remained undiscovered and unsuspected. I have neither father, mother nor sister. My only brother was killed today. I closed his eyes about an hour before I was wounded. I shall soon be with him. I wish you to bury me with your own hands that none may know after my death that I am other than my appearance indicates."(18)

Miss Edmonds found a chaplain to pray with the soldier and remained with her until she died. Then Miss Edmonds procured the help of two soldiers on burial detail and together they made a grave in the shadow of a mulberry tree, "near the battlefield, apart from all others." Miss Edmonds carried the soldier herself to the burial place and, "…gave her a soldier's burial, without coffin or shroud, only a blanket for a winding sheet. There she sleeps in that beautiful forest…"

There is an irony with this story that cannot pass untold. When Miss Edmonds discovered the lady soldier it was not as a female nurse, it was in the uniform of a male nurse with the 2nd Michigan Infantry, for Sarah Emma Edmonds was disguised as Private Franklin Thompson.

There is documentation for about one hundred such cases of female soldiers in the Civil War and it is estimated that the number could have been as great as four hundred. Most of them were in Union regiments. The women had to go to great lengths to hide the fact that they were female. It was easier at that time to pass the "physical" because, obviously, it was not very thorough. "If the 'young man' looked healthy, had two front teeth to tear the cartridge, 'he' was immediately signed up, because of the desperate need of soldiers."(19) However, discovery meant instant discharge from the unit and possible prosecution for fraudulent enlistment.

Miss Edmonds was a Canadian by birth. As she was growing up she tried to fullfill her father's wish for a son. She was quite a tomboy. She left home rather than be forced into a marriage arranged by her father. She arrived in the United States dressed as a young man. She assumed the name Franklin Thompson and got a job with a Connecticut publishing house. She went west to Flint, Michigan, to represent the firm. She was looked upon by her friends in the community as a, "good looking, likable, successful young man, who made money, dressed well, drove his own horse and buggy, and had many 'lady friends.'"(20)

It was under the same name of Franklin Thompson that she enlisted in Company F, 2nd Michigan Infantry, at the outbreak of the war. After serving as a field nurse for a few months she was accepted into the Secret Service of the United States.(21) At the time of the Battle of Antietam Sarah was absent from her regiment for reasons that have never been fully explained. That Sarah Emma Edmonds was disguised as a Union soldier is a matter of fact. Whether the anecdote about the discovery of the lady soldier is true, or is an invention of an overactive Victorian imagination, will forever be another of the mysteries of Antietam.

Give Us a Drink

Lieutenant Origen G. Bingham of the 137th Pennsylvania saw no action at Antietam other than the burial of the Confederate dead. In a letter home he wrote:

> "Our regiment has been detailed to bury the dead, the most disagreeable duty that could have been assigned to us; tongue cannot describe the horrible sight which we have witnessed; the Union soldiers were all buried when we arrived on the field the rebel dead lay unburied and hundreds still remain so… I would not describe to you the appearance of the dead even if I could, it is too revolting. You can imagine the condition of the bodies when I tell you that they were slain on Wednesday and it is now Sunday…I was up at the Provost Marshalls office this morning for permission to buy some liquor for our boys to keep them from getting sick when at their disagreeable labor…"(22)

Although there are no accounts of Union troops throwing bodies down wells at Antietam, whiskey again appeared with the burial details. It should come as no surprise that the soldier would want a drink to numb the senses and make it more bearable. As Private S.M. Whistler of the 130th Pennsylvania remembered at the dedication of their monument at Bloody Lane:

Rebel dead awaiting burial at Antietam. (USAMHI)

"In the burial of the dead on this particular part of the field, the 130th Regiment, by reason of having incurred the displeasure of its brigade commander, was honored in the appointment as undertaker-in-chief. The weather was phenomenally hot, and the stench from the hundreds of black bloated, decomposed maggoty bodies, exposed to a torrid heat for three days after the battle, was a sight truly horrid and beggaring all power of verbal expression. The fact that the Confederate dead were so much darker than your own was attributed to the fanciful cause that they had eaten gunpowder at breakfast the morning of the battle. Over head floated large numbers of those harpies of the air, buzzards, awaiting an opportunity to descend to earth to partake of the cadaverous feast. Just over there in Muma's field in one ditch you placed 185 Confederate corpses, the one on top of the other, and indecorously covered them from sight with clay.(23)

The Civilians

Some local residents of the Sharpsburg area also helped with the burial of the dead. Across from Miller's Cornfield on the Nicodemus farm worked a twenty-four year old hired hand named Alexander Davis. After the battle he gathered fifteen Massachusetts soldiers for burial. He found these and other dead at various places on the farm, including some near the barn, some near the spring house, and one near the front door of the house. Although Davis did not use the Nicodemus well as a sepulcher for dead Confederates, he did find a novel use for it. After he finished burying the dead, he filled the well with cartloads of broken guns, swords, cartridge boxes, canteens, and other relics of the battlefield.(24)

In addition to large numbers of human casualties, there was also a large number of dead horses at Antietam. Local farmers were contracted to collect and burn the carcasses. The pall of smoke, together with the stench of the corpses, forced the local inhabitants into their houses, with

Battle of Antietam—The 130th Pennsylvania Regiment of Volunteers burying the Rebel dead, Friday, Sept. 19—This spot was the scene of one of the most desperate conflicts of the day. From a sketch by our special artist, Mr. F. H. Schell. *Leslie's Illustrated,* October 19, 1862.

their doors and windows closed in an attempt to escape the nauseating odor. Citizens as far away as Keedysville were bothered by the stench from the battlefield.(25)

For days after the battle, the area was swamped with civilian sight-seers and souvenir hunters. Otho Nesbitt came twenty miles on horseback from Clear Spring, Maryland, to see the battlefield. On September 19, he penned the following in his diary:

"I rode on to the battle field where the Rebels formed their line of battle, they were not buried...nearly all lying on their backs. The line I suppose was a mile long or more...Along the turnpike and the fences on each side they were laying thick...They were all swelled up and black and purple in their faces...The men were brought to the place of burying and laid on their backs...a blanket thrown over them till the grave or trench was ready and then put in."(26)

Bloated and twisted bodies of Confederate dead along the Hagerstown Pike at Antietam. The dead soldier on the right still has a knapsack strapped to his back. (LC)

Many of the civilians were Northern people looking for relatives and loved ones. In the days following the battle, many Union soldiers were recovered by family and sent home for burial. A makeshift mortuary was set up in the Dunkard Church where the new art of embalming was offered to those who could afford it. Martin E. Snavely, a local farmer, remembered hauling a six-horse load of coffins, containing embalmed Union dead, from the church to the railroad depot at Hagerstown.(27)

Taken Home

Union Maj. Gen. Jesse Lee Reno had been killed late in the day at Fox's Gap. His body was taken to Baltimore, where it was embalmed by the inventor of the process, William E. Chenowith. Earlier in the war, Chenowith had been on maneuvers with the Union Army. One day he was annoyed by the odor of a dead dog, and poured formaldehyde over the carcass to keep it from smelling. Two weeks later he passed by the same spot and was surprised to find that the dog's skin had been preserved perfectly with no discoloration. He began experimenting with arterial use of formaldehyde and

Dunker Church was used as a makeshift mortuary after the battle. (MCMOLLUS)

Gen. Jesse L. Reno killed in action at South Mountain. (DCT)

acquired a patent for the process. (By the end of the war the embalmer would become one of the normal camp followers). Thus embalmed, General Reno's remains were placed in an air tight coffin for shipment by rail to Boston.(28)

Not all the bodies had the luxury of returning home. Different railroads had different rates and requirements, which many families could not afford. James Weeks had traveled from Illinois to Maryland in search of his brother-in-law, William Cullen Robinson of the 83rd New York. On September 23 at the "School House Hospital" in Keedysville, he found him. In a letter home James wrote:

> "I arrived at the hospital about an hour after he died…They said he must have fired a great many rounds as his lips were very black from biting the cartridges off…When I got here the Surgeon had sent his knapsack containing his wallet, letters, his watch, and in fact all his effects. I found a match box in his pocket and one of his comrades gave me his knife…I bought a rough coffin (the best I could get) and washed his face and neck and combed his hair smooth and covered him round with a large clean sheet and they dug a deep grave on a little knoll on the bank of the Antietam Creek. And I buried him there…It was almost impossible to bring him home with me as I should have had to come way back to Baltimore and purchase a metallic coffin (for him as they won't allow any other to pass over the line) and by the time I should have got back he would have been so much decayed that they would not keep him for me."(29)

Bowen B. Moon had a different experience with the railroads. Arriving at Sharpsburg in the last days of September, 1862, to retrieve the body of his brother-in-law William A. Salisbury of the

Tombstone of Pvt. W. A. Salisbury. He is not buried under it! (SRS)

34th New York Regiment, Moon learned from a soldier of the 34th the exact spot where William had been buried. At a cooper's shop (a maker of wooden barrels), Moon found:

> "…several carpenters making coffins. These coffins were solid and substantial, but I was told that to get an elegant coffin I would have to send to the town of Frederick or Baltimore and it would be several days before it would arrive. Of course duty required me to take one of the substantial coffins that many were using there."

On October 2, 1862, at 8:00 a.m. Moon and a hired man arrived at William's grave. For $10.00 the man had agreed to exhume the body and haul it to Hagerstown. As Moon remembered:

> "The man I employed carefully removed the dirt until he came to [a] blanket that had been placed over three dead placed in one grave. Separating the blanket in the middle there I beheld the dead brother 'sleeping the sleep that knows no wakening.' It was just two weeks subsequent to the battle, and the features and contours of the face was easily recognized."(30)

Moon left William's headboard at the gravesite. The hired man had so many orders to fill that he could not provide Moon a ride to Hagerstown, and so he walked the ten miles.

Moon did succeed in loading the coffin on a freight train in Hagerstown, but he ran into problems in the state of New York where he was informed the railroad "did not carry dead bodies that had begun to decompose." Moon procured a compound which caulked the cracks in the coffin, and he enlisted the aid of some Union soldiers standing nearby to carry it. With the help of a bribe to the baggage manager and the threatening demeanor of the soldiers, Moon had the coffin loaded on the train and returned home without further incident.(31)

Some of the Union dead were taken back home personally by a relative rather than trusting to the railroads. Private William Kay of the 8th Pennsylvania Reserve Infantry Regiment had been mortally wounded at the Battle of South Mountain. He died four days later on September 18, 1862, in a "hospital" in Middletown, Maryland. William's father, Isack Kay, traveled by wagon the seventy miles from their home in Yellow Creek, Pennsylvania. Isack had his son placed in a wooden coffin and packed in salt for the trip home. William was buried in the family plot of the White Church Cemetery.(32)

Few of the Confederates made it back home for burial, and most of these were officers. The average Confederate citizen could not travel north into enemy territory to retrieve the dead relative. Those who dared did so at their own risk. Maryland was south of the Mason-Dixon line, but it was controlled by the Union Army.

Confederate Brig. Gen. Samuel Garland Jr. had been killed early in the fighting at Fox's Gap. He received his mortal wound less than a mile from the field where General Reno received his later that day. Garland's body was taken to the Mountain House at Turner's Gap and thence to Boonsboro. At the cabinet shop of John C. Brining his body was embalmed (the local cabinet maker made coffins as well and therefore was also the local undertaker). His remains were then taken to Lynchburg, Virginia. On the afternoon of September 19, he was placed in the family tomb.

See Me Buried

Captain Chalmers Glenn of the 13th North Carolina had also been at Fox's Gap with his "servant" Mat. They had been raised together since childhood, and on the morning of September 14, Captain Chalmers had a premonition. "Mat" he said, "I shall be killed in this battle. See me buried, then go home and be to your mistress and my children all that you have ever been to me." Captain Chalmers was killed and Mat buried him somewhere at Fox's Gap. Mat returned home and, as the story goes, died of a broken heart less than a year later.(33)

But this was the exception. Indeed, at one place in Maryland, the Confederates were burned rather than buried. Towering above Harpers Ferry, West Virginia, are the lofty cliffs of Maryland Heights. On September 13, 1862, a battle had transpired for the possession of the heights as part of General Stonewall Jackson's siege of Harpers Ferry. The Confederates won the heights, but they had to abandon the position two days later. They had no time to bury the dead. After Antietam, Union burial details buried their troops in one mass grave, as one Union veteran remembered, " a hole on the top

Gen. Samuel Garland Jr. was Killed at Fox's Gap. (DCT)

of the mountain." The area around the heights is stony and almost soiless; and so, when it came to burying the Confederates, the details took the easy way out. Brush and logs were gathered and the dead Confederates were cremated.(34)

Most of the Confederates killed during the Maryland Campaign were buried by Union soldiers already exhausted from burying their own dead; Federals who felt badly toward the enemy for killing friends and comrades; and troops who worked haphazardly under the effects of alcohol. Hence, it is no surprise that almost three-fourths of the Confederates that were buried at South Mountain and Antietam are unknown Civil War soldiers missing in action.

Oliver T. Reilly was seven years old at the time of the Battle of Antietam. Days after the battle he visited the field with his father and remembered, "...dead soldiers that had crawled into the bushes, died there, and had not been buried yet. Some of those that were buried had their feet out, some their hands, and some were buried so shallow that their heads could be seen."(35)

Weeks after the battle, Christian M. Keedy visited the field and observed, "soldiers that had been laid together on top of the ground." (Perhaps among the last to be "buried" by exhausted men). Fence rails had been placed around them and "dirt thrown over them, and the hogs had rooted the shoes off with the feet in them and it was a common thing to see human bones lying loose in gutters and fence corners for several years, and frequently hogs would be seen with limbs in their mouths."(36)

Months later on May 14, 1863, John Koogle, a farmer in the Middletown Valley, was traveling with a friend. His diary entry for that day is short, but it speaks volumes: "Today is Ascension Day. Henry and I were over the South Mountain battlefield, some citizens were burying bones."(37)

Maryland and Pennsylvania farmers visiting the battlefield of Antietam while the National troops were burying the dead and carrying off the wounded, Friday, Sept. 19. From a sketch by our special artist, Mr. F. H. Schell. From *Leslie's Illustrated*, October 18, 1862.

Every Memorial Day

Private Henry Struble, Company C, 8 Pa. Reserves, was wounded at the Battle of South Mountain. He was taken to a field hospital and placed beside another wounded soldier. The other man was thirsty so Struble lent him his canteen. They were separated and never saw each other again. Struble survived his wound but the other man died. When the burial detail buried the soldier, they assumed the canteen was his and used the name on the canteen: Henry Struble. The real Henry Struble returned to his home in Youngwood, Pennsylvania. He became mayor in 1898. Every Memorial Day Henry would send flowers to decorate his grave at Antietam. Henry Struble passed away in 1912. The identity of the man below Henry's tombstone is known only to his Maker.

Henry Struble's tombstone marks the grave of an unknown soldier. (SRS)

"Simon" stands vigil over the rows of Union dead in Antietam National Cemetery. (SRS)

2

The Antietam National Cemetery

"One of the striking indications of civilization and refinement among a people, is the tenderness and care manifested by them towards their dead, in the location and erection of suitable resting places for their remains, and their embellishment and ornamentation in an appropriate and becoming manner, thus robbing the grave of its terrors and death of its repulsiveness; by appealing to the sense with all that is beautiful in Nature and Art."(1)

With these words the trustees for the Antietam National Cemetery described their feelings and their reasons for the cemetery's creation. Humans have beliefs and rituals concerning the treatment of their dead. Hasty burial in shallow trenches is not one of them.

The Cornfield

Three years after the Battle of Antietam, in September, 1865, John Trowbridge was touring the battlefield. Trowbridge stopped at the "Cornfield" and observed that the trees were still scarred and that there were rotting knapsacks still littering the ground. Trowbridge also observed a farmer plowing the field with three horses abreast and, "…loose headboards, overturned by the plow and lying half imbedded in the furrows."

Trowbridge struck up a conversation with the farmer and questioned him about the burial trenches:

"'A power of them in this here field !…I always skip a Union grave when I know it, but sometimes I don't see 'em, and I plow 'em up.'…Torn rags strewed the ground. The old ploughman picked up a fragment. 'This here was a Union soldier. You may know by the blue cloth'…We found many more bones of Union soldiers rooted up and exposed."

Trowbridge's battlefield guide, Lewy Smith, related an anecdote to Trowbridge about his last visit to the "Cornfield." Smith said that he had seen a ploughman in the field and, "...everytime he came to a grave he would just reach over his plow, jerk up the headboard and stick it down behind him again as he plowed along; and all the time he never stopped whistling his tune."(2)

It soon became apparent to everyone that a more permanent resting place was needed for the Antietam dead.

Maryland, My Maryland

The Antietam National Cemetery was created by the Maryland State Legislature. State Senator Lewis P. Fiery, a pro-Union native of Washington County, introduced a resolution in 1864 for the purpose of acquiring a parcel of land to contain the remains of both Union and Confederate soldiers who fell in the battle of Antietam. A committee appointed by the state visited Sharpsburg and surveyed the battlefield area for an appropriate site. The site selected is now the location of the Antietam National Cemetery. Afterwards, on March 10, 1864, the State of Maryland appropriated five thousand dollars towards the purchase of the site; however, a clear title to the land was delayed because one of the heirs was incompetent and an inmate of a Virginia lunatic asylum.(3)

During the resulting lull, the Maryland legislature passed an act repealing the original act. Then in March, 1865, additional legislation passed to provide for the purchase of ten acres of land. Other states were invited to appoint a trustee and, together with four trustees from Maryland, they formed "a body politic in law, under the name, style and title of the Antietam National Cemetery." An additional seven thousand dollars was appropriated. Thomas A. Boult, Augustus A. Biggs, Edward Shriver, and Charles C. Fulton were appointed as the Maryland trustees. It was their duty, and the duty of the trustees of all the states joining the corporation, to remove the remains of all soldiers of the Battle of Antietam. The remains of Confederate soldiers were to be buried in a portion of the ground separate from the Union soldiers.

Brother Against Brother

To many Marylanders, the idea of burying Union and Confederate soldiers in the same cemetery did not seem unusual. Maryland had truly been a state where brother fought against brother, and

Antietam Cemetery in 1866. (LC)

father against son. Twenty thousand Marylanders had fought for the Confederacy, while fifty thousand had fought to preserve the Union. Western Maryland had largely been pro-Union, while Baltimore and Eastern Maryland were pro-Confederate. During the Battle of Antietam batteries and regiments from the state could be found in both armies.

The Board of Trustees

Eventually eighteen other states, all Union, joined the Antietam National Cemetery corporation. They included Connecticut, Delaware, Illinois, Indiana, Iowa, Maine, Massachusetts, Michigan, Minnesota, New Hampshire, New Jersey, New York, Ohio, Pennsylvania, Rhode Island, Vermont, West Virginia, and Wisconsin. When the cemetery was completed, these states had contributed over $90,000.00 and had changed the purpose and scope of the cemetery.

Aaron Good was employed to help make a list of burial places. As a resident of Sharpsburg, he had already devoted his time to identifying the dead and locating their graves. The community of Sharpsburg had been overwhelmed by the Battle of Antietam and, as stated before, quick burial in shallow trenches had been the rule. Although some bodies had been embalmed, and some bodies had been buried in natural conditions that preserved the remains, by 1865 only skeletons remained in most of the trenches. Some trenches had been plowed over and some had been eroded to the point where bones were exposed.

The work of exhuming and reinterring the Union dead began in October, 1866, under the direction of Lieutenant John W. Sheree. Although Lieutenant Sheree was with the Office of the Quartermaster General, which was responsible for the exhumations and reinterments, he was wrongly labeled as being in command of the "Burial Corps." This misnomer would persist to the point where even the press would use it to describe Lt. Sheree's activities. In fact there never existed an entity entitled the "Burial Corps." But since this was the accepted usage for Lt. Sheree and his operations the term "Burial Corps" will be used to describe events from here on.

It was Lt. Sheree's duty to hire hands to perform the actual exhumations and to oversee the operations. Most of the men employed for the task were local day laborers and farmers, and were usually paid at the rate of one dollar a day. Additional manpower and material were brought up the C & O Canal from Washington, D.C. At the urging of the trustees, and the authorities in Washington, the scope of the cemetery was expanded to include all the Union dead who fell in Maryland.(4)

One Thousand Coffins

In October, 1866, the Sharpsburg correspondent for *The Boonsboro Oddfellow* reported: "On Sunday morning about 60 men, with wagons, camp equipage, etc., arrived here (Sharpsburg) and have commenced digging graves for intering the dead in the National Cemetery. One thousand coffins have arrived…A wagon train has also just arrived from the canal, laden with provisions for the men, who are encamped near the Cemetery…"(5) These men worked until January, 1867, when winter weather forced them to wait until spring.

Elias Spong was one of the members of the burial corps. During this first period of exhumations, he worked in the area of Miller's "Cornfield." He unearthed one soldier that he remembered being too heavy for his size. Upon closer inspection, he found that the dead soldier had a twelve pound cannonball in him. It had had just enough force to enter but not pass through the poor soul.(6)

Spong also remembered an unusual sight among the dead in the vicinity of Burnside Bridge. Although most of the dead by this time were just bones, the workers found one soldier wrapped in his blanket who was well preserved. He had a beard over a foot long and hair down over his shoulders; otherwise he looked almost the same as when he had been buried.(7) It should be noted that Spong was deceived by a common misconception. There is a myth involved that claims the fingernails and hair continue to grow after death. Since all cellular activity ceases at death this is

Union soldier gazes at the graves of the 51st New York killed at Burnside Bridge. (DCT)

not true. If the body that Spong saw at the Burnside Bridge had long hair and a beard, it was because the dead man had had them in life, and not because they grew after death.

Preserved bodies were the exception to the rule, however, and since the men of the burial corps had been working with bones, they would not be able to recognize individuals. Miss Edmond's lady soldier, for example, might not have been recognized as a female by the daylaborers contracted by the government. If she was found, and if she was not identified in some way, she would simply have been buried under an "unknown" tombstone. Assuming that she was reinterred, there is the possibility that one of the graves at the Antietam National Cemetery contains a female veteran of the Civil War.

On November 22, 1866, J. M. Mentzer, the editor of the Oddfellow, reported:

"Up to this time about 1,200 dead have been removed. They are placed in substantial coffins...In raising the dead every grave is carefully examined, and strict search is made for relics which may in any manner serve to identify the remains. So far about two-thirds have been fully recognized. There is no difficulty in identifying those buried in the different Church-yards—the head-boards being yet in good condition. Those buried in fields, (in many cases) have been plowed over and the boards destroyed. Yet many are identified by memoranda kept by the farmers and others living in the neighborhood. In some cases relics found in the graves afford the most satisfactory evidence."(8)

Photographs of loved ones and notes in bottles with the dead soldier's identity were not uncommon "memoranda." One of the notes read: William C. Stickney, Co. C, 7th Me. Vol. died Sept. 26, at 11 o'clock P.M.—Residence, Springfield Maine."(9)

Mentzer could not help noticing that another body had been found in an unusual state of preservation and he attributed this to the fact that the body had been embalmed. He noted that the body of Lt. Oliver W. Sanford, of Wisconsin, "was found to be in a most wonderful state of preservation, having almost the same appearance as when he died. Those who knew him in life would doubtless recognize him now."(10)

Met With Kindness

As the reinterments progressed, Mentzer observed:

> "…The burial Corps has met with kindness from the persons residing in the neighborhood, on whose properties the bodies were buried, with but two exceptions. One person contended that there were none buried on his place, but the guides and those who were present at the battle knew better, and a large number of bodies were dug up in his garden. He had cultivated his cabbages over the shallow graves of the slain, and stoutly contended that there were none there! Another treated the members of the Corps rather roughly, and asserted that none were buried on his farm. But the contrary fact was known, and a number of bodies were taken up from beneath a farm road that he had made over the loyal dead!"(11)

Since Western Maryland was largely pro-Union, members of the burial corps were met with kindness on the part of the local civilian population. However, it is noteworthy that some farmers did not think much of the burial corps and just wanted to be left alone. If some of the local population resented the men exhuming the loyal Union dead, undoubtedly a larger number resented the men who would try to recover the treasonous Confederate dead years later.

Lee's Rock

The work of grading the site and building the wall around the cemetery continued throughout the winter of 1866-67. The lime for the masonry was burned on the site. It was burned at an expense of fifteen cents per bushel, less than half the cost at a limekiln. Sand came from the bed of the Potomac River. Stones for the wall were quarried about a quarter mile from the cemetery and the granite for the cap-stones came from Keedysville. Grading of the cemetery posed a problem when it came to the question of what to do with a local landmark known as "Lee's Rock."

Colonel Henry Kyd Douglas was a resident of the area and had served on Confederate General Stonewall Jackson's staff during the war. Years later he recalled:

> "Near where General Lee was standing was a clump of trees. During or after the war, the trees were cut away and a large rock discovered. Rumor soon gave to this bowlder the name of 'Lee's Rock,' and when the land was cleared away for the present National Cemetery this rock was left standing for historic reasons. But, as usual, fame brought trouble and envy. People who visited the Cemetery were curious to see the rock upon which Lee had stood, viewing the progress of the battle. This souvenir of Lee was most obnoxious to the extremely loyal and its removal was demanded. Bitter complaint was made to the Trustees, a mixed body of soldiers and politicians, and the debate therein grew warm and men lost their tempers. The conservative members protested against such narrowness and rather liked the idea of having it there as a historical memento, but the ultraist declared that no such relic of rebellion ought to stand amid the graves of the Union dead. The latter prevailed and Lee's Rock was broken up: dug up, scattered, obliterated."(12)

To provide the reader with an example of the emotions evoked by Lee's Rock, consider the following by J. M. Mentzer:

> "A great many visitors are arriving here daily to see the great Antietam National Cemetery—many of whom are attracted to a mound of stone bearing the name of 'Lee's Rock,'(so called,) which is enclosed in the Cemetery, and which has been literally

battered and chiseled…Visitors from the South pound off a pound or two by way of a remembrance of the old Rebel Chief—and real live Yankees, who never have been 'lionized,' choose to kick off a chunk occasionally to take to their 'Down East' homes, where the war was not;'—and God or Mahomet only knows what wondrous tales may yet be told or even printed about a little piece of ordinary limestone, which, but for the war, would have been broken up on Col. Miller's turnpike or made to serve for the foundation of some country Jail, (like that of Boosboro, for instance.) Lee's Rock!—Bah!!!"(13)

According to Mentzer, the rock would have been dismantled and hauled away by the curious anyway, had it been left alone.

Lee's Rock was removed, however, much to the bemusement of some of the locals. As Douglas remembered, "We Rebels looked on, while the fury seethed, in silent amusement, and when it was all over, revealed the truth that Lee never saw that rock; if he had seen it he could not have climbed up on it; if he had done that he could not have seen anything on the outside of the trees."(14)

The existence of the rock has never been disputed, but whether General Lee actually stood on it to observe the battle will always remain a mystery. Visitors to the cemetery who wish to see the spot for themselves should proceed to the Pennsylvania section and look for Mrs. Bryant's monument (the wife of a former superintendent). According to Oliver T. Reilly, who was to become one of the most popular local battlefield guides in the years after the war, Mrs. Bryant's monument marks the location of Lee's Rock.

The monument of Mrs. Elizabeth Bryant, wife of the former superintendent, J. M. Bryant, marks the location of the Lee Rock. (SLS)

A Change of Plans

In April, 1867, the burial corps resumed its work. At the urging of the trustees and the Federal Government, the scope of the cemetery had changed to include the Union dead from the entire state of Maryland. In May of that same year, the editor of the *Middletown Valley Register,* George C. Rhoderick, noted the arrival of the burial corps:

> "...for the purpose of removing to the Antietam Cemetery the remains of the Union Soldiers who fell in the battles of South Mountain and Monocacy. Quite a large number lie buried in the cemetery here...in addition to those who fell in the sanguinary conflicts on our own soil, a large number who yielded up their lives in the bloody struggles that took place in the Shenandoah Valley, were also buried here."(15)

In July, J. M. Mentzer observed the passage of the burial corps through Boonsboro on its way to Cumberland, Maryland, some sixty miles to the west. The corps took with it five hundred coffins. Some weeks later Mentzer saw it return with about four hundred of the coffins filled.

By September, 1867, the work of exhuming and reinterring the Union dead was completed. Up to that time, 4,695 Union soldiers (2,903 known, 1,792 unknown) had been reinterred, with one third of the graves quarried out of solid rock. In addition to the Union dead that fell in Maryland, the trustees also managed to have the remains of eleven soldiers reinterred from Fulton County, Pennsylvania.(16)

The Dedication

On Tuesday, September 17, 1867, five years after the Battle of Antietam, the cemetery was officially dedicated. Because Congress had not yet authorized the funding for durable headstones at national cemeteries, the trustees had to settle for temporary wooden headboards. The stone markers would not be put in place until 1873. The soldier's monument that now stands in the center of the cemetery was also absent. The crowd in attendance ranged between ten and fifteen thousand. Among the dignitaries present were President Andrew Johnson, Governor Swann of Maryland, former Governor Bradford of Maryland, General George B. McClellan, General Ambrose Burnside, General Ulysses S. Grant, and Governor John W. Geary of Pennsylvania.

Superintendent's residence, Antietam National Cemetery. (DCT)

U. S. flag put on the cemetery wall by an unknown stone mason. (SRS)

A Loyal Governor

Although absent at the Battle of Antietam because of a wound received earlier at the Battle of Cedar Mountain, Geary returned to duty to command a division in the XII Corps. He was well liked and by war's end, had been awarded the rank of Major General. Geary was one of those soldiers who turned a successful military career into a successful political career. In 1866 he had been elected to his first of two terms as a Republican governor of Pennsylvania.

Governor Geary was not scheduled to speak, but, as J. M. Mentzer reported:

"...the crowd called loudly for Gov. Geary...The shouts were deafening and continuous. Gov. Swann attempted to speak and command silence, but the shouts of the people completely drowned his voice and compelled him to take his seat. 'Geary! Geary! we want to hear a loyal Governor speak,' shouted the masses as this living tide of humanity swayed with excitement and patriotic emotions. Another attempt was made by Swann to still the tumult, but his voice was unheard."(17)

Governor Geary was allowed to speak. He requested that the crowd permit the program to continue, and afterwards, if they still desired, he would speak:

"...President Johnson was introduced, amidst very faint applause from a few Maryland and Virginia rebels...the programme of speakers did not please the majority. Swann, Johnson, Bradford did not command the respect of the 'boys in blue,' and the loyal hearts gathered to do honor to the dust of the fallen heroes. This was evidenced throughout the entire proceedings, and the almost wild enthusiasm for Gov. Geary, or any known truly loyal man who made his appearance. This was not the case with Johnson, Swann, or Bradford."(18)

In a more subdued tone, Rhoderick agreed with Mentzer about the President's reception:

"The President met with a cool reception from the masses. His entrance into the enclosure excited but faint applause, and was in wide contrast with the frequent and deafening cheers subsequently given Gen. Geary, the loyal Governor of Pennsylvania, who finally gratified the crowd with a speech. Several regiments of the 'Boys in Blue' formed the escort, but they were evidently no admirers of the President."(19)

Although the cornerstone for the Soldier's Monument was laid with full Masonic ceremony, many in the crowd were disappointed. The war was not long past and sentiments still ran strong. Governor Thomas Swann was a Virginian by birth and this provided reason enough for some in the crowd to resent his being a speaker at a ceremony for loyal Union dead. President Johnson was not popular either; in a few months he would escape impeachment by one vote.

The Government Takes Over

In 1879 the Antietam National Cemetery was transferred from its trustees to the War Department. The operation and maintenance of the cemetery had become too much for the trustees to pay for. It was rumored that the cemetery had been allowed to fall into a state of disrepair and the weeds allowed to grow so that the government would feel compelled to take over the ownership. Antietam Cemetery was one of the few national cemeteries that had not been originated by the Federal Government. On August 1, 1879, title for the cemetery was secured by the War Department. The United States government then became responsible for its maintenance and the payment of outstanding debts.

The statue that commands the center of the Antietam National Cemetery, known locally by the nickname "Simon,"(20) was not placed there until 1880. Although completed in 1874 at a cost of $35,000, it had been placed on exhibit at the Centennial Exposition in Philadelphia in 1876. After the Centennial it was shipped by boat to Washington D.C. in two pieces. The original dedication had been planned for 1879; however, due to an accident one piece had to be retrieved from the bottom of the Potomac River and this resulted in delaying the dedication until the following year.(21) The monument was officially dedicated on September 17, 1880. By this time the permanent headstones were in place.

Due to a general reorganization of the government in 1933, the Antietam National Cemetery passed into the care of the U. S. Park Service. The cemetery was used as a veteran's cemetery until 1953 when this practice stopped because of a lack of space; however, some of the

Dedication of the Soldier's Monument September 17, 1880. (DCT)

veterans also contracted to have their wives buried with them. A visitor to the cemetery can find twenty-five such couples. The most recent interment of a wife, Mrs. Luther Stunkle, occurred in November 1989.

Still to be Found

From time to time the remains of Union soldiers are found and reinterred at the cemetery. In 1910, O. T. Reilly was witness to such a reinterment:

> "Charles Smith, who resided at the East Woods, was digging some dirt along the Smoketown road…he dug out the remains of a Union soldier supposed to be a member of the 12th or 13th Massachusetts Regiment, on the east side of the hill north of the Mansfield monument. The man had fallen against the bank with out-stretched arms and that is the way he was found, and on the finger bone was found a ladies' gold ring, and old daguerreotype , brass picture frame, a padlock, and some Massachusetts State coat of arms buttons were with the bones. Mr. Smith reported to the Superintendent of the National Cemetery and the body was taken there and buried as unknown."(22)

As recently as March, 1989, some remains were found. The partial remains of four individuals were accidently unearthed by an amateur relic hunter in the area near Bloody Lane. Only chest cavities were found. The skulls and the long bones had presumably been reinterred at Antietam National Cemetery by the burial corps in 1866-67. The men of the burial corps, for the most part, had been dealing with only bones and it is conjectured that these remains somehow were lost or misplaced by the details. New York State cuff buttons, Catholic crucifixes, medals, and rosary beads were found with the remains. Also found were unfired 69 caliber buck-and-ball ammunition and this, along with the other artifacts, indicated that the remains were from soldiers of the Irish Brigade. On September 17, 1989, the remains were placed in a plain pine coffin and buried with full military honors in front of the New York section at the cemetery.(23)

Monument to members of the Irish Brigade whose remains were found in 1988. (SRS)

HERE LIE THE PARTIAL REMAINS OF FOUR UNKNOWN UNION SOLDIERS OF THE IRISH BRIGADE, KILLED SEPTEMBER 17, 1862, DURING THE BATTLE OF ANTIETAM, WHILE ASSAULTING THE CONFEDERATE POSITIONS IN "BLOODY LANE." AFTER THE WAR, PORTIONS OF THEIR BODIES WERE REMOVED AND INTERRED IN THIS NATIONAL CEMETERY. THESE ADDITIONAL REMAINS WERE DISCOVERED WITHIN THE BATTLEFIELD IN 1988 AND REINTERRED SEPTEMBER 17, 1989.

Inscription on the Irish Brigade Monument. (SRS)

One Nation

About two hundred fifty veterans of the Spanish-American War, World War I, World War II, and the Korean Conflict can be found in the cemetery. Although there are no Confederates in this cemetery, among these 20th Century veterans can be found the sons of the South. There are two from Alabama, one from North Carolina, and six from Virginia who, together with their Northern brothers, gave that "last measure of devotion" for their country, a United States of America.

Antietam National Cemetery allowed veterans of all wars to be placed within its confineds. Pictured here are the grave markers of a father and son. The father served in WWI and the son in WWII. Both died on February 2. (SRS)

Six black WWI veterans were buried in a separate section during the days of segregation. (SRS)

Sergeant George A. Simpson

George Simpson was the color sergeant of the 125th Pennsylvania Infantry Regiment when it entered the action near Dunkard Church. He was shot in the temple and fell dead while carrying the regiment's new flag. Over 200 men were killed or wounded that day, including his brother Randolph, who was shot through the breast but survived to witness the dedication of the regiment's monument on September 17, 1904. The sister of these two men had the honor of unveiling the monument that depicted George holding the regimental colors. Sergeant Simpson is the only soldier buried in the Antietam National Cemetery who has a monument on the battlefield.

Tombstone of Sergeant George A. Simpson (S.R.S.)   Monument of the 125th Pennsylvania Infantry (S.R.S.)

A Dog Story

Captain Werner Von Bachelle commanded Company F of the 6th Wisconsin Volunteer Infantry which belonged to the famed "Iron Brigade." He was killed on September 17, 1862, at the Battle of Antietam while leading his men through the "Bloody Cornfield." Bachelle was always accompanied by his pet Newfoundland dog. The dog had been trained to perform military salutes and other tricks. The Newfoundland was his constant companion and was by his side when he was killed. On the morning of September 19th the burial details found the dog lying dead upon Bachelle's prostrate form. The animal had perished guarding the body of his master. The men of the 6th Wisconsin buried the dog with Captain Bachelle. The two remained together for at least five years. One can only speculate as to whether or not the day laborers who comprised the "Burial Corps" five years later would have recognized the dog's remains from Captain Bachelle's. And, assuming that they did distinguish the dog from the good captain, would they have reinterred its remains at the national cemetery as well. No one knows for sure as no record of the dog's reinterment exists. However, it cannot be discounted that there exist the possibility that under stone #858 along with Captain Bachelle rest the remains of his faithful Newfoundland.

The statue of "Hope" Washington Confederate Cemetery, Hagerstown, Maryland. (SRS)

3

The Washington Confederate Cemetery

At the end of 1867 the Confederate dead of the Maryland Campaign of 1862 still remained where they had originally been buried. The only exceptions were three unknown rebels who had been buried on the site of the Antietam Cemetery and "...removed by unknown persons."(1)

South Mountain

While conducting research for a historical pamphlet, Mr. John Watts DePeyster made a visit to Fox's Gap in 1867. He noted that the Confederates buried in and around the vicinity of Wise's cabin had corn growing over their trenches in 1866 and speculated that the corn crop of 1867 would "doubless obliterate every vestige of their last resting place." He also noted that the graves had no stones or markers to designate them as such. In the short five years since the soldiers' burial, either nature or the souvenir hunter had removed what few markers there had been.(2)

DePeyster described Daniel Wise as "a fine looking old mountaineer." He noted that the cabin was completely riddled with grape-shot and bullets. He sat in Wise's cabin for a while to jot down some notes. Although he made no mention of the well, he did note that, "In a little garden immediately adjoining and west of the house, a small plot not over fifty feet square, fifty-eight Rebels lie buried." Fifty square feet is not a large area. A plot of ground seven feet by seven feet would yield forty-nine square feet. Surely, DePeyster was looking at the well site, and if he could not bring himself to make mention of the well, it might have been due to the fact that it was too soon after the war for any bad press about the "Boys in Blue." In the years between the Civil War and the turn of the century, five presidents came from Ohio. Since the winners write the history, stories about drunken Ohioans dumping bodies down a well were not acceptable. Better to perpetuate a legend about an old man than to sully the reputation of the Union. Ironically, Daniel Wise would

Unpublished photograph of the Daniel Wise cabin. Courtesy Doug Bast.

never know about the legend because the first mention would come in a regimental history published after his death.(3)

DePeyster observed that in many localities along South Mountain there were many hasty graves "from which the Spring and Winter rains have washed away the scanty earth and left the bones exposed." He talked to a farmer that lived in another area of the South Mountain Battlefield who complained that the bones of the Rebel dead on his ground were continually washed out by heavy rains and that it was more than he could do to "keep them decently covered." Touched by what he saw that summer of 1867, DePeyster took it upon himself to reinter some of the Rebel dead: "For my part, I paid Mr. Wise the trifle he asked to reinter some of those near the 'Old Sharpsburg Road,' for it seemed a profanation to leave the bones to bleach unheeded and uncovered."(4)

DePeyster and his companions ended their visit on a lighter note. While visiting another farm on South Mountain he noted that the grounds were "filled with graves." And while talking to the wife of the farmer, DePeyster observed that she "seemed to take a sort of pride in residing in a spot which many persons might have shunned as a sort of Golgotha. One of the party asked her if she did not mind living in the midst of so many dead. 'Oh no,' she replied, 'They are very quiet neighbors.'"(5)

Antietam

Conditions at Antietam were similar to those at South Mountain. Many of the Confederate trenches were eroded and bones were exposed. It was not uncommon to see dogs and livestock roaming about with human bones in their mouths. Many of the trenches had simply been plowed over in preparation for the season's plantings. Ironically the Confederate dead found a friend in the governor of a Union state.

"Make Suitable Arrangements"

In a letter to the Trustees of the Antietam Cemetery dated December 3, 1867, Governor R. E. Fenton of New York called their attention to the sad condition of the Confederate dead. He reminded the Trustees that the fourth section of the Maryland Acts of Assembly called for, "The remains of the soldiers of the Confederate army to be buried in a part of the grounds separate from those of the Union army." Governor Fenton noted that the Southerners, although misguided and misled, were still Americans and that they should not be remembered with enmity or unkindness. Governor Fenton ended by saying:

"...the Trustees of the Antietam Cemetery, especially in view of the fact that the Southern States have not thus far been in a position to contribute to the general fund, should either set apart a sufficient plot of ground within the cemetery walls for the burial of the Confederate dead, or make suitable arrangements for an enlargement of the present enclosure, if necessary, to the attainment of the end proposed."(6)

The Board of Trustees adopted a resolution to "set apart for the burial of the Confederate dead who fell in the battle of Antietam in the first invasion of Lee the southern portion of the grounds not occupied, and separate from the ground devoted to the Union dead." In the following January session, the Maryland Legislature appropriated $5,000 to assist in the execution of the resolution. There the matter rested until the following May.(7)

Resolutions

On May 6, 1868, the superintendent of the Board of Trustees for the Antietam Cemetery reported that the unoccupied portion of the southern grounds was not sufficient for the burial of the Confederate dead. The purchase of additional ground bordering the south side of the cemetery was recommended. The Board passed a resolution to make the purchase and a committee was appointed to carry out the resolution.

On June 17, 1868, the Board passed a resolution postponing all action with reference to the removal of the Confederate dead until the next meeting. At the next meeting on November 18, the Board passed a resolution postponing all action until the annual meeting to be held in December. At this meeting, held on December 9, 1868, the Board "resolved to continue the resolution postponing all action for the burial of the Confederate dead."(8)

Bowie's List

After this December meeting the Trustees for the State of Maryland contacted Governor Swann. They informed him of the condition of the Confederate dead and requested that some action be taken to protect the graves of the dead until they could be reinterred elsewhere. It was still assumed that the next site would be additional ground adjoining the Antietam National Cemetery. Due to illness Governor Swann was forced to retire and the request passed along to his successor, Governor Oden Bowie.

In 1869 Governor Bowie requested Thomas A. Boult to prepare a list of the burial places of the Confederate dead. Boult employed the services of Moses Poffinberger and Aaron Good, both of Sharpsburg, for this purpose. They visited every trench and grave they could find. They mounded up and recovered those trenches that had been eroded over the intervening years. From their notes the list was compiled. On May 1, 1869, it was published under the official title of "A Descriptive list of the Burial Places of the Remains of Confederate Soldiers, who fell in the battles of Antietam, South Mountain, Monocacy, and other points in Washington and Frederick Counties, in the state of Maryland." Today it is simply referred to as "Bowie's List."

Some of the entries in Bowie's List are chilling commentary on the aftermath of war. Most visitors to the Antietam Battlefield are familiar with the action in and around the "Cornfield." Within four hours on the morning of September 17, 1862, half of the day's casualties occurred in this area. One of the entries for the "Cornfield" reads: "Eighteen trenches supposed to contain two hundred and ninety unknown...Maj.Tracy, 27th Ga.; in east end of trench containing one hundred and fifty. Buried in D. R. Miller's fifty-acre field...the trenches can all be seen, although the field has been plowed; buried shallow; bones exposed in places; trappings, etc. can be seen. Nine trenches supposed to contain two hundred and twenty-five unknown. Buried in D.R. Millers field...buried shallow, exposed. Eight trenches supposed to contain three hundred and five unknown...bones exposed."(9)

Elsewhere in Bowie's List is the succinct entry, "58 unknown, In Wise's well on South Mountain."(10)

Missing In Action

Although some civilian labor had been locally contracted, most of the Confederate dead had been interred by Union burial details. As stated previously, Confederates usually were buried after the Union dead. The details were already exhausted from their work and, quite naturally, desired to finish quickly. Hence many Confederate trenches were more haphazard and shallow than their Union counterparts. Those who died later in the field hospitals received better burials and, for the most part, retained their identities.

Mr. Poffinberger and Mr. Good did not find them all since they were making their search seven years after the battle. If only four years after the battle, farmers were growing cabbages and making roads over the trenches of the loyal Union dead, a much worse fate occurred to the graves of the treasonous Rebels, with some farmers disavowing any knowledge of Confederate dead on their property, just as some had tried to do with the men reinterring the Union dead.

Remember that Michael Deady recorded in his diary that the details had buried four hundred and fifty Confederates in the vicinity of Fox's Gap. Bowie's list accounted for only two hundred in the Fox's Gap area. Either Deady was grossly overestimating the number of dead he helped bury or Governor Bowie's men missed many of them, and we are also faced with the prospect of Civil War MIA's still to be found.

Not Wanted

By 1870 the trustees of the Antietam National Cemetery had taken no action toward the burial of the Confederate dead. Some of the trustees argued that since the Southern states had not contributed any money, they had no right to bury their dead in the cemetery; however, it was still too early after the war for ill feelings to have faded. To many veterans of the North, burying Confederates at Antietam would have been the same as burying the Japanese at Arlington after World War II.

The simple truth was that the Trustees for the Antietam National Cemetery did not want any Confederates buried there. It certainly follows that if the Trustees were not going to allow a rock that General Lee supposedly stood upon to remain in their cemetery, they were certainly not going to allow dead Confederates.

Maryland, My Maryland

The State of Maryland decided to proceed on its own. The General Assembly of 1870 enacted Chapter 213, an act that repealed the act of 1868 which appropriated the sum of $5,000.00. In the act the assembly gave the following reason: "the sum of five thousand dollars was appropriated to the removal and burial of the Confederate dead...in the Antietam National Cemetery; the said appropriation so made is yet unappropriated, by reason of the persistent refusal of the trustees of said 'Antietam National Cemetery' to allow the remains of said Confederate soldiers to be intered therein." The legislation then set up the charter for the creation of the Washington Confederate Cemetery.

The charter provided for "the burial and final resting place of the remains of the Confederate dead, and all other of both armies in the late war." The charter further required that the cemetery should be located within one mile of Hagerstown.(11)

The first trustees of the Washington Confederate Cemetery were appointed. They were Colonel Henry Kyd Douglas, Major George Freaner, both of Washington County, and James H. Gambrill, of Frederick County. It was their responsibility to oversee the exhumation and reinterment of the Confederate dead to the site chosen for the cemetery.

Hagerstown

Two more years passed until a suitable location was found. In 1872 a site was chosen and $2,400 of the $5,000 appropriation was spent for two and three-fourths acres of land at Rose Hill Cemetery in Hagerstown. There were practical reasons for choosing an existing cemetery. As reported in the *Hagerstown Mail:*

> "To have purchased a separate lot; to have enclosed and improved it and placed it in order for the reception of the dead, would probably have consumed the whole amount of the appropriation...Then, too, in a few years, without constant and especial attention (which could not have been given) the lot would have been overgrown with weeds and briars. As it is, it will have the perpetual attention of the custodian of Rose Hill Cemetery and will always be kept in order."(12)

Henry Mumma and Antietam

All that remained was to find a way to do the exhumations as economically as possible with the funds available. As the trustees reported on December 9, 1873:

> "...it was our desire to adopt a plan by which we could collect and bury the greatest number of dead with the small sum of $2,600 left in our hands. Believing that any contract for the removal of the dead to Washington Cemetery per capita would soon exhaust the fund, we deemed it best to select a reliable and energetic agent who would employ hands, purchase lumber, have coffins made, and the bodies exhumed and moved with strict regard to economy and the due execution of our trust. Such a man we found in Mr. Henry C. Mumma, of Sharpsburg, and the faithful manner in which he performed his duties fully justified our confidence in him and the plan we adopted."(13)

In September, 1872, ten years after the battle of Antietam, Mumma and his workers started the job of exhuming and reinterring the Confederate dead. Mumma was paid an amount that averaged one dollar a head. From the *Hagerstown Mail*, we find:

> "Up to Saturday evening last, one hundred and ninety eight dead bodies had been delivered, most of which were then intered. They are substantially enclosed—the remains of two persons, when unknown—being simply the bones—fill a single box about 3 1/2 feet long and about a foot square. In one of the sections some over curious persons had, on Sunday last, descended into a trench which was not yet covered...and had broken off the lid—thus exposing the bones...In this collection was a camp spoon containing the letter 'R' and a couple of old knives...Most of those now buried are unknown."(14)

The unknown were buried in rows and marked thus. Those who could be identified were buried according to their state.

It was also noted by the Hagerstown press that there were a large number of graves scattered throughout the area and an appeal was made to the local citizenry: "It is the wish of those who have charge of the matter that those who have knowledge of such graves report them...or take up the bodies themselves and convey them to the cemetery, where they will (if they require it) have reasonable compensation for expense incurred."

Coxon's Map

The job of actually laying out the positions and locations of the gravesites fell to the custodian of the Rose Hill Cemetery, Joseph Coxon. Together with the County Surveyor, S. S. Downin, they laid off the site and compiled a map of the burial places. This map would later be known as "Coxon's Map" and would be the source for the metal plaque that now stands at the cemetery. With the exception of one flat solitary headstone, of Colonel S.E. Lumpkins, this plaque is the only marker at the Washington Confederate Cemetery. It shows the locations of almost 2,500 soldiers. The area in front of this plaque was used to bury boxes of amputated limbs.(15)

The Work Remaining

By the end of 1872 the work of removing the Confederate dead from Antietam was drawing to a close. As reported by the trustees:

> "...we removed from the battlefield of Antietam and vicinity to Washington Cemetery 1721 dead bodies and have yet the sum of $413.34 remaining in the Treasury. This balance is to be expended in sodding the graves and in other necessary work in the cemetery so far as it will reach. It will not be sufficient to purchase, in addition, the ordinary headboards with which the graves should be marked...We think it proper to add that from the best information we can obtain, there are yet about 500 bodies of Confederate soldiers in the vicinity of South Mountain and in other places in Washington County, which our means would not enable us to reach..."(16)

Another $5,000 was appropriated by the Maryland legislature in 1874. Virginia and West Virginia each appropriated an additional $500, bringing the total for 1874 to $6,000. Colonel W. A. Morgon, of West Virginia, and Major R. W. Hunter, of Virginia, were elected to represent their states as trustees of the cemetery, along with the original three.

It is interesting that Pennsylvania appropriated $3,000 toward the removal of the Confederate dead from the field of Gettysburg to Washington Cemetery, but because the people of Virginia had already removed the greater portion of them to Richmond, the Pennsylvania authorities withheld the funds. No other state has ever offered funds for the Washington Confederate Cemetery.

South Mountain

Work resumed for the reinterment of the South Mountain dead. In July, 1874, George C. Rhoderick of Middletown, Maryland, noted in his newspaper, "Several men arrived in this place on Tuesday last, and proceeded to disinter the remains of the few Confederate dead who were buried here during the war...Among the bones in one of the graves was found a small metal inkstand, which was in a good state of preservation and was still about half full of ink."(17)

The men spoken of were Henry C. Mumma and his workers. Mumma had been rehired by the trustees to finish the work. As reported in the *Hagerstown Mail:*

> "[Mumma] has been most successful in his work, and is at this time continuing its prosecution with vigor. He was in town on Tuesday last, and had at that time, since the resumption of operations...recovered and brought to the Cemetery for interment 255 bodies, at the remarkably small cost of $1.65 per head. Some of these bodies we have heretofore noticed as having been taken from the historical well on South Mountain battle-field, where they were thrown by Gen. Reno's command."(18)

Only known depiction of Daniel Wise on South Mountain battlefield. (SRS)

For years after the war, the mistaken belief existed among many of the visitors to the battlefields that the dead from Wise's well had been taken home. This was due to local self-appointed battlefield guides, who in order to make their tours more interesting, not only used the local legends but embellished them with each telling.

One can only speculate on the actual exhumation of the bodies from the well since no written account, other than that of the Hagerstown press, has yet been found. Daniel Wise was still living at the cabin when Mumma was exhuming the South Mountain dead. It is reasonable to assume that Wise wanted the dead on his property removed. It is also likely that Mumma had a copy of Bowie's list, and since he was being paid per body, would have retrieved all the remains he could find. It must have taken time to excavate the well, and one might hypothesize the dead from the well were among the last taken off the mountain. If one looks at Coxon's Map, on the burial area periphery, where the last remains were buried, one finds this inscription, "29 Boxes, 58 Bodys Unknown." It is circumstantial evidence, but it is the best evidence available that this is where the dead Confederate soldiers from Wise's well are buried.

Missing

By August, 1874, the work was finished. Mumma had brought the remains of 2,240 Confederate soldiers to the cemetery within a cemetery at Rose Hill. It is reasonable to assume that Mumma's experiences were similar to those who completed the Union reinterments, with some farmers welcoming him, and some not. By adding the number of those killed outright to the number who died from their wounds, a figure of four thousand Confederate dead is the result of the Maryland Campaign of 1862. Even if a certain number were transported home for burial, one must conclude there are yet a large number of the dead to be found.

Hope

On February 28, 1877, a monument was placed at the cemetery. Historian J. Thomas Scharf observed "upon the top is a marble figure more than five feet in height, representing Hope leaning upon her anchor, with flowing robes, and upon her brow is set a star (perhaps the single star of the Confederacy)."(19) It was also described in *Frank Leslie's Illustrated Newspaper*, "The monument is nineteen feet high. The pedestal is of gray Richmond granite. The plinth, of Scotch (Aberdeen) granite, light brown of various shades, dappled with black and gray, and very highly polished. It was prepared as it is in Scotland. The figure is of white marble (Italian)."(20)

According to the trustees of the Confederate Cemetery some weeks before the dedication, "The Monument is not as imposing as we could wish, but it is the best we could do with the means at our disposal and the plan we determined upon for the future…The entire cost, including freight, transportation from depot here, and erection amounts to $1440."(21)

The Dedication

The Washington Confederate Cemetery was officially dedicated on Tuesday, June 15, 1877. Special trains were running from Washington, Baltimore, and Shepherdstown. Former Confederate Major General Fitzhugh Lee, nephew of Robert E. Lee, was chosen to dedicate the cemetery. As Scharf observed:

> "In Hagerstown the day was universally given up to the celebration. Many of the citizens kept open house and invited persons to lunch or dine with them. Although it was Tuesday, the county 'public day,' very little business was transacted. It is thought that at least six thousand people visited the cemetery during the day, and that there were five thousand present at one time."(22)

Due to a train accident, the contingent from Frederick County, Maryland, was not able to attend.

Around 2:00 p.m., a procession formed in the Hagerstown square and proceeded down South Potomac Street toward the cemetery. Various dignitaries and area groups formed a parade, among them the Martinsburg Band and Drum Corps, the Berkeley Light Infantry, the mayor and city council of Hagerstown, the fire department of Hagerstown (their engines decorated with flowers), the Keedysville band, and many more. It was noted that the delegations from Williamsport, Funkstown, and Sharpsburg "were noticeably large, and carried masses of beautiful flowers."

A choir of sixty people was at the cemetery. Various groups provided music and various speakers, oratory. Colonel Henry Kyd Douglas was the master of ceremonies. Rev. Levi Keller, of Funkstown, delivered the opening prayer in which he "thanked Almighty God for the restoration of love and unity between the late contending armies."

After a historical sketch of the cemetery, delivered by Major George Freaner, and the dedication dirge by the choir, General Lee, the principal orator of the day, was introduced. General Lee spoke from a written manuscript which the local press expected to receive for publication; however, General Lee thought it was prepared too hastily and withheld the manuscript from publication. All that survives of the General's address is that remembered the day after by the Hagerstown press:

> "Gen. Lee, the orator of the day…delivered an eloquent address, in which…he said that the people of the two sections now had a common country, and that it behooved his hearers to love and cherish it, and to banish discord and strife. Fraternal harmony must prevail. We should look hopefully forward to the future…General Lee's manner was earnest and impressive and he was listened to with profound attention by all of the vast assembly whom his voice could reach."(23)

After the oratory the graves were strewn with flowers and the procession was reformed for the march back to town.

The Only Tombstone

The only individual marker at the Confederate Cemetery belongs to a Georgia Officer. Colonel Samuel E. Lumpkin had been wounded at the battle of Gettysburg. After the retreat to Hagerstown, the Colonel died of typhoid fever, probably contracted due to weakness from loss of blood after an amputation. He was buried in a Presbyterian cemetery with Myrtle planted on his grave. In 1913, when the church decided to expand, the body was reinterred. On June 20, 1913, The Trustees of the Confederate Cemetery paid $3.25 to Rose Hill Cemetery for the reinterment of Colonel Lumpkin. The marker was purchased the following year from the firm of C. E. Darner for the sum of twelve dollars.(24) It is a sad irony that the only man to have a tombstone at the Washington Confederate Cemetery should have his name, and the name of his state misspelled.

Colonel James

The story of Colonel James is a good example of the labyrinth of puzzles and contradictions one finds when looking through the "Fog of War" and "Mist of Time" to follow the stories associated with people and events that transpired over a century and a quarter past.

Prewar photograph of Colonel Samuel Lumpkin. (SRS)

The only tombstone in Washington Confederate Cemetery bears the misspelled name of Col. Lumpkin. (SRS)

Charles F. Walcott, a member of the 21st Massachuetts Regiment, was involved in the afternoon's combat during the Battle of South Mountain at Fox's Gap (known as the Battle of Boonsboro in the South). His regiment fought in the area around Wise's cabin. Walcott kept a diary which he used for the basis of a regimental history written in 1882. In that history, Walcott recounted an incident that happened the night of September 14, after the fighting was over:

> "I had an interesting conversation with a wounded Rebel officer during the night. About midnight I heard a call for help, and going to the spot saw some one moving rapidly away from a man lying on the ground. The prostrate man told me that he was Lieutenant-Colonel James of the 15th South Carolina, that he was shot through the body when our men made the last assault, and had pretended to be dead, hoping that he should feel able to try to escape before morning, but found himself growing weaker, and knew that he should die. He said that he had called for help, because a prowling rascal had turned him over and taken his watch."

It was a cold night, so Walcott got a blanket for Colonel James and:

> "gave him a drink of whiskey. As I sat by him he told me that when his regiment was ordered to cross the Potomac the colonel had refused to go, saying that the regiment had enlisted to defend the South, and not to invade the North, but that he had sprung to the front, and telling the colonel that he was a coward, had called on the men to follow him, but had led them to their death...the brave fellow died before morning."(25)

As stated previously the buttons from Colonel James' uniform were made into jewelry for Frank Firey's sister.(26) Firey also related that in the following year, "as Lee's army was marching to Gettysburg, passing by our farm in Maryland, my father chanced to talk with several Confederate soldiers of a South Carolina Regiment." Firey told the soldiers of burying Colonel James. In disbelief one of the soldiers exclaimed, "Colonel James! My God! He was the Colonel of our regiment, and his brother is the captain of our company."

The soldiers ran away to summon Captain James. Frank Firey went on to recount that a "tall muscular man with blue eyes...wearing a handsome gray uniform," returned to talk with his father and, "As he talked with my father about his brother the tears rolled down his cheeks, and his tall frame shook with emotion. My father chanced to mention having cut the buttons from Colonel James uniform..." Captain James asked if he could have the buttons and Miss Firey immediately consented. Captain James then remarked that he wished to take up the remains of his brother and send them home.

Unfortunately, at the time of the Gettysburg Campaign, Fox's Gap was occupied by Union troops and this prohibited Captain James from seeking the remains of his brother. As he was leaving, Captain James said, "When we return from Pennsylvania or when the war is over, I will, with your kind assistance, secure the remains of my brother and take them home for burial." But, as Frank Firey noted, "On its return from Gettysburg Lee's army marched diagonally through our farm in Maryland. Captain James was not among the host that passed by, and the poor fellow never returned for the remains of his brother." Mr. Firey was writing his comments in 1915.(27)

In 1867, during his trip to South Mountain, DePeyster had noticed the grave of Colonel James in the vicinity of Wise's cabin. He noted that to the east of the cabin was buried "a Major or Colonel E. S. James, according to one account, of a South Carolina, but more likely of a Georgia regiment. He was killed near a little log barn, just south of the Wise log house under a single large tree." As mentioned before, DePeyster noted that "his grave, as well as those of his men, has neither stone nor board to designate it."(28)

In Governor Bowie's descriptive list, on page 49 appears the entry: "Lt. Col. E. S. James, N. C., forty-seven unknown, In Wise's lot on east side of house and lot on top of South Mountain."

Colonel James was a member of Drayton's Brigade, Longstreet's Corps, and as such was among the first of the Confederate forces to arrive at South Mountain from Hagerstown. During the afternoon's fighting on September 14, 1862, they were posted in the mountain roads in the area of Wise's cabin. They were severely mauled by a flanking fire delivered by the 17th Michigan in their charge on the stone wall bordering the Wood Road leading to Fox's Gap. Drayton's Brigade suffered some of the worst casualties of that day.(29)

Drayton's Brigade was composed of four regiments: the 50th Georgia, 51st Georgia, 15th South Carolina, and 3rd South Carolina. George Shoulter James was a Lieutenant-Colonel in the 3rd South Carolina Regiment. Because there were also North Carolina troops involved in the combat at Fox's Gap, it explains how a Union officer, such as Walcott, would confuse the two states. Walcott admits in his footnotes that he recorded the story in his diary on the following day and that there could be mistakes. DePeyster thought it likely that Colonel James was from Georgia since there were also Georgia troops in Drayton's Brigade. Whatever the cause, Colonel James was misidentified as from a North Carolina regiment, and this is what was recorded in Governor Bowie's List.(30)

It is also likely a crude wooden headboard marked the grave of Colonel James, and a roughly carved "G. S. James" could be mistaken for "E. S. James." By 1867, the headboard was gone. It was probably Daniel Wise who showed the grave to visitors and also identified it as that of a Rebel colonel. It is assumed that this is how Colonel James was entered into Bowie's List. With no headboard over his grave, and no buttons left on his uniform, it is possible Colonel James was just another unknown in a mass grave. Mr. Muma and his men had no way to identify one set of remains from another when they did the exhumations. Although Colonel James' name appears in Bowie's List, it does not appear on Coxon's Map at the Washington Confederate Cemetery in Hagerstown.

Hence either Colonel James was exhumed and taken home (explaining why his name does not appear on Coxon's Map), or he was reinterred as an unknown in Hagerstown. In light of what Firey wrote, it seems unlikely Colonel James was "taken home."

In itself, this story has little significance, but it may be more than just the tale of another Confederate soldier who lost his identity on a battlefield far from home. There is a strong possibility that Lieutenant-Colonel G. S. James gave the order for the first shot of the American Civil War. It has long been accepted through legend that Mr. Edmund Ruffin fired the first shot at Fort Sumter in Charleston Harbor, South Carolina.(31) This first cannon fire has often been dubbed as the shot that started the Civil War; however, this legend has its detractors.

Lieutenant General Stephen D. Lee was a Captain in the South Carolina army and an aide on the staff of General Beauregard at the beginning of the war. In 1883, in a letter to the Southern Historical Society, Stephen Lee wrote:

> "I wish to correct an error which has almost passed into an historical fact. It is this: That Edmund Ruffin, of Virginia, did not fire the first gun at Fort Sumter, but that Capt. George S. James, of South Carolina, Afterward killed when a Lieutenant-Colonel at Boonsboro', Md. did fire it… Mr. Edmund Ruffin (who was much beloved and respected) was at the iron battery on Morris Island. I always understood he fired the first gun from the iron battery, but one thing is certain—he never fired the first gun against Fort Sumter. George S. James did."(32)

Colonel James did not actually pull the lanyard that fired the cannon, but he was in command of the batteries responsible for the first shot, and he would have given the order to fire.(33)

Thus, there exists the possibility that somewhere in one of the "unknown" burial sections of the Washington Confederate Cemetery, intermingled within the small confines of a three foot coffin and with the bones of another unknown soldier, rests the remains of the man who gave the order to fire the first cannon shot at Fort Sumter.

Still Out There

As at Antietam, from time to time the remains of Civil War soldiers still turn up. In 1893 Carlton M. Younkins was digging postholes for a fence on his farm below Fox's Gap. As later reported in *The*

Valley Register, while at this work, he brought up some human remains, including "a skull, a rib, and a few small bones." It was noted that the skull was in a fine state of preservation with nearly all the teeth still in place.(34) Since it could not be identified as Union or Confederate, it was taken to Hagerstown. So the irony exists, although there are no Confederates at Antietam, there may be a Union soldier at Hagerstown.

In 1902 Henry Burgen, then supervisor of the Chesapeake and Ohio Canal, while making repairs to the canal near Antietam, accidently dug up the remains of two soldiers. They were determined to be Confederate soldiers from Georgia. This was ascertained by buttons found with the remains. Lodged in one of the skeletons was the fragment of a shell and around the ankle bone of the other was tied a blue silk ribbon. They were reinterred at Hagerstown.(35)

About a mile southwest of Sharpsburg, on the right of Route 34 toward Shepherdstown, West Virginia, stands the old Captain D. Smith farmstead. It was one of the most noted Confederate field hospitals. In 1907 Franklin Otto was renting the farm from his brother, and while plowing the fields, uncovered the remains of several soldiers. This was nothing new to Otto. He would often

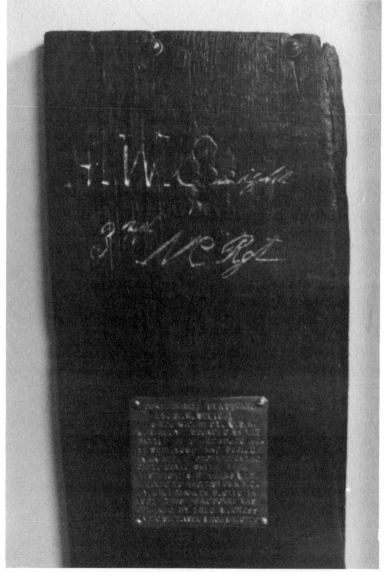

Hand carved head board of Lt. A. W. Spraight 3rd. North Carolina Regiment. Many Southern identifications were lost when the head boards were removed or deteriorated over the years.

talk with visitors and tell them of the many skeletons he found over the years. He also would show some of the headboards he had in the house. Among them was one that had carved into it, "A. W. Spraight, 3rd N. C. Reg."(36) The remains were discovered in the northeast corner of the old orchard, and a check with Bowie's list revealed that A. W. Spraight, along with sixteen others, had been "Buried in Capt. David Smith's orchard, northeast corner, were buried deep; the orchard has been plowed and graves plowed over, but can all be pointed out. Some of the boards have been preserved at the house. Some unknown were also buried here."(37) Somehow they were able to identify the remains of Mr. Spraight and, along with the other sixteen "unknowns," he was reinterred at Hagerstown. Coxon's Map shows his name in the North Carolina section. It is curious to note that although Mr. Spraight's place of burial was listed in 1869, it was not until 1907 that he was found and reinterred.(38)

O. T. Rielly of Sharpsburg remembered when the government was building the road in front of the Poffenberger's farm, and "six Confederates were dug up near by; five of them lay side by side and the sixth one was laid across the others...One was dug up when the Massachusetts State Monument was put up, besides many others in different places since, which is proof that many others of the unaccounted for lie buried in the fields, some never to be found."(39)

To be reinterred at the Antietam National Cemetery, the remains must be proven to be those of a Union soldier. Since the charter for the Washington Confederate Cemetery simply calls for "all other of both armies," the remains of any Civil War soldier yet to be found may be reinterred there, regardless of what side he fought for.

Brass plate describing the history of Spraight's head board. This and the previous photograph are courtesy of Doug Bast.

Confederate monument Mount Olivet Cemetery, Frederick, Maryland. (SRS)

4

Mount Olivet Cemetery

The wounded Confederate soldier of the Maryland Campaign of 1862 usually followed one of two paths after the battles. Those taken prisoner at South Mountain or Antietam recuperated from their wounds in a field hospital. These hospitals were established in the churches and barns of the local community. Those that could be transported were taken east to Frederick, Maryland (sometimes with a stop-over at Middletown), and then on to Baltimore as prisoners of war. Those who were fortunate to withdraw with the Confederate Army made their way across the Potomac River to Shepherdstown, Virginia (West Virginia was established in 1863). Some of these wounded perished and were buried in the local cemeteries, including Mount Olivet at Frederick, Maryland, and Elmwood at Shepherdstown, West Virginia.

Mount Olivet

On October 4, 1852, the Mount Olivet Cemetery Company was incorporated and thirty-two acres of ground purchased. During and after the Civil War, both Union and Confederate soldiers were buried here. Most of the Union soldiers were reinterred at Antietam; however, there remain about one hundred Union soldiers buried in the lots of relatives.(1)

In 1870, as the Maryland State Legislature appropriated funds for the Washington Confederate Cemetery, two thousand dollars was also appropriated for the reinterment of Confederate remains to Mount Olivet. Some Confederate dead already rested at Mount Olivet, and the legislature believed two thousand dollars would be enough to reinter those scattered about Frederick County.

Jacob Englebrecht was a citizen of Frederick City. He was a prosperous storekeeper who was keenly interested in his community. In his diary entry for late September, 1862, he noted that he went to Mount Olivet to help bury a Union soldier. He wrote there were:

> "...none but the Hearse & two to drive,...I helped to carry him in the grave, the graves was a long trench about 7 feet wide & about 20 or 30 feet long, the last coffin being partly

uncovered, we put him next to the last, about one inch apart, & left ready for the next one—they bury some days 8 or 10—those of the Rebel army are buried in another row. the Same way & up to that time numbered Sixty (I counted them) Some of the headboards were marked with their names. one was - 'Lieut. Col. T. C. Watkins 22 Regt. South Carolina."(2)

In addition to the Confederate dead of the Maryland Campaign there were also Confederate dead from the Battle of Monocacy. On July 9, 1864, the Confederate forces of Lieutenant General Jubal Early fought the Federals under the command of Major General Lew Wallace. The Confederates won the battle but it was a hollow victory. General Early's plans of marching on the Union capital at Washington, D.C. were delayed by the battle. General Grant was able to reinforce Washington with extra troops. General Early's troops marched to within sight of the capital but were unable to proceed any farther. The Battle of Monocacy has thus been called the "Battle that saved Washington."

Confederates who died in the hospitals of Frederick received better treatment than those of the Maryland Campaign buried by Union burial details, and since the Confederates retained possession of the field after the Battle of Monocacy, most of the Confederates buried at Mount Olivet were identified.

The Last Line

Along the western boundary of Mount Olivet are the headstones of 304 Confederate soldiers (seven Confederate soldiers are either located elsewhere or "possibly removed").(3) Of these 304 headstones only 29 bear the inscription "Unknown." Beginning at the north-east end of this line and walking along it toward the south-west, the dead are chronological from the Maryland Campaign up through the Battle of Monocacy.

The only exception to this rule is the first headstone. It is not number one. It has no number because it was placed there in 1907 after the others. It marks the spot of Sergeant Damascus Wetherly, who was reinterred from Braddock, Maryland. Although listed as a private with the 2nd Florida in the cemetery's records, it is more likely he was a sergeant with Cobb's Georgia Legion (part of Cobb's Brigade, McClaws Division) since this regiment, and not the 2nd Florida, fought at Braddock on the day before the Battle of South Mountain and since Sergeant Wetherly was from Georgia and not Florida. The grave at Braddock had been cared for by Mrs. John H. Williams. After her death, resort development changed the face of Braddock and it became necessary to do away with the "country graveyard." In 1907 Sergeant Wetherly was reinterred at Mount Olivet by the Fitzhugh Lee Chapter of the United Daughters of the Confederacy. He was placed at the beginning of the Line.(4)

After Sergeant Wetherly the tombstones are marked consecutively from 1 to 303. At the end of the line there are two monuments. One monument is so worn by the passage of time as to be almost unrecognizable. It is a memorial to the 408 (so says the monument) Confederate dead of the Battle of Monocacy.

The other monument bears the names of all the men of Frederick County known to have fought with the Confederate Army in the Civil War. It was erected in 1936 through the efforts of William J. Grove, G. Raymond Shipley, G. Mantz Besant, Albert Brown, Lewis A. Rice, and Glen H. Worthington.(5) Worthington had been a little boy at the time of the Battle of Monocacy. He hid in the cellar of the family's house as the fighting raged over the family's farm. Later in life Worthington wrote "Fighting for Time," which is considered a classic on the Battle of Monocacy.

The First Maryland Monument for the Unknown

In 1879, the residents of Frederick County with Confederate sympathies felt that something should be done to honor those who died for the "Lost Cause." An organization called the "Confederate Monument Association" was formed and funds sought for the erection of a monument. Over

Monument to 408 unknown Confederate dead from the Battle of Monocacy, July 9, 1864, (SRS)

Monument containing the names of men from Frederick County "Who Fought For Southern Rights." (SRS)

$1,500.00 was eventually raised and the project was brought to fruition when the monument was unveiled on Thursday, June 2, 1881.(6)

As reported by the pro-Union Frederick *Examiner*, "The day throughout was disagreeable...the rain fairly poured down, but notwithstanding a great number of persons attended." Some of those in attendance included members of the Winchester Light Infantry under command of Captain John Williams, the Frederick Riflemen under command of Lieutenant S. F. Thomas, the Linganore Guards of Unionville, members of the Society of the Army and Navy of the Confederates States of Maryland, the Murry Confederate Association, and the Charles Monumental Band of Baltimore.(7)

It was estimated that some 300 people gathered in a pouring rain in front of City Hall for the march to Mount Olivet. The rain was still falling so there was little ceremony. Four young ladies, among them the daughter of James H. Gambrill (trustee for Washington Confederate Cemetery), pulled the cord which held a veil over the statue. Flowers were then placed at the foot of the monument.

The monument is in the form of a private Confederate soldier standing at parade-rest. It was designed by Carl Conrads of Hartford, Connecticut, and was made in Italy of Carrara marble. The figure stands upon a granite pedestal five feet square. Among the inscriptions around the base is the following: "To the unknown soldiers whose bodies here rest." It was reported by the Fitzhugh Lee chapter of the U. D. C. to be the first monument erected to Confederate unknown.

After the brief ceremony the procession marched back to City Hall, and the exercises planned for the cemetery were held there. Among the speakers was Confederate General Bradley T. Johnson, a native of Frederick. His father, Baker Johnson, was the brother of Maryland's first Governor, Thomas Johnson. Bradley had entered the Confederate Army as a captain in the 1st Maryland Infantry Regiment. He had participated in the Maryland Campaign, and by war's end had achieved the rank of brigadier general.

During the Maryland Campaign, the office of the Frederick *Examiner* had been ransacked by Confederate soldiers.(8) Hence, nineteen years later, when reporting General Johnson's speech, the editor of the *Examiner* could only bring himself to write the following:

"Gen. Johnson says that 'which was true twenty years ago, is true today.' Certainly it is. Twenty years ago it was wrong for the Southern States to go into rebellion against the national authority, it is just as wrong now, to say that it was right then."(9)

Lieut. Col. Thomas C. Watkins

On Sunday morning, September 14, 1862, the 22nd South Carolina Regiment left Hagerstown for Boonsboro and South Mountain. Lieut. Col. Thomas C. Watkins commanded the regiment. It arrived at Boonsboro about 4:00 P.M. and was immediately marched up the mountain to Turner's Gap and put into battle. It was a desperate time for the Rebel Army. The Confederates were outnumbered and the Union Army threatened to overrun the Confederates on the Mountain. The 22nd South Carolina went into battle northeast of Turner's Gap along the ridge to the north of what is today called Dahlgren Road. Below them were the Pennsylvania Reserves.(10)

In his official report of the battle, Maj. M. Hilton wrote:

"...we came in contact with the enemy and immediately opened on them, the enemy occupying a very favorable position against us. After engaging them for about half an hour, we were ordered to fall back, which we did some 30 yards, though in some confusion, Lieut. Col. T. C. Watkins calling to the men to rally to their colors and to fall into line. While thus exposing himself, and having succeeded in forming the regiment in line of battle, he fell, struck by a musket-ball in the head. Thus fell a brave and skillful

Tombstone (center) of Lt. Colonel T. C. Watkins 22nd South Carolina Regiment who died of wounds received at Turner's Gap, September 14, 1862. (SRS)

officer at the head of his command, encouraging and rallying his men with the last breath of life."(11) The Confederates withdrew from the mountain that night and left their dead and wounded on the field.

Watkins' family had always assumed that he had been buried somewhere on the battlefield of South Mountain. As far as they knew Lieut. Col. T. C. Watkins was "Missing In Action," a Civil War MIA. Thomas's son, John C. Watkins, was only ten years old at the time of the battle. Imagine, then, his surprise , when in May, 1910, at the age of fifty-eight, while on a visit to Frederick, Maryland, he accidently came across his father's grave at Mount Olivet. Lieut. Watkins did not die on the battlefield. He was taken to Frederick, where he died on September 26, 1862, two days before Jacob Englebrecht noticed his headboard.(12)

John Watkins said that he was very much touched and gratified to find his father's grave resting in a beautiful cemetery, guarded by the Confederate monument and cared for by the Daughters of the Confederacy. Unfortunately, his mother had died not knowing of her husband's resting place.

Lieut. Col. Watkins tombstone is number 45 in the line at Mount Olivet.

Other Monuments

At the entrance to Mount Olivet visitors will notice a monument to Francis Scott Key, the author of our national anthem, "The Star Spangled Banner." Mr. Key is entombed beneath the monument.

Of special note elsewhere in the cemetery is a monument to another legend of the Maryland Campaign, Barbara Fritchie. In a poem by John Greenleaf Whitter that describes an event pur-

Francis Scott Key Monument. (SRS)

Barbara Fritchie Monument. Her relatives said it never happened. (SRS)

ported to have taken place as the Confederates were leaving Frederick on September 10, 1862, "Dame Barbara" was immortalized for defending the Stars and Stripes. While waving the flag from her attic window she uttered the following defiant words at Confederate General Stonewall Jackson, "Shoot if you must, this old gray head, but spare your country's flag..." Although it has been shown many times that Jackson did not pass by Fritchie's house and that "Dame Barbara" was ninety-six years old and bedridden at the time, this legend has persisted.

Reverend Freeman Ankrum best summed up the situation when he wrote, "A Quaker poet who likely never saw the city, a ninety-six year old lady, and a Confederate general who never saw either, poet or lady, made as fine an advertising project as any city could desire."(13)

Nevertheless, against vigorous protest from the Fitzhugh Lee chapter of the U. D. C., Barbara Fritchie was reinterred at Mount Olivet and a monument was erected over her grave. On September 9, 1914, it was dedicated; however, many relatives and friends refused to attend. When asked why they simply replied, "she didn't do it."(14)

General T. J. "Stonewall" Jackson. (DCT)   Barbara Fritchie. (DCT)

Monument to the unknown dead at Shepherdstown, West Virginia. (SRS)

5

Elmwood Cemetery

As early as Saturday, September 13, 1862, elements of the Army of Northern Virginia arrived at Shepherdstown. By Monday afternoon the 15th, the walking wounded from South Mountain had begun to collect in the small town. Eventually the entire army would pass through as it retreated after the Battle of Antietam. The more severely wounded were left in town. Those that died and were not sent home were buried in the local graveyard, Elmwood Cemetery.

In 1867 the Southern Soldier's Memorial Association of Shepherdstown, West Virginia, was organized. They purchased ground at Elmwood in 1868 for the purpose of reinterring Confederate dead. In addition to those already in the cemetery, others were collected for reinterment and on Memorial Day, June 6, 1870, the Confederate Cemetery at Elmwood was officially dedicated.(1)

A crowd of 3,500 persons attended. It had been raining for a week and it threatened more rain that morning. But about noon the clouds broke and the day became quite pleasant; however, the threat of rain that morning had kept the number in attendance lower than expected. It was noted that there was a large number of persons from Washington County, Maryland.(2)

Rev. Dr. Bittle gave the opening prayer and Captain Dulaney's Band of Sharpsburg played the dirge. A monument was unveiled and Captain Joseph McMurran provided the oratory. On the west face of the monument was the following inscription, "To the unknown dead, though nameless, their deeds are not forgotten." As reported in the Sheperdstown *Register*, Captain McMurran noted:

> "...It is one of the noblest instincts of our nature that leads us to honor the good and brave...this monument is the first of the kind in this valley, and it is right that it should be, as it stands on the south bank of the classic Potomac...a way mark to inform travelers that they are entering the southland...We dedicate it in the spirit of peace."(3)

The benediction was given by Rev. W. G. Gross and, after strewing the grave with flowers, the crowd retired to a nearby grove. Other addresses were delivered by Judge Edward White, of

Cast iron Confederate grave marker located in Elmwood Cemetery. This was a popular item offered for sale in veterans magazines after the war. (SRS)

Clarke County, Virginia, and W. H. Travers, of Charlestown, West Virginia. Music was provided by Captain Dulaney's Band and Captain Criswell's Cornet Band of Shepherdstown.

The dead of Elmwood's Confederate Cemetery are listed as 106 known, with name and command, and 56 unknown. Elsewhere throughout the Cemetery are located an additional 90 known Confederate dead. Once again it should come as no surprise that there are more known than unknown since this was friendly territory.

The Shepherdstown Cavalry

A visitor to Elmwood Cemetery will notice that quite a few of the local Confederate veterans served with Company F of the 1st Virginia Cavalry. Originally organized as the Shepherdstown Cavalry in 1858, it was composed largely of farmboys from the local area. It is said to have been among the first units to arrive at Harper's Ferry following news of John Brown's raid. At the outbreak of the Civil War it became Company F, 1st Virginia Cavalry and served as such until the end of the war.(4)

General Kirkland

In the back area of the cemetery there is a granite monument that marks the resting place of Brigadier General William Whedbee Kirkland, C.S.A.

The general was from North Carolina. He was appointed to West Point but never graduated. He served in the United States Marines until 1860. At the beginning of the Civil War he joined the Confederate Army as a Captain of infantry. Later he became Colonel of the 21st North Carolina Infantry.

Kirkland led his regiment at the battle of First Bull Run and took part in Gen. Stonewall Jackson's Valley Campaign. He was wounded at the First Battle of Winchester. He rejoined his regiment in time for the Gettysburg Campaign, and was later wounded at the Battle of Bristoe Station. Promoted to Brigadier General on August 29, 1863. The general was again wounded at Gaine's Mill in 1864 but continued in the army until near the close of the war.

General Kirkland's monument. The general was
wounded three times during the war and still lived into
the next century. (SRS)

After the war Gen. Kirkland settled in Savannah, Georgia. Later he moved to Shepherdstown
and lived on the Wild Goose Farm operated by his son-in-law R.D. Shepherd. He was invalided
near the turn of the century and spent the last years of his life in a soldier's home in Washington
D. C.(5)

He Rode With Stonewall

Near the grave of Gen. Kirkland in the rear area of the cemetery rest the remains of Henry Kyd
Douglas. His boyhood home, "Ferry Hill," is located on the Maryland side of the Potomac River
overlooking the bridge that leads into Shepherdstown. After the war he settled in Hagerstown
where he became one of the first trustees for the Washington Confederate Cemetery. In addition to
these duties, Douglas practiced law, was the head of the First Regiment, Maryland National
Guard, was Associate Judge of the Fourth Circuit Court, and served four years as Adjutant General
of Maryland. A popular and effective speaker, he was often called upon to deliver oratory at many
public occasions. He was appointed a Brigadier General of Volunteers in the Spanish American
War but his health did not permit his participation. Henry Kyd Douglas never married. He died in
1904 at age sixty-four in his home on Potomac Avenue in Hagerstown. It was often said by those
who knew him that they "never knew a man who more deserved the too often used words: A
soldier and a gentleman."(6)

In September, 1937, the Henry Kyd Douglas Camp of the Sons of Confederate Veterans
dedicated a memorial to the men of the Shepherdstown area who had served in the Confederate

Henry Kyd Douglas. Confederate staff officer and post war Adjutant General of Maryland. (SRS)

Monument to Henry Kyd Douglas. Douglas wrote the classic "I Rode With Stonewall." (SRS)

Army. It is located at Elmwood Cemetery. It is made of white concrete and has five bronze tablets that hold the names of five hundred and seventy-seven men who served in the famous "Stonewall Brigade."

The grandson of Gen. Robert E. Lee, Dr. George Bolling Lee, was present for the unveiling.(21) Although no record exists, it is likely that in his heart Dr. Lee echoed the feelings of his other relative who had spoken sixty years earlier at Hagerstown, Fitzhugh Lee, when he reminded those in attendance that we were one country and that it was in our best interest to work together.

Elmwood Cemetery showing the monument to Confederate unknown in the center. The long monument to the left contains five bronze tablets listing the names of men who served in the famous Stonewall Brigade. (SRS)

Stonewall Brigade Monument, Elmwood Cemetery. (SRS)

Epilogue

On Memorial Day of 1989 I went to the Antietam and Hagerstown cemeteries to pay my respects. At Antietam there were little American flags waving in front of each headstone. One is immediately impressed by the enormity and expanse of the cemetery. And one cannot but be impressed by the sacrifice of those soldiers beneath those flags.

At Hagerstown I was also impressed. I was impressed by the loneliness and the emptiness of two acres of neatly mowed grass. I was also moved by their sacrifice. They never stopped being Americans. While we may or may not agree with the motives behind their sacrifice, we cannot deny their "last full measure of devotion" as well.

For those of my generation there is something particularly disquieting about the phrase "missing in action." As I stood in front of "Hope," I took a moment to reflect on those Civil War MIA's in front of me.

I walked over to a spot I frequent regularly, where there are twenty-nine boxes that contain the remains of fifty-eight unknown, and I laid a wreath which I personally dedicated to all those Americans who lost their identities in our wars. I looked around. In one corner of the Washington Cemetery stood a lone Texas flag to commemorate the nine identified Texans laid there. At another spot where some Virginians were buried, was a wreath. If you didn't know where to look you could miss the only headstone there, since it is the type that is flush with the ground. And that was it.

Maryland has been called "America in miniature." Within our borders we have two cemeteries that symbolize the tragedy of the American Civil War. The Antietam National Cemetery is where the flags of the victors wave, and the Washington Confederate Cemetery is where the vanquished lay in unmarked rows, Americans all.

Notes

Chapter 1

1. Murfin, James V.; *The Gleam of Bayonets*, p.241
2. Some historians choose to call the fighting on September 14, 1862, The Battles on South Mountain. There was also a battle at Crampton's Gap six miles south of Fox's Gap. There are those who would group Crampton's Gap with the siege of Harper's Ferry, September 13-15. My use of the term "South Mountain" refers to the fighting at Fox's Gap, Turner's Gap, and the area Northeast of Turner's Gap along the Dahlgren Road to Frostown. My casualty figures are compiled from the Official Records, Gen. Carmen's manuscript, and the *Middletown Valley Register*

South Mountain	Union	Confederate	Totals
Killed	362	376	738
Wounded	1,633	1,472	3,105
Missing	104	909	1,013
Total	2,099	2,757	4,856

There were almost 25,000 Union troops engaged at South Mountain against less than 10,000 Confederate troops, this means that the Union troops suffered 8% casualties of those engaged versus almost 28% of the Confederates engaged. Had it not been for Antietam, South Mountain would have been remembered as a glorious victory for the Union.

Antietam	Union	Confederate	Totals
Killed	2,108	1,546	3,654
Wounded	9,549	7,754	17,303
Missing	753	1,018	1,771
Total	12,410	10,318	22,728

At Antietam there were 55,956 Union troops engaged (22% casualties) and 37,351 Confederate troops engaged (28% casualties).

3. Lord, Francis A.; *They Fought for the Union*, pp. 256-257
4. Wren, James; Diary at Antietam Battlefield Library, entry for 9/15/1862
5. *Confederate Veteran*, May 1908, p.208 and p.230
6. Compton, Samuel; Memoir, manuscript at Duke University p. 99-100
7. Lord, Edward O.; *History of the Ninth Regiment, New Hampshire Volunteers*, p. 91

8. Noyes, George F.; *The Bivouac and the Battlefield*, p. 181
9. Ellis, Thomas T.; *Leaves From the Diary of an Army Surgeon*, p. 259
10. *Confederate Veteran*, January 1915, p. 71
11. *Confederate Veteran*, January 1896, p. 27
12. Trowbridge, John T.; *The Desolate South*, p.23
13. Deady, Michael; Diary, manuscript at Haye's Presidential Center, entries 9/16/1862-9/18/1862
14. Clugston, John McNutty; Diary, manuscript at Haye's Prsidential Center, entry for 9/18/62
15. Eby, Cecil D.; *A Virginia Yankee in the Civil War, The Diaries of David Hunter Strother*, p. 112
16. Eby, p. 113
17. Racine, J. Polk; *Recollections of a Veteran or Four Years in Dixie*, p. 47-48
18. Edmonds, S. Emma E.; *Nurse and Spy in the Union Army*, pp. 271-272
19. Lammers, Pat; "Women Spies of the Civil War," United Daughters of the Confederacy Magazine
20. Donnet, G.L.; *Noble Women of the North*, pp. 48-49, Hanging File Antietam Battlefield Library
21. During her tour of duty for the Secret Service Sarah assumed many disguises that helped her get behind enemy lines without detection. She blackened her skin with silver nitrate, donned a black wig, and adopted African-American mannerisms to pose as a servant boy. Another disguise was that of an old Irish peddler woman. She actually cut slits in her face to look older. About a year after the battle of Antietam Sarah came down with malaria. Rather than be hospitalized and risk discovery Sarah applied for a furlough. Her request was denied so she decided to desert. She nursed herself back to health. Years after the war her ill health led her to apply for a pension from the government. She was able to convince the 48th Congress that she had been Frank Thompson. Congress granted her a pension of $12.00 a month. Later at a reunion of the 2nd Michigan infantry her fellow soldiers were dumfounded to find that Frank was Sarah.
22. Bingham, Origen G.; Letter at Western Maryland Room of Washington County Free Library
23. Whistler, S. M.; *Pennsylvania at Antietam*, p. 164
24. Cross, Fred Wilder; *Antietam*, manuscript at Antietam Battlefield Library
25. Cross and Frassanito, William A.; *Antietam: The Photographic Legacy of America's Bloodiest Battle*, p. 256
26. Nesbitt, Otho; *Maryland Time Exposures 1840-1940*, pp. 276-279
27. Reilly, O.T.; *The Battlefield of Antietam*
28. Spaur, Michael L.; "What's in the Name? Reno Monument Road," Frederick News Post, January 2, 1980
29. Weeks, James; Letter at the Western Maryland Room of the Washington County Free Library. In his book *Drums along the Antietam* Rev. Johm W. Schildt writes, "The author feels that Cullen Robinson was buried on a hill overlooking the Little Antietam in Keedysville. The body was supposed to be sent to Palmyra, New York. However, there is no record of the young man's burial in that city. In the spring of 1971 another James Weeks, the great-great-grandson of the James Weeks who came to Keedysville in 1862, came trying to find the grave of William Cullen Robinson. Thus far the search has been fruitless. There is no record of his burial in the National Cemetery, unless he is one of the unknown. Most likely, Cullen Robinson who served in the Ninth New York Militia, known as the Eighty-Third New York [Regiment], lies buried overlooking the Little Antietam. Such is the tragedy and horror of war."
30. Moon, Bowen B.; Letter at Antietam Battlefield Library. If one looks at the Antietam Cemetery roster they will find a numbered headstone for William A. Salisbury. It is number 827 in the New York section. Mr. Moon removed his brother-in-law and left the headboard with the other two bodies. We do not know who is under headstone number 827, but we do know that it is not William A. Salisbury.
31. Mr. Moon's letter is headed "Russia, N. Y. Sept. 3, 1907"

32. Bates, Samuel P.; *Pennsylvania Volunteers Vol. 1*, and oral history of Kay family as told to author by Isack Kay's greatgrandson, Mr. Joseph E. Hamilton.

33. Glenn, E. T. B.; "Death of Captain Glenn," *Camp-fire Sketches and Battlefield Echoes of 61-65*, p. 350. If Captain Glenn was reinterred at Hagerstown, he was done so as unknown, since his name does not appear on either Bowie's List or Coxon's Map. Indeed, as of this writing, the author has not been able to identify one Confederate soldier at Hagerstown as being reintered from South Mountain. They all are unknown. As the reader will discover, the only Confederate as yet identified from South Mountain rest at Mt. Olivet Cemetery in Frederick, Maryland.

34. Frye, Susan W. and Dennis E.; *Maryland Heights*, pp. 65-66

35. Reilly

36. Reilly

37. Koogle, John; Diary, manuscript at Middletown Historical Society

Chapter 2

1. Author Unknown, *History of Antietam Cemetery*, p.5

2. Trowbridge, John T., *The Desolate South*, pp. 25-26

3. Snell, Charles W. and Brown, Sharon A.; *Antietam National Battlefield and National Cemetery, Sharpsburg, Maryland: An Administrative History*, pp. 1-2

4. Snell and Brown, p. 16

5. *Boonsboro Oddfellow*, J. M. Mentzer Publisher, October 11, 1866

6. Reilly

7. Reilly

8. *Boonsboro Oddfellow*, November 22, 1866

9. *Boonsboro Oddfellow*, November 22, 1866; Mr. Stickney may be found in the Maine section of the Antietam Cemetery, tombstone #3172

10. *Boonsboro Oddfellow*, November 22, 1866; Oliver W. Sanford was from Mineral Point, Wisconsin. He enlisted into Company I of the 2nd Wisconsin on April 22, 1861. He was soon promoted to 1st Sergeant. On March 25, 1862, he was promoted to 2nd Lieutenant. He was mortally wounded at Antietam and died on October 13, 1862. He is buried in the officer section near "Simon," Stone #853.

11. *Boonsboro Oddfellow*, December 13, 1866

12. Douglas, Henry Kyd; *I Road With Stonewall*, pp. 166-167

13. *Boonsboro Oddfellow*, October 11, 1866

14. Douglas, p.167

15. *Middletown Valley Register*, G. C. Rhoderick publisher, May 17, 1866

16. *History of Antietam Cemetery*, p. 202

17. *Boonsboro Oddfellow*, September 10, 1867

18. *Boonsboro Oddfellow*, September 10, 1867

19. *Middletown Valley Register*, September 20, 1867

20. The local oral history for the origin of the nickname goes back to a Nineteenth century hero known as Simon Pure. The story goes that because the statue was of white granite it reminded the local children of something pure. The children dropped the last part of the name and started calling the statue Simon.

21. Otto, Betty and Anibal, Charles; *Antietam National Cemetery*, p. 4

22. Reilly

23. Potter, Stephen R.; U.S. Park Service Handout

Chapter 3

1. *A Descriptive List of the Burial Places of the Remains of Confederate Soldiers*, hereafter referred to as Bowie's List, p. 45
2. De Peyster, J. Watts; *The Decisive Conflicts of the Late Civil War, or Slaveholders' Rebellion*, p. 55
3. Walcott, Charles F.; *History of the Twenty-First Regiment Massachusetts Volunteers*, p. 194: "…The burial of a portion of the rebel dead was peculiar enough to call for special mention. Some Ohio troops had been detailed to bury them, but not relishing the task, and finding the ground hard to dig, soon removed the covering of a deep well connected with the Wise's house on the summit, and lightened their toil by throwing a few bodies into the well. Mr. Wise soon discovered what they were about, and had it stopped; and then the Ohians went away, leaving their work unfinished. Poor Mr. Wise, anxious to get rid of the bodies finally made an agreement with General Burnside to bury them for a dollar apiece. As long as his well had been already spoiled, he concluded to realize on the rest of its capacity, and put in fifty-eight more rebel bodies, which filled it to the surface of the ground."
4. De Peyster, p. 56
5. De Peyster, p. 56
6. Bowie's List, p. 8
7. Bowie's List, pp. 8-9
8. Bowie's List, p. 8
9. Bowie's List, p. 35
10. Bowie's List, p. 51
11. *Laws of the State of Maryland, 1870*, pp. 370-374
12. *The Hagerstown Mail*, September 6, 1872
13. Report of the Trustees of Washington Cemetery at the Western Maryland Room of the Washington County Free Library
14. *The Hagerstown Mail*, September 6, 1872
15. Clem, Richard E.; "Confederates Buried in Hagerstown," *Cracker Barrel*, p. 16
16. Report of the Trustees of Washington Cemetery
17. *Middletown Valley Register*, July 31, 1874
18. *The Hagerstown Mail*, June 26, 1874
19. Scharf, J. Thomas; *History of Western Maryland*, p. 1102
20. *Frank Leslie's Illustrated Weekly*, July 7, 1877
21. Report of the Trustees of Washington Cemetery
22. Scharf, p. 1102
23. *The Hagerstown Mail*, June 15, 1877
24. Clem, Richard E.; "2,000 Confederates Buried Here, but Just One has Marker on Grave," *Cracker Barrel*, pp. 12-15
25. Walcott, pp. 191-192
26. *Confederate Veteran*, January 1915, p. 71
27. *Confederate Veteran*, January 1915, pp. 71-72
28. De Peyster, p. 55
29. Carmen, Ezra; The Maryland Campaign, manuscript at Western Maryland Room of the Washington County Free Library
30. Bowie's List, p. 49
31. Ward, Geoffrey C., Burns, Ric, and Burns, Ken; *The Civil War*, Alfred A. Knopf, New York, 1990, p.39; This is the most recent history of the Civil War that repeats this legend.
32. Lee, Stephen D.; "Who Fired the First Gun at Sumter?" *Southern Historical Society Papers*, p. 501
33. Halsey, Ashley, *Who Fired the First Shot*, pp. 27-36, Hawthorn Books Inc., New York, 1963
34. *Middletown Valley Register*, May 19, 1893
35. *Confederate Veteran*, May 1902, p. 221

36. Cross, *Antietam*
37. Bowie's List, p. 16
38. Cross observed the headboard as reading "A. W. Speight, 3rd N. C. Reg." The entry in Bowie's List reads, "A. W. Spraight, 3rd N. C.," and this is the same as the spelling on Coxon's Map. God only knows which is correct!
39. Reilly

Chapter 4

1. Williams, T. J. C.; *History of Frederick County Maryland*, p. 227
2. Englebrecht, Jacob; Diary at Western Maryland Room of Washington County Free Library, p. 190
3. Mount Olivet Cemetery Records
4. *Confederate Veteran*, June 1907, p. 255
5. Haines, Elsie White; *The Frederick Post*, Sidelights August 6, 1962
6. Williams, p. 395
7. *The Frederick Examiner*, June 8, 1881
8. *The Frederick Examiner*, September 24, 1862
9. *The Frederick Examiner*, June 8, 1881
10. Carmen, Ezra; *The Maryland Campaign*, manuscript at the Western Maryland Room of the Washington County Free Library
11. Hilton, M.; *The War of the Rebellion: Official Records*, Vol. XIX p. 948
12. *Confederate Veteran*, July 1910, p. 329
13. Ankrum, Freeman; *Maryland and Pennsylvania Historical Sketches*, p. 64
14. Anson, Cherrill, unlabeled and undated newspaper article from the hanging file of the C. Burr Artz Library, Frederick, Maryland

Chapter 5

1. *Confederate Veteran*, May 1902, p. 113
2. *The Shepherdstown Register*, June 11, 1870
3. *The Shepherdstown Register*, June 11, 1870
4. *Elmwood Cemetery Death Roster*, Antietam National Battlefield Library
5. Warner, Ezra J.; *Generals in Gray*, pp.171-172 and *The Daily Mail*, September 15, 1962
6. Green, Fletcher M.; *I Rode With Stonewall*, pp.356-358, and *Confederate Veteran*, March 1904, p. 125
7. *The Shepherdstown Register*, September 23, 1937

Bibliography

Books:

Ankrum, Freeman; *Maryland and Pennsylvania Historical Sketches*, Masontown, Pennsylvania, 1947

Bates, Samuel P.; *Pennsylvania Volunteers*, Harrisburg, Pennsylvania, 1869

De Peyster, John Watts; *Decisive Conflicts of the Late Civil War, or Slaveholder's Rebellion*, New York, 1867

Douglas, Henry Kyd; *I Rode With Stonewall*, the University of North Carolina Press, 1940

Eby, Cecil D., editor; *A Virginia Yankee in the Civil War, the Diaries of David Hunter Strother*, the University of North Carolina Press, 1961

Edmonds, Sarah E.; *Nurse and Spy in the Union Army*, Hartford, Connecticut, 1866

Ellis, Thomas D.; *Leaves From the Diary of an Army Surgeon*, New York, 1863

Frassanito, William A.; *Antietam: The Photographic Legacy of America's Bloodiest Day*, Charles Scribner's Sons, New York, 1978

Halsey Jr., Ashley; *Who Fired the First Shot? and other untold stories of the Civil War*, Hawthorn Books Inc., New York, New York, 1963

King W.C. and Derby, W. P. editors; *Camp-Fire Sketches and Battlefield Echoes of 1861-65*, Boston, Massachusetts, 1886

Lee, Stephen D.; *Southern Historical Society Papers*, Vol. XI, 1883

Lord, Edward O.; *History of the Ninth Regiment New Hampshire Volunteers*, Concord, New Hampshire, 1895

Lord, Francis A.; *They Fought for the Union*, Bonanza Books, New York, 1960

Murfin, James V.; *The Gleam of Bayonets,* Louisiana State University Press, 1965

Noyes, George F.; *Bivouac and Battlefield,* Harper & Brothers, 1863

Racine, J. Polk; *Recollections of a Veteran or Four Years in Dixie,* Elkton, Maryland, 1894

Reilly, Oliver T.; *The Battlefield of Antietam,* Hagerstown Bookbinding and Printing, Hagerstown, Maryland, 1906

Scharf, J. Thomas; *History of Western Maryland,* Reprint, Baltimore, Maryland, 1968

Snell, Charles W. and Brown, Sharon A.; *Antietam National Battlefield and National Cemetery, Sharpsburg, Maryland, An Administrative History,* U.S. Department of the Interior, National Park Service, 1986

State of Maryland, *A Descriptive List of the Burial Places of the Remains of Confederate Soldiers,* published by direction of His Excellency, Oden Bowie, Governor of Maryland, Free Press, Hagerstown, Maryland, 1869

Trowbridge, John T.; *The Desolate South,* Little, Brown and Company, Boston, 1956

Trustees, *History of Antietam National Cemetery,* Baltimore, 1869

Walcott, Charles F.; *History of the Twenty-First Regiment Massachusetts Volunteers,* Boston, Massachusetts, 1882

War of the Rebellion: A Compilation of the Official Records of the Union and Confederate Armies, Volume XIX, Part I-Reports

Ward, Geoffrey C.; *The Civil War,* Alfred A. Knopf, New York, 1990

Warren, Marrion E.; *Maryland Time Exposures 1840-1940,* The John Hopkins University Press, 1984

Warner, Ezra J.; *Generals in Gray,* Louisiana State University Press, 1959

Whistler, S. H.; *Pennsylvania at Antietam, Report of the Battlefield Memorial Commission of Pennsylvania,* 1906

Williams, T.J.C.; *History of Frederick County Maryland,* L.R. Titsworth & Co., 1910

Magazines:

Confederate Veteran:
    Confederates Buried at Shepherdstown, April 1911
    Confederate Cemetery at Frederick, MD., July 1910
    Confederate Dead in Maryland, December 1897
    Dead Angle-Rules for Burial of the Dead, May 1908
    Grave of Sergeant Damascas Wetherly, June 1907
    M. Deady, January 1896 and August 1923
    Monument at Shepherdstown, W. VA., February 1902

On the Battlefield of South Mountain, January 1915
Rules for Burying Dead of the Enemy, May 1908
Two Georgia Martyrs of Sharpsburg, May 1902

Cracker Barrel:
Confederates Buried in Hagerstown by Richard E. Clem, July 1983
Georgia Officer is Only Confederate With Own Marker at Hagerstown by Richard E. Clem, June 1984

The United Daughters of the Confederacy Magazine:
Women Spies of the War Between the States by Pat Lammers, February 1982; Hanging File at the Antietam Battlefield Library

Manuscripts:

Bingham, Origan G.; Letter Hanging file at the Western Maryland Room of the Washington County Free Library

Carmen, Ezra; *The Maryland Campaign,* Copy at the Western Maryland Room of the Washington County Free Library

Clugston, John McNutty, Diary, Courtesy of the Rutherford P. Hayes Presidential Center, Freemont Ohio

Compton, Samuel, Memoirs, Duke University Manuscript Department, Durham, North Carolina

Cross, Fred Wilder; *Antietam,* Courtesy Mr. Doug Bast, Boonsboro, Maryland, and Antietam Battlefield Library, Sharpsburg, Maryland

Deady, Michael; Diary, Courtesy of the Rutherford P. Hayes Presidential Center, Freemont, Ohio

Englebrecht, Jacob; Diary, Copy at the Western Maryland Room of the Washington County Free Library

Koogle, John; Diary, Courtesy of the Middletown Historical Society, Middletown, Maryland

Moon, Bowen B.; Letter at Antietam Battlefield Library

Weeks, James; Letter, Hanging file at the Western Maryland Room of the Washington County Free Library

Wren, James; Diary at Antietam Battlefield Library

Miscellaneous:

Elmwood Cemetery Death Roster, Antietam Battlefield Library

Hanging File, Antietam Battlefield Library

Hanging File, C. Burr Artz Library, Frederick, Maryland

Otto, Betty, and Anibal, Charles; *Antietam National Cemetery*, Pamphlet by the National Park Service

Potter, Stephen R., Initial Report of Archaeological Excavation of Irish Brigade Remains at Antietam National Battlefield, Summer 1988, Handout by National Park Service

Trustees of the Washington Confederate Cemetery, Report, December 9, 1873, Hanging file at Western Maryland Room of the Washington County Free Library

U.S. Census for 1850, 1860, and 1870

U.S. Soldier Monument, Handout by National Park Service

Newspapers:

Frank Leslie's Illustrated Newspaper, copy in hanging file at Western Maryland Room of the Washington County Free Library

The Boonsboro Oddfellow, Washington County Free Library, Hagerstown, Maryland

The Frederick Examiner, C. Burr Artz Library, Frederick, Maryland

The Frederick Post, C. Burr Artz Library, Frederick, Maryland

The Hagerstown Daily Mail, Washington County Free Library, Hagerstown, Maryland

The Hagerstown Mail, Washington County Free Library, Hagerstown, Maryland

The Shepherdstown Register, Shepherdstown Library, Shepherdstown, West Virginia

The Valley Register, Middletown, Maryland

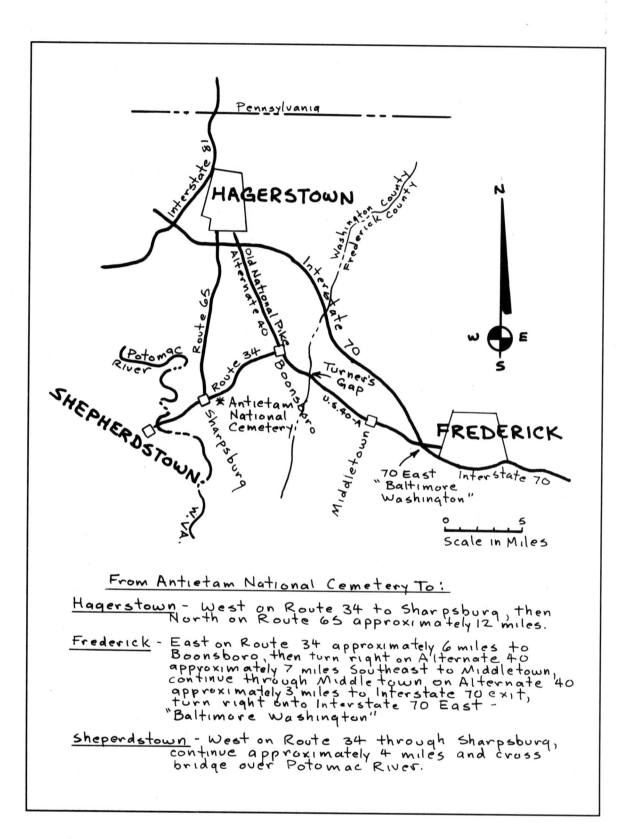

From Antietam National Cemetery To:

Hagerstown - West on Route 34 to Sharpsburg, then North on Route 65 approximately 12 miles.

Frederick - East on Route 34 approximately 6 miles to Boonsboro, then turn right on Alternate 40 approximately 7 miles Southeast to Middletown, continue through Middletown on Alternate 40 approximately 3 miles to Interstate 70 exit, turn right onto Interstate 70 East - "Baltimore Washington"

Sheperdstown - West on Route 34 through Sharpsburg, continue approximately 4 miles and cross bridge over Potomac River.

Introduction to Cemetery Rosters

A complete list of the known Civil War soldiers in the four cemeteries discussed in this book follows this introduction. Most of the material for the rosters was provided by the staff of the Antietam National Battlefield. Without their help, these rosters would have been a difficult undertaking indeed. All rosters have been alphabetized to facilitate ease of use.

The roster for the Washington Confederate Cemetery does not provide much more than a soldier's name and home state. Because of the nature of the burials, it is next to impossible to determine the exact location of an individual even if one is identified. Those fortunate enough to find someone at Elmwood or Mt. Olivet will fare better in their search for information. Individual graves are easily identifiable at these cemeteries.

By far, the Antietam roster provides the most information on the individuals buried there. The last category will provide the reader with the location the soldier was removed from and any comments that were included. Smoketown should be considered synonymous with Antietam. At the time of the battle, Smoketown was a small hamlet close to the battlefield. Many field hospitals were established there. Locations outside of Maryland are identified with the appropriate state abbreviation.

When known, following the place of exhumation will be the name of the battle that the soldier participated in. When the place of burial and the battle are the same, only one name is use. Other information, such as a age or place of origin, has been provided in the space available. Standard abbreviations are used for individual rank and regimentation.

If you desire further information on an individual in the rosters you can contact the superintendent of Antietam at the following address:

Antietam National Battlefield
P.O. Box 158
Sharpsburg, MD 21782-0158

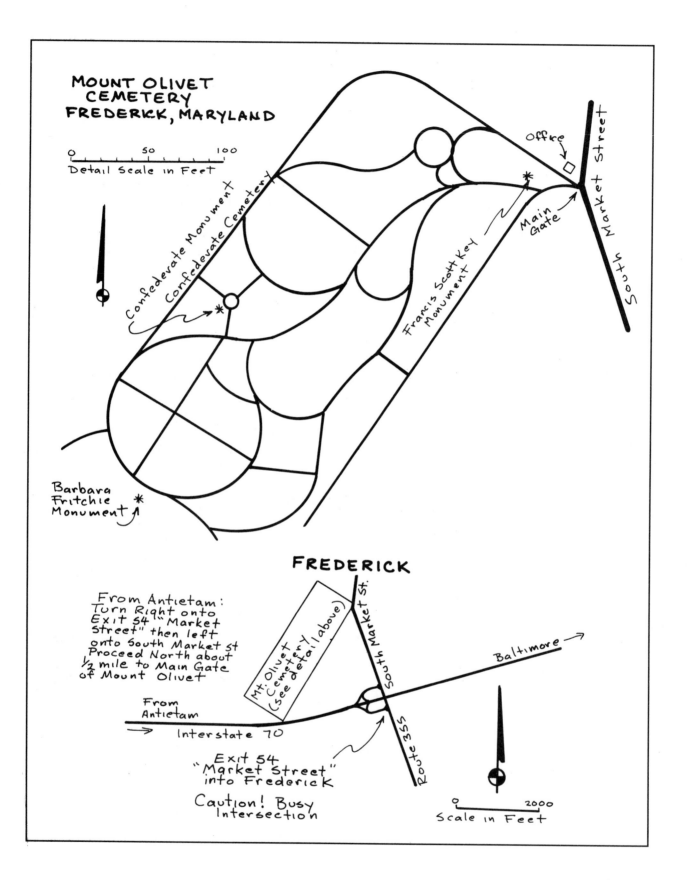

MOUNT OLIVET
CEMETERY
FREDERKK, MARYLAND

0   50   100
Detail Scale in Feet

Confederate Monument
Confederate Cemetery

Office

South Market Street

Francis Scott Key Monument

Main Gate

Barbara Fritchie Monument

FREDERICK

From Antietam:
Turn Right onto
Exit 54 "Market
Street" then left
onto South Market St
Proceed North about
½ mile to Main Gate
of Mount Olivet

Mt. Olivet Cemetery (See detail above)

South Market St.

Baltimore

From Antietam
Interstate 70

Exit 54 "Market Street" into Frederick

Caution! Busy Intersection

Route 355

0   2000
Scale in Feet

Mt. Olivet Cemetery

List of Confederate soliders who were interred at Mt. Olivet, Frederick, Maryland.

Name	Rank/Co.	Regiment	Date of Death	Grave No.
Adams, Elihu	Pvt. B. 3	3 Ark. Inf.	10-27-1862	147
Albright, David	Pvt A.	7 LA. Inf.	3-17-1863	193
Albright, Geo. M. G.	Capt. F.	53 NC Inf.	7-16-1863	204
Allen, Alexander,	Pvt. H.	17 VA Cav.	7-16-1864	249
Allen, William	Pvt. H.	G. 8 VA Cav.	5-11-1864	279
Anderson, Benj. J.	Lieut. D.	19 VA	10-20-1862	139
Anderson, James L.	Lieut. E.	6 GA	10-16-1862	122
Anderson, James P.	Pvt. F.	9 LA Inf.	7-17-1864	251
Anselen, Amos K.	Pvt. F.	8 LA Inf.	11-19-1862	170
Ard, E. F.	Pvt. G.	15 SC	2-25-1863	190
Bachus, John W.	Pvt. A.	12 Battn. GA L. Art.	9-1-1864	290
Baker, H. C.	Pvt. H.	30 NC Inf.	12-17-1862	184
Bankston, Green B.	Pvt. D.	6 GA Inf.	10-9-1862	99
Barker, J. M.	Pvt. D.	22 SC	9-22-1862	Area O
Barkley, C. H.	Pvt. G.	12 NC Inf.	9-30-1862	69
Belcher, Wesley	Pvt. C.	22 VA Cav.	7-17-1864	253
Bell, B.W.	Pvt. K.	1 NC Inf.	11-2-1862	159
Biggs, Wm. F.	Pvt. K.	2 Miss. Inf.	10-13-1862	118
Blanton, A.	Pvt. F.	15 SC	10-1-1862	72
Boatwright, G. W.	Pvt. E.	12 Battn. GA L. Art.	7-12-1864	243
Boger, Jacob	Pvt. A.	20 NC Inf.	11-4-1862	160
Boles, J. Francis	Pvt. K.	48 NC Inf.	11-16-1863	168
Bonds, John	Pvt. B.	20 NC Inf.	11-26-1863	173
Bourne, W. J.	Pvt. F.	12 Battn. GA L. Art.	8-13-1864	282
Bowers, J. A.	Pvt. I.	15 SC	10-10-1862	105
Bowles, G. R.	Sgt. F.	42 VA	7-13-1863	203
Box, Joseph	Pvt. K	26 GA Inf.	10-14-1862	126
Boyd, Abraham	Pvt. C.	36 GA Inf.	7-28-1863	208
Brooks, John B.	Pvt. E.	18 GA Inf.	10-12-1862	112
Brown, R. M.	Pvt. B.	2 SC	11-7-1862	162
Bryant, Thomas	Pvt. B.	14 NC Inf.	10-19-1862	135
Budd, Joseph	Pvt. K.	Hampton SC Legn.	9-28-1862	57
Byrd, Daniel	Pvt. C.	5 NC Inf.	10-8-1862	94
Cadles, W. H.	Pvt. D.	12 Battn. GA L. Art.	7-22-1864	260
Castel, Barney	Pvt. D.	North GA Vol.	9-23-1862	29

Name	Rank/Co.	Regiment	Date of Death	Grave No.
Cavanaugh, J. P.	Pvt. F.	17 SC	10-14-1862	119
Chisolm, Octavus	Corp. E.	5 LA Inf.	8-2-1864	274
Churchill, C.	Corp. E.	5 LA Inf.	9-23-1862	31
Claig, Jno. F.	Pvt. D.	16 VA Cav.	7-12-1864	247
Clark, C. W.	Pvt. H.	13 GA Inf.	8-2-1864	273
Clay, Moses	Sgt. E.	12 GA	7-10-1864	230
Coleman, Wm. D	Pvt. D.	21 VA	7-26-1864	264
Coleman, William J.	Pvt. G.	60 GA Inf.	10-7-1862	90
Collins, A.D.	Pvt. H.	17 SC	10-2-1862	78
Collins, Ziba J.	Sgt. K.	61 GA Inf.	7-24-1864	263
Corbet, Manning	Pvt. G.	50 GA Inf.	10-1-1862	73
Corfro, J.	2 Lt. I.	1 NC	9-20-1864	27
Cottingim, M. M.	Pvt. A.	2 Miss. Inf.	11-18-1864	169
Cowan, George H.	Pvt. K.	3 NC Inf.	10-17-1862	146
Creamer, J. B.	Pvt. G.	27 GA Inf.	10-17-1862	127
Cross, George W.	2 Lt. K.	20 NC	8-13-1864	283
Crumby, H.	Pvt. C.	5 AL Inf.	9-28-1862	58
Curry, Daniel	Pvt. K.	6 LA Inf.	7-16-1864	250
Dancy, W.	Pvt. G.	18 NC Inf.	8-24-1863	214
Daniel, G. N.	Pvt. E.	19 GA	9-10-1862	4
Davidson, R.	Pvt. C.	4 Tex	2-3-1863	189
Davis, John C.	Pvt. B.	5 FL Inf.	10-26-1862	145
Davis, Joseph A.	Sgt. I.	AL Inf.	9-23-1862	42
Davis, Wm. A.	Pvt. A.	12 Battn. L. Art	8-15-1864	285
Davis, Wm. F.	Pvt. A.	60 GA Inf.	7-10-1864	227
Denny, A. T.	Pvt. B.	13 GA Inf.	10-13-1862	115
Dilworth, Isaac K.	Sgt. G.	17 VA	7-18-1864	257
Dix, T. S.	Pvt. K.	13 GA Inf.	7-12-1864	242
Dunn, Thomas J.	Pvt. E.	18 Miss Inf.	6-19-1863	200
Eason, G.S.	Pvt. H.	15 AL	10-21-1862	141
Eason, James	Pvt. H.	30 NC Inf.	7-18-1864	255
Easteds, M.	Pvt. E.	27 SC	9-27-1862	48
Eidson, Wm.	Pvt. A	38 GA Inf.	10-6-1862	91
Evans, J. L.	Pvt. B.	51 GA	10-11-1862	103
Fitske, J. R.	Pvt. I.	12 AL	10-19-1864	132
Fontenot Hyplite	Pvt. F.	8 LA Inf.	8-5-1864	276
French, Wm.	Pvt. A.	17 VA Cav.	7-27-1864	265
Fulghum, J. T.	Pvt. E.	12 Battn. GA L. Art.	7-19-1864	256
Fuller, B. H.	Pvt. D.	12 Battn. GA L. Art.	8-20-1864	286
Gammel, Marcelus	Pvt. G.	3 Ark. Inf.	12-5-1862	178
Gardner, Alex. S.	Pvt. A.	Nelson's 31 Battn. VA Art.	7-9-1864	217
Gay, Isaac H.	Pvt. G.	38 GA Inf.	7-12-1864	244
Gill, Wm. J.	2 Lt. D.	30 NC Inf.	10-13-1862	144
Goode, Wm. T.	Pvt. K.	2 Miss. Inf.	1-15-1863	187
Goodman, Wm. F.	Pvt. D.	48 VA Inf.	7-12-1864	239
Gossett, H.	Pvt. D.	53 NC	7-7-1863	202
Grantsham, J. B.	Pvt. G.	6 FL	10-23-1862	139
Green, Alfred, R.	Pvt. E.	33 NC Inf.	10-6-1862	89
Griffin, A.C.	Pvt. B.	5 SC	9-30-1862	66
Griggs, Lewis	Pvt. K.	43 NC Inf.	7-23-1863	205
Groves, J.P.	Capt. B.	1 (Nelligan's) LA Inf.	7-18-1864	254
Haggard, Wm.	Pvt. A.	Nelson's VA Battn.	7-9-1864	216
Hales, Owen	Corp. F.	61 GA Inf.	11-19-1864	294
Hall, John	Pvt. K.	14 NC Inf.	9-10-1862	3
Hamby, W. P.	Pvt. K.	27 SC	10-27-1862	148

Name	Rank/Co.	Regiment	Date of Death	Grave No.
Hamric, Thomas H.	Pvt. M.	6 AL Inf.	9-26-1862	46
Hargrove, J.H.	Pvt. D.	12 NC Inf.	10-10-1862	102
Harman, William	Pvt. D.	37 VA	11-9-1862	164
Harper, Thomas W.	Pvt. H.	2 FL Inf.	10-9-1862	98
Harris, Robert	Sgt. C.	2 Miss Inf.	10-9-1862	96
Hartley, W. G.	Pvt. C.	6 GA Inf.	10-24-1864	144
Harvey, Daniel W.	Corp. A.	21 VA Inf.	7-10-1864	221
Hawkins, W. John	Pvt. A	38 GA	10-28-1862	150
Heath, T. B.	Pvt. E.	12 Battn, GA L. Art.	7-29-1864	268
Henry, Marcus H.	Corp. B.	23 NC Inf.	10-18-1862	130
Hernickel, F. C.	Sgt. D.	16 Miss Inf.	10-9-1862	97
Hesterley, R. Y.	Pvt. B	12 AL Inf.	10-11-1862	111
Hicklin, Joseph H.	Pvt. B	6 SC	10-25-1862	142
Hicks, Jacob	Pvt. F.	21 NC Inf.	9-26-1862	51
Higgins, Joseph	Pvt. I.	6 LA Inf.	7-28-1864	269
Hill, William	Pvt. H.	26 AL Inf.	10-5-1862	83
Hobson, Geo. W.	1 Lt. A.	Nelson's Battn. VA Art.	7-9-1864	Not Located; possibly removed.
Hodnett, H. H.	Pvt. K.	13 GA Inf.	7-14-1864	245
Hogan, James	Pvt. C.	12 AL Inf.	10-3-1862	79
Holder, Abel	Pvt. H.	20 NC Inf.	7-10-1864	231
Horne, J. B.	Pvt. C.	3 NC Inf.	9-26-1862	49
Howell, M. D.	Pvt. H.	26 AL Inf.	3-15-1863	192
Hudson, H. J.	Pvt. D.	12 Battn. GA L. Art.	7-31-1864	272
Hughs, R. P.	Pvt. D.	50 GA Inf.	11-5-1862	174
Hunt, Wm. P.	Corp. B	12 NC Inf.	9-26-1862	54
Ingles, Charles	Pvt. B.	8 LA Inf.	9-15-1862	10
Ivey, Thomas J.	Pvt. E.	31 GA Inf.	9-10-1864	292
Jackson, Lemuel	Pvt. H.	49 GA Inf.	10-13-1862	109
Jackson, Lewis M.	Pvt. F.	20 NC Inf.	7-10-1864	235
Jernigan, Joseph	Pvt. F.	20 SC Vols.	10-4-1862	82
Johns, James M.	Pvt. G.	5 FL Inf.	10-5-1862	86
Johnson, J. E.	Pvt. G.	Miss Tigers	7-15-1862	1
Joiner, Malichi, Jr.	Pvt. E.	12 Battn. GA L. Art.	7-19-1864	259
Jones, Allen	Pvt. D.	18 GA Inf.	10-17-1862	129
Jones, David G.	Pvt. E.	51 GA Inf.	10-6-1862	93
Jones, Samuel J.	Pvt. G.	6 AL Inf.	9-28-1863	64
Keel, John D.	Pvt. G.	West LA. Art.	7-10-1864	219
Kelly, A.D.	Pvt. A.	26 AL Inf.	10-10-1862	87
Kelly, Daniel, M.	Pvt. B.	3 NC Inf.	6-19-1863	199
Kennedy, A. V.	Pvt. H.	Hampton SC Legn.	6-19-1863	181
Kinnehorn, Thoms	Pvt. F	12 Battn. GA L. Art.	7-28-1864	264
Kirkley, D. M.	Pvt. G.	2 SC Inf.	12-7-1862	179
Knight, John H.	Pvt. B.	12 Battn. GA l. Art.	7-11-1864	237
Knupp, George	Pvt. B.	7 VA	10-21-1862	136
Lafitte, Francis	Corp. F.	9 LA Inf.	7-12-1864	240
Lanhart, Joseph	Pvt. D.	16 Miss Inf.	12-15-1862	182
Lane, John T.	Capt. G.	4 GA Inf.	7-25-1863	206
Lane, Joshua	Pvt. F.	27 NC Inf.	11-27-1862	175
Langford, J. D.	Pvt. G.	13 LA	7-10-1864	229
Langford, J. Ross	Pvt. F.	10 GA Inf.	3-15-1863	191
Langford, John	Pvt. E.	60 GA Inf.	8-10-1863	212
Laws, Anderson	Pvt. E.	23 NC Inf.	10-28-1862	154
Legrest, William S.	Pvt. G.	9 AL	9-30-1862	65
Lenk, G.W.	Pvt. B.	9 LA Inf.	7-10-1864	225

Name	Rank/Co.	Regiment	Date of Death	Grave No.
Lewis, Henry D.	Pvt. E.	1 NC Inf.	11-11-1862	165
Lewis, W. A.	Pvt. G.	13 GA Inf.	7-31-1864	271
Liden, John	Pvt. D.	7 LA Inf.	11-6-1862	161
London, H. S.	Pvt. D.	15 NC Inf.	1-1-1863	186
Lowe, George H.	Pvt. D.	5 LA Inf.	9-1-1864	291
Lucas, George H.	Pvt. D..	14 VA Cav.	8-28-1864	289
Lynch, Hosea W.	Pvt. F.	13 GA Inf.	8-13-1864	284
Mabry, Solomon P.	Pvt. G.	6 AL Inf.	5-22-1863	194
McBride, Wm. C.	2 Lt. H.	9 LA Inf.	7-22-1864	262
McClung, G. A.	Pvt. K.	14 VA Cav.	8-11-1864	280
McCowan, J. M.	Pvt. F.	15 SC	9-21-1862	25
McDonnell, Dennis	Pvt. C.	7 LA Inf.	7-11-1864	234
McGahery, J. J.	Pvt. C.	Providence, AL	9-23-1862	26
McGee, James	Pvt. H.	1 NC Inf.	10-4-1862	85
McGee, Patrick	Pvt. A.	4 GA	7-10-1864	226
McGuire, Patrick	Pvt. C.	7 LA Inf.	7-10-1864	224
McKay, D. F.	Pvt. B.	11 Battn. GA Art.(Sumner)	9-20-1862	59
McKee, Levi T.	Pvt. G.	42 Miss. Inf.	8-13-1863	213
McKenny, C. C.	Pvt. C.	5 GA	9-23-1862	38
McLead, Wm. H.	Pvt. E.	61 GA Inf.	10-6-1862	92
McNair, Jas L.	Pvt. C.	31 GA Inf.	7-25-1863	207
McNeil, James	Pvt. C.	8 FL Inf.	11-13-1862	167
McPherson, Wyat H.	Pvt. H.	50 GA Inf.	10-27-1862	149
Madden, Charles D.	Pvt. C.	12 SC	10-28-1862	156
Mash, M. S.	Pvt. A.	12 NC Inf.	10-28-186	Not Located; Possibly removed.
Mason, J. K.	Pvt. K.	22 SC	10-11-1862	107
Michaels, John A.	Pvt. K.	27 GA	10-16-1862	123
Mikles, John A.	Pvt. E.	12 AL Inf.	10-3-1862	77
Miles, Wyatt S.	Sgt. H.	3 Ark. Inf.	10-14-1862	116
Miller, A.	Pvt. H.	4 NC	9-23-1862	32
Miller, George	Pvt. F.	21 GA Inf.	7-12-1864	238
Miller, George W.	Pvt. E.	8 LA Inf.	7-27-1864	266
Miller, Henry	Pvt. C.	3 MD	10-3-1862	75
Miller, S. F.	Pvt. G.	18 NC	9-15-1862	24
Mitchel, J. A.	Pvt. C.	26 GA	10-14-1862	Not Located; Possibly removed.
Monk, Hinton	Pvt. A	24 NC Inf.	10-14-1862	
Montgomery, Marshall F.	Pvt. G	8 LA Inf.	7-10-1864	233
Moore, Frank A.	Pvt. D.	6 GA Inf.	10-10-1862	104
Morris, Joseph W.	Capt. D.	16 VA Cav.	9-9-1864	300
Moss, T. L.	1 Lt. G.	61 GA Inf.	10-22-1862	
Murick, john	1 Lt. C.	17 NC	9-26-1862	43
Murphy, John	Pvt. E.	27 GA Inf.	10-21-1862	137
Myers, Clarkson W.	Corp. B.	14 NC Inf.	10-18-1862	128
Nickles, John T.	Pvt. I.	3 AL Inf.	10-11-1862	108
Nix, John T.	Pvt. F.	50 GA Inf.	10-4-1862	88
Osteen, John R.	Capt. G.	50 GA	9-23-1862	30
Owen, A.	Sgt. G.	19 GA Inf.	10-28-1862	153
Owen, H. J.	Sgt. I	14 Tenn. Inf.	10-30-1862	157
Padgett, A. M.	Sgt. M.	7 SC Inf.	1-3-1863	185
Page, Joseph A.	Pvt. A.	Nelson Battn. VA Art.	7-9-1864	218
Park, A. G.	Corp. G.	17 VA Cav.	7-15-1864	248
Parker, Wm. A.	Pvt. H.	4 Tex. Inf.	12-18-1862	183
Patten, Samuel	Pvt. G.	31 GA Inf.	8-27-1864	288

Name	Rank/Co.	Regiment	Date of Death	Grave No.
Peadro, Samuel M.	Lieut. D.	16 VA Cav.	8-27-1864	303
Pence, Leroy	Corp. F.	60 GA Inf.	9-12-1864	293
Penn, E. M.	Lieut. A.	22 SC Inf.	9-12-1862	Not Located; Possibly removed.
Perry, N.	Pvt. F.	22 NC Inf.	10-23-1862	138
Phillips, Lewis S.	Pvt. E.	3 NC Inf	10-30-1862	155
Pinson, John G.	Pvt. A.	12 Battn. GA L.Art.	8-22-1864	287
Pitcher, J. M.	Pvt. B.	9 LA Inf.	7-20-1864	258
Pitts, Raisin	Pvt. B.	6 AL	9-26-1862	44
Pondrick, A. W.	Pvt. F.	4 GA	10-11-1862	124
Pope, John W. B.	Pvt. E.	31 GA Inf.	7-10-1864	220
Potter, Alex	Pvt. E.	12 AL	9-25-1862	41
Powell, W. H.	Pvt. I.	3 SC Inf.	5-2-1863	197
Power, Fleming	Pvt. K.	6 GA Inf.	1-29-1863	188
Preston, Thos. C.	Sgt. E.	14 VA Cav.	8-2-1864	275
Raper, Alex	Pvt. H.	12 AL Inf.	9-27-1862	47
Ray, James	Pvt. I.	3 NC Inf.	10-17-1862	125
Reeves, Laomi	Pvt. B.	3 NC Inf.	11-6-1862	163
Reeves, Robert	Pvt. G.	27 GA Inf.	10-12-1862	198
Register, John S.	Pvt. A.	6 AL Inf.	9-16-1862	2
Rentz, John W.	Adjt. A.	AL Inf.	10-10-1862	106
Ricard, Stephen	Pvt. C.	5 AL Inf.	7-10-1864	221
Roberts, E.	Pvt. E.	10 LA Inf.	9-26-1862	50
Roberts, G. L.	Sgt. K.	26 GA Inf.	7-22-1864	261
Roberts, G. R.	Pvt. B.	23 Miss Inf.	10-2-1862	74
Robertson, E. H.	Corp. G.	14 NC Inf.	11-2-1862	158
Robertson, J. S.	Corp. H.	26 AL	9-28-1862	55
Roe, George W.	Pvt. B.	26 GA Inf.	8-8-1864	278
Rooker, David T.	Pvt. A.	5 NC Inf.	9-24-1862	33
Roundtree, Thos. J.	Pvt. K.	7 SC Inf.	12-8-1862	180
Royster, James M.	Pvt. C.	47 NC	7-29-1863	209
Sanders, W. J.	Pvt. G.	9 LA Inf.	7-30-1864	270
Searborough, William D.	1Lt. I.	1 NC Inf.	9-20-1864	13
Selden, Braxton	Pvt. H.	9 VA Cav.	8-3-1863	210
Sexton, John M.	Pvt. A.	4 VA	8-6-1864	277
Sharp, O. D.	Pvt. H.	1 NC Inf.	11-21-1862	172
Shaw, J. G.	Corp. D.	60 GA Inf.	7-10-1864	228
Shines, James	Pvt. F.	51 GA	9-27-1862	52
Shiver, Evan T.	Pvt. A.	35 A.C. Inf.	10-8-1862	95
Shuman, Andrew	Pvt. E.	50 GA	9-25-1862	40
Shuman, Emanuel	Pvt. E.	50 GA Inf.	9-24-1862	34
Sietz, John	Pvt. F.	7 SC Inf.	10-1-1862	61
Sloan, David	Pvt. F.	50 GA Inf.	9-27-1862	53
Smith, Baxter M.	Pvt. K.	8 FL Inf.	9-28-1862	60
Smith, C. N.	Pvt. F.	45 NC	7-11-1864	241
Smith, R.	Pvt. E.	14 SC	9-5-1862	6
Somerhall, W. W.	Pvt. E.	3 SC Art.	9-19-1862	28
Stacy, Joseph	Pvt. F.	27 NC Inf.	11-12-1862	166
Stamps, Wm. M.	Pvt. A.	12 Battn. GA L.Art.	7-17-1864	252
Stanford, Zedediah	Pvt. A.	12 Battn. GA L.Art.	7-11-1864	246
Stedman, B. M.	Pvt. G.	48 NC Inf.	10-19-1862	134
Stembridge, Benjamin	Pvt. E.	6 GA Inf.	10-6-1862	84
Stephens, John	Pvt. B.	51 GA	10-12-1862	110
Stewart, Joseph	Pvt. E.	3 Battn. SC Inf.	10-4-1862	81
Stewart, R.	Pvt. F.	14 NC Inf.	10-2-186	71

Name	Rank/Co.	Regiment	Date of Death	Grave No.
Strickland, M. T.	Pvt. G.	50 GA Inf.	12-4-1862	177
Suit, Johnson	Pvt. D.	6 AL Inf.	8-28-1863	215
Sullivan, Michael	Pvt. K.	6 LA Inf.	4-22-1863	196
Summerall, J. M.	Pvt. G.	50 GA	9-19-1862	12
Swiler, Henry L.	Pvt. D.	7 LA Inf.	9-19-1862	301
Tamming, Andrew J.	Pvt. D	7 LA Inf.	7-10-1864	232
Tegil, S.	Pvt. D.	4 AL	10-6-1862	Not Located; Possibly removed.
Thigpen, Amos	Pvt. B.	3 NC Inf.	11-19-1862	171
Todd, Aquilla	Corp. F.	5 NC Inf.	12-11-1862	176
Trawick, Orthnold	Pvt. F.	50 GA Inf.	9-28-1862	56
Trulock, Charles	Pvt. F.	50 GA Inf.	9-27-1862	16
Turberville, S.	Pvt. E.	1 SC Inf. P.A.	10-1-1862	67
Tuck, F. M.	Pvt. C.	Holcombe SC Legion	9-30-1862	63
Wallace, J. J.	G	18 SC Inf.	10-13-1862	113
Waller, Wiley J.	Pvt. E.	23 NC Inf.	10-13-1862	120
Watkins, T. C.	Lt. Col.	22 SC Inf.	9-26-1862	45
Watts, W. B.	Pvt. C.	1 SC Rifles	8-8-1863	211
Weatherly, D.	Pvt. D.	2 FL Inf.	8-8-1862	
Webb, James D. Jr.	Corp. D.	5 AL Inf.	2-26-1865	295
West, Henry H.	Pvt. A.	3 NC Inf.	7-6-1863	201
West, William T.	Pvt. K.	51 GA	10-14-1862	121
White, Stephen R.	Pvt. H.	8 FL Inf.	10-17-1862	131
Wiley, William	Pvt. F.	50 GA Inf.	9-23-1862	23
Williams, Charles F.	Pvt. G	8 LA Inf.	10-2-1862	76
Williams, P. K.	Corp. E.	2 GA Inf.	4-21-1863	195
Winbish, Peter	Pvt. I.	24 VA Inf.	10-22-1862	143
Wise, W. R.	Corp. K.	13 GA Inf.	7-11-1864	236
Womack, Elbert	Pvt. G.	48 NC Inf.	10-14-1862	117
Wooldridge, J. R.	Pvt. C.	60 VA Inf.	3-23-1865	296
Young, Burrel L.	Pvt. A.	23 GA Inf.	10-1-1862	151
Young, C. C.	Pvt. A.	18 SC Inf.	10-1-1862	70

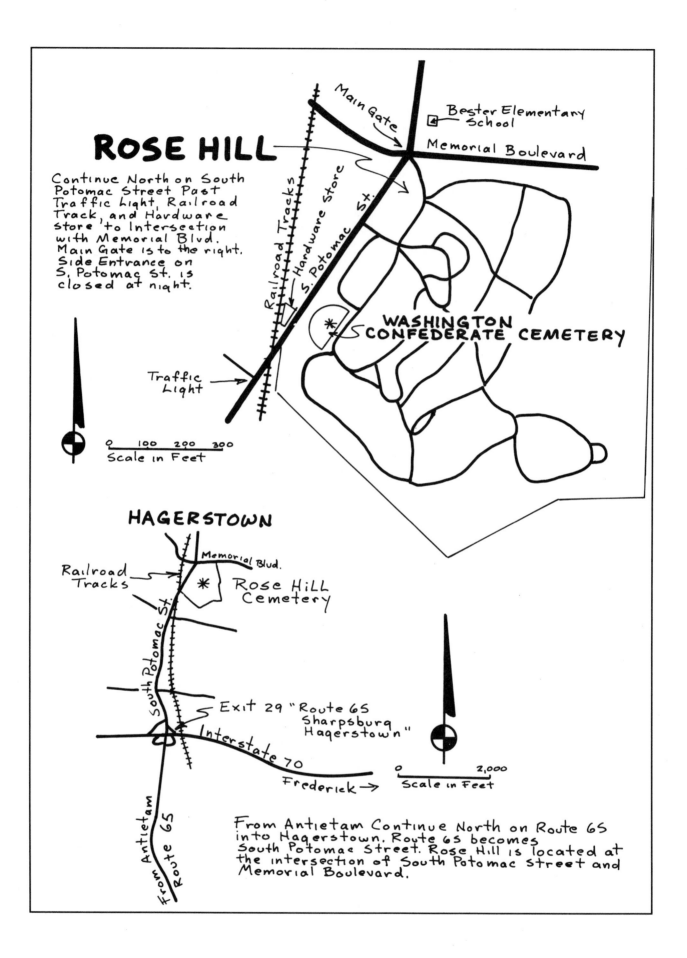

ROSE HILL

Continue North on South Potomac Street Past Traffic Light, Railroad Track, and Hardware Store to Intersection with Memorial Blvd. Main Gate is to the right. Side Entrance on S. Potomac St. is closed at night.

Main Gate

Bester Elementary School

Memorial Boulevard

Railroad Tracks

Hardware Store

S. Potomac St.

WASHINGTON CONFEDERATE CEMETERY

Traffic Light

0   100   200   300
Scale in Feet

HAGERSTOWN

Memorial Blvd.

Railroad Tracks

Rose Hill Cemetery

South Potomac St.

Exit 29 "Route 65 Sharpsburg Hagerstown"

Interstate 70

Frederick →

From Antietam

Route 65

0   2,000
Scale in Feet

From Antietam Continue North on Route 65 into Hagerstown. Route 65 becomes South Potomac Street. Rose Hill is located at the intersection of South Potomac Street and Memorial Boulevard.

Washington Cemetery

Name	State
A., E. H.	Georgia
Abernalty, Lt.	South Caroilina
Able, Gor	Virginia
Albright, C. M. Captain	North Carolina
Allen, G. W. C.	Georgia
Allen, Jno.	Virginia
Alsop, H. P.	Virginia
Anderson, J.	Virginia
Anderson, J.	Virginia
Anderson, M. O.	Virginia
Anker, M.	Louisiana
Anslin, A. N.	Louisiana
Argenbright, J. H.	Virginia
Arges, John	Georgia
Argo, J. E. Georgia Legion	Georgia
Ascott, J.	North Carolina
Ayers, W. B.	North Carolina
Ayres, J. E. Colonel	North Carolina
B., M. M.	Virginia
Barer, J. C. Sergeant	Mississippi
Barnes, J. R.	North Carolina
Barnes, W. W.	North Carolina
Bass, C. T.	North Carolina
Batten, J.	North Carolina
Bayly, W.	Georgia
Beeks, J. C. Captain	Georgia
Bell (Ball or Boll), B. W.	North Carolina
Bincks, J.	South Carolina
Binn, C. C. Lieutenant	Georgia
Black, John	Virginia
Black, T. H.	Louisiana
Blalock, M.	Mississippi
Blanton, Ambrose	South Carolina
Booker, Chas.	Virginia
Booker, J.	Virginia
Boon, J.	Texas
Bowers, J. A.	South Carolina
Boynton	Georgia

Name	State
Bozman, J. Lieutenant	South Carolina
Braddox, Dr. Colonel	12th Alabama Regiment
Braddox, Dr.	South Carolina
Brantley, H. B.	Georgia
Brazeall, W. S.	Texas
Brook, G. W.	Virginia
Brown, Corporal	Virginia
Brown, Dozier	Georgia
Bruster, W.	Georgia
Bryant, Thos.	North Carolina
Bryant, W. B.	Mississippi
Bryson, J.	Virginia
Burdett, L. G.	Alabama
Burgan	Louisiana
Butler, J. E.	Georgia
Butler, L.	Mississippi
Butler, Phil	Louisiana
Byrd, F.	South Carolina
C (or G.), B. T.	Virginia
C., J.	South Carolina
Campbell, J. H. Q.	Georgia
Campbell, W. O.	Mississippi
Canas (or Caras), Aug.	Louisiana
Canon, E.	Virginia
Carmichael, J. C.	North Carolina
Carter, B. A.	Virginia
Cary, Jesse	South Carolina
Cerve (or Cerne), N.	Georgia
Cherry, Sergeant	Virginia
Clark, C. H.	Mississippi
Clark, C. H.	Mississippi
Clark, F. H.	Louisiana
Clark, W.	Louisiana
Cobb, J. W.	Georgia
Cochran, J. D.	Mississippi
Coleman, C. W.	North Carolina
Coleman, M.	Georgia
Collins, H. T.	Georgia
Colly, J. A.	Virginia
Colwell, Colonel	27th Georgia Regiment
Conghlin (or Coughlin), D.	Virginia
Conough, J. P.	South Carolina
Cook, Captain	Mississippi
Cork, E. W. Lieutenant	Louisiana
Coughty, Thos.	Alabama
Coughty, Thos.	Georgia
Cowan, Geo. H.	North Carolina
Cox, William	South Carolina
Craine, J. S.	South Carolina
Crave, H.	Virginia
Crawford, R. B.	South Carolina
Credit, Stephen	Georgia
Daney, W.	North Carolina
Davis, R. B.	Mississippi
Davis, R. F.	Alabama

Name	State
Davis, W. J.	Texas
Denson, J. L.	Arkansas
Denson, J. N.	Arkansas
Dobson, E. F. Lieutenant	South Carolina
Doluglas, A.	Texas
Dunlap	South Carolina
Dunlap, J.	North Carolina
Duplices, P. N.	Louisiana
Dye, Jas.	Virginia
Dyerer, H.	Texas
Easteds, M.	South Carolina
Ervin, J. S.	Mississippi
F. (or R), J. B.	Georgia
Farner, J. A.	Virginia
Farris, J. M.	South Carolina
Flemming, J. G. Lieutenant	North Carolina
Fontent	Louisiana
Foult (or Fonlt), C. A.	North Carolina
Foult, G. A.	North Carolina
Frances, E. S.	Virginia
Franck, Lieutenant	South Carolina
Franklin, W.	South Carolina
Frazier, E. L.	South Carolina
Frye, J.	North Carolina
Fuller, J. M.	Mississippi
Gardner, B.	Louisiana
Gardner, C. D.	Mississippi
Garner, W.	North Carolina
Garnett, J.	Louisiana
Garr, J. R. Georgia Legion	Georgia
Garton, C. F.	Louisiana
Gillman, H. G. G.	South Carolina
Gilmore, B. F.	Georgia
Goin, E. B.	South Carolina
Golickly, C.	South Carolina
Gones	Mississippi
Gosnell, C.	South Carolina
Gosnell, W. W.	Louisiana
Gower, A. W.	Georgia
Green, Benj.	Virginia
Griffin, N. T.	South Carolina
Grigg, L.	North Carolina
Gritten, R.	South Carolina
Grubne, M.	Georgia
Gunn, E. N.	Georgia
H., J. M. B. E. B.	Mississippi
Hagens, J. G.	Georgia
Hall, James	Arkansas
Haller, G.	Louisiana
Hanger, G. M.	Virginia
Hanks, Jno.	Georgia
Harnes, John Lieutenant	Virginia
Harper, J. R.	North Carolina
Harris, J. R. Corporal	South Carolina
Harris, R.	Georgia

Name	State
Harty, Kirby	North Carolina
Hasper	North Carolina
Head, Jesse D.	Arkansas
Hedrick, W. W.	Alabama
Heintz, L. Captain	Louisiana
Henry, Z. P.	Texas
Herring, B. P.	North Carolina
Herring, D. P.	North Carolina
Hickman, H.	Mississippi
Hicks, Jacob	North Carolina
Hightower, R. B.	Georgia
Hill, J. N.	North Carolina
Hill, W. S.	South Carolina
Hobbs, T.	Georgia
Hogue, Wesley J.	Arkansas
Holder, A.	North Carolina
Homes, Lieutenant Colonel	Georgia
Hoords, R.	Georgia
Horne, J. H.	North Carolina
Hudson, J. P.	Louisiana
Hudson, J. S.	Georgia
Hugney, N. M.	South Carolina
Hunt, Wm. P.	North Carolina
Hyall, E. L.	Arkansas
Jackson, S. M.	North Carolina
Jenkins	North Carolina
Jeste, W. J.	Georgia
Johnson, H.	South Carolina
Johston, A. J.	Virginia
Judd, W.	Louisiana
Just, J. H.	Virginia
Kearney, J. S.	Louisiana
Keesee, Benton Sergeant	Arkansas
Keeser, C. M.	Virginia
Kelly, Danl.	North Carolina
Kennedy, A. V.	South Carolina
Kessler, T.	Mississippi
Kirkpatrick, E. R.	Mississippi
Kountz, A. J.	North Carolina
Kriegner, J. O. Lieutenant	21st Miss. Regiment
Laferty, F.	Louisiana
Lane, W. H.	North Carolina
Lans, W. E.	North Carolina
Laprope, B. C.	Georgia
Late	Georgia
Leak, J. M.	Virginia
Leggit, E. B.	Louisiana
Legrist, Wm. S.	South Carolina
Light, Jas.	Georgia
Lindsey, W. R.	South Carolina
Little, W. R.	South Carolina
Little, W. E.	South Carolina
Low, Jos. M.	Georgia
Lucus, J. A.	Virginia
Lumpkin, Samuel Lt. Colonel	44th GA Inf.

Name	State
Lunder	Virginia
M., J. L.	Virginia
M., J. P.	Louisiana
Malicott (or Maticott), C.	Virginia
Marrow, T. H.	Virginia
Martin, C. R.	Louisiana
Marting, J. H.	South Carolina
Marton, N.	Mississippi
Mason, Jno. R.	South Carolina
Matering, Broks.	Georgia
matering, R. C.	Alabama
Mathews, B.	Georgia
Mathony, B.	Georgia
Matson	Louisiana
Maxcey, Jas. F.	Georgia
Maxwell, Saml.	South Carolina
McCoy, J. H. Corporal	Georgia
McCoy, S. T.	South Carolina
McDugle, J.	Mississippi
McFarland, Captain	Louisiana
McNeedy, A. Sergeant	South Carolina
McWilliams, J. J.	Georgia
Miller, Alfred D.	North Carolina
Miller, G. W.	Louisiana
Mitchell, John D. H.	Georgia
Mone, B. T.	Virginia
Montgomery, M.	Louisiana
Morgan, J. C.	South Carolina
Morton, R. Captain	Mississippi
Nair, J. W.	North Carolina
O'Brien, W.	Georgia
Oger, P.	Louisiana
Oliphant, P. N.	North Carolina
O'Neal, J. B. Lieutenant	South Carolina
Paget, A. M.	South Carolina
Pallet (or Pullet), F. L.	North Carolina
Penn, E. M. Lieutenant	South Carolina
Perring, Henry	Virginia
Perry, Nathaniel	North Carolina
Petty, Newton	South Carolina
Phelps, J.	Texas
Pheton, Joe (or Jas)	Virginia
Phifer, J. H.	Louisiana
Pratt, Jas. P.	Georgia
Price, R. E.	Louisiana
Pruitt, J. C.	Mississippi
Rate, J. B.	Virginia
Reading, J.	Georgia
Reed, J. W.	Virginia
Reeder, N. Captain	Georgia
Reno, W. A.	Virginia
Rice	South Carolina
Rice, A. J.	Georgia
Rigson, J. L.	North Carolina
Riley, J.	Georgia

Name	State
Riley, Davidson Co.G. 4th Texas	Texas
Ring, J. A.	Alabama
Roa, J. G.	Virginia
Roach (could be Shadreck Deralh "Shacky" Roach)	South Carolina
Roberts, J. M. Lieutenant	Mississippi
Roberts, J. M. Lt.	21st Miss. Regiment
Robinson, E. H.	North Carolina
Robinson, S. Lieutenant (Possibly L.T.S.)	Louisiana
Rodney, Ruben	Louisiana
Rohrer, J. C.	Mississippi
Rooker, Davis F.	North Carolina
Royston, J. M.	North Carolina
S., T. J.	Georgia
Sander, Thos.	Georgia
Savill, L. D. (or O.)	Louisiana
Scoggins	Louisiana
Shellers, J. W.	Mississippi
Sessions, Johnathan	Mississippi
Seyton, Sergeant	Mississippi
Shadburn, Dr.	Louisiana
Shinp, E.	North Carolina
Shiwater, T. Corporal	Virginia
Shorouhart, W. N.	Georgia
Shuber, M. J.	South Carolina
Shuttler (or Shuffler), Jno.	North Carolina
Sidly, John	South Carolina
Sigman, R.	North Carolina
Sigmore, R.	North Carolina
Simmons, C.	Mississippi
Slaughter, J. L.	Georgia
Smith, C. N.	North Carolina
Smith, E. B.	Louisiana
Smith, J. B.	Mississippi
Smith, S. J.	North Carolina
Smith, W.	Georgia
Snead, W. A.	Virginia
Snires, J. R.	Alabama
Sotton, Elias	North Carolina
Sowbro (or Sourbro), Wm.	North Carolina
Spalding, J.	Alabama
Spofford (or Spotford), G.T.	Mississippi
Spraight, A. W.	North Carolina
Spratling, J.	Alabama
Starr, H. A.	South Carolina
Stedman, B. M.	North Carolina
Stoan, J. (or Sload), 10th LA	Louisiana
Stokes, J.	Virginia
Stone, W.	North Carolina
Stoner (or Stover) Lt. Colonel	North Carolina
Strider	North Carolina
Strong, Colonel	Louisiana
Strong, Colonel	South Carolina
Stubbs, J.	South Carolina
Tall, R. B.	Texas
Tallicum, A.	South Carolina

Name	State
Taylor, R. N.	Mississippi
Teter, D. W.	Virginia
Thompson, J., 10th LA	Louisiana
Thompson, J. H.	North Carolina
Tillywill, Solomon	South Carolina
Towley (or Towdey or Townley), Ezra	Mississippi
Turner, H.	Mississippi
W., H. H.	Georgia
W., S. R.	North Carolina
Wagner, R. A.	Mississippi
Wagner, W.	Louisiana
Walker	South Carolina
Walker, M.	Virginia
Wallace, John	South Carolina
Walton	Virginia
Ward, W. H.	Georgia
Ward, W. H.	Mississippi
Watey, G.	Virginia
Waton, W. Sergeant	Virginia
Watts, W. B.	South Carolina
Waty, G.	Virginia
Weaver, Jno. W.	Alabama
Wells, Thos.	Mississippi
West, H.	North Carolina
West, W. C.	Mississippi
Whatley, George C., Cpt.	10th AL Inf.
Wicker, W. B.	Virginia
Wiles, J.	North Carolina
Wiley, J. A.	North Carolina
Williams, Duncan	North Carolina
Williams, J.	Georgia
Williams, J. M.	Mississippi
Willingham, W. F.	South Carolina
Wilson, T. J.	Virginia
Winston, W. D.	Virginia
Wise, J. T.	South Carolina
Wolf, A. F.	Texas
Wood, E.	Virginia
Wood, H. H.	Virginia
Wright, James	South Carolina
Wright, J. C.	Georgia
Wright, J. W.	Mississippi
Wright, W.	Georgia
Young, C.	Georgia
Young, John C.	South Carolina

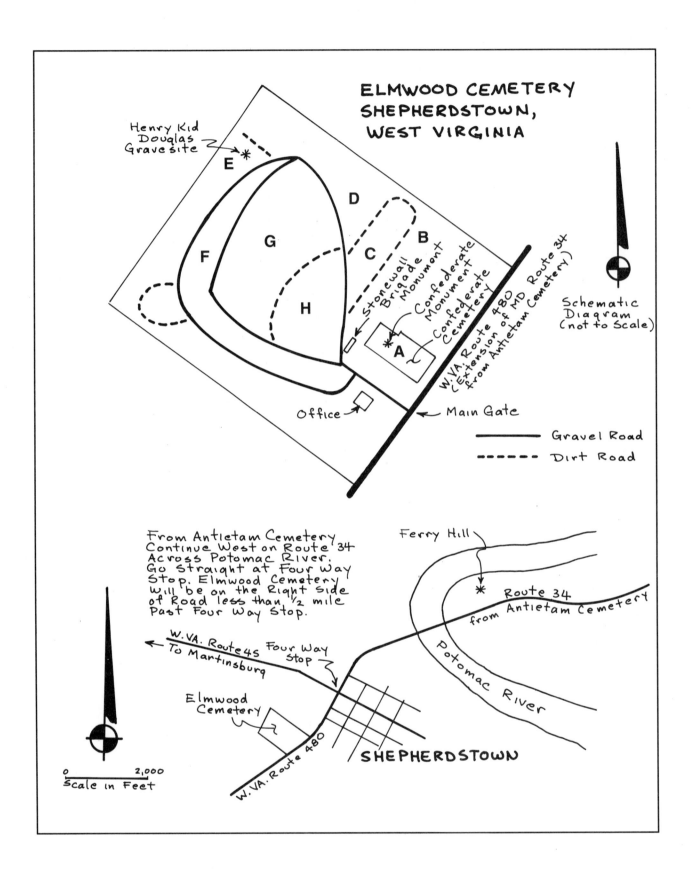

ELMWOOD CEMETERY SHEPHERDSTOWN, WEST VIRGINIA

Henry Kid Douglas Gravesite

E

D

B

F G C

Stonewall Brigade Monument

Confederate Monument

Confederate Cemetery

H

A

W.VA. Route 480 Route 34 (Extension of MD Route 34 from Antietam Cemetery)

Schematic Diagram (not to Scale)

Office

Main Gate

——————— Gravel Road

- - - - - - - Dirt Road

From Antietam Cemetery Continue West on Route 34 Across Potomac River. Go Straight at Four Way Stop. Elmwood Cemetery will be on the Right side of Road less than ½ mile Past Four Way Stop.

Ferry Hill

Route 34 from Antietam Cemetery

Potomac River

W.VA. Route 45 To Martinsburg

Four Way Stop

Elmwood Cemetery

W.VA. Route 480

SHEPHERDSTOWN

0   2,000
Scale in Feet

Elmwood Cemetery

Shepherdstown, West Virginia

Name	Rank/Co.	Regiment	Death Date	Grave No.	Comments
Adams, George E.	B	2 VA Inf.	9-29-1905	H	Stonewall Brigade, Age 62
Adams, William A.	D	12 VA Cav.	6-16-1906	H	Born Dec. 28, 1839
Agnew, J. C.		5 SC		A-K6	
Allen, Joseph	K	6 NC		A-C5	
Anderson	Sgt. Maj.	5 FL		A-P7	
Banks, M.	C	Hampton Leg.		A-K7	
Banks, Washington	D	12 VA Cav.	1897	B	Laurel Brigade, Born 1819
Barnhart, Adrian		20 NC		A-L5	May be Reinhart, Addison
Barnhart, Geo. W.	B	3 VA Inf.	8-29-62	H	KIA 2nd Manassas, Born July 28, 1842
Barnhart, H. F.	B	2 VA Inf.	1915	H	Stonewall Brigade, Born 1837
Baudy, J.		21 MS		A-Q4	May be Bundy, J.
Beazley, James A.	Lt.C	9 VA Cav.	9-15-62	A-C1	KIA Boonsboro, May be Beasley
Billmeyer, Milton J.	Capt. F	1 VA Cav.	8-31-1907	B	Born Oct. 10, 1834
Billmeyer, Robert L.	F	1 VA Cav.	3-9-1907	B	Born Sept. 25, 1843
Billmyer, John T.	Lt.F	1 VA Cav.	3-6-74	B	Stuart's Brigade, Age 44
Boswell, George M.		Union Army	3-18-1932	D	Grand Army of Republic Marker
Boyd, H. W.	Lt. C.	5 TX		A-N4	
Bundy, J.					See Baudy, J.
Burbank, E. D.					See Durank, E. D. B.
Burke, George F.	F	1 VA Cav.		B	
Burke, Redman	Capt.	12 VA Cav.	11-11-62	A-B7	From Jefferson Co. WV
Butler, Dr. Vincent M.	Capt. B	2 VA Inf.	4-22-64	B	Stonewall Brigade, Born Dec. 21, 1820
Butler, William	B	2 VA Inf.	5-6-63	G	Stonewall Brigade, Born Sept. 25, 1811
Camerson, Alexander B.	2nd Lt. B	2 VA Inf.	8-29-62	B	WIA Manassas 8-28-1862, Age 29
Cameron, Henry F.	Sgt. B	2 VA Inf.	10-11-88	B	Stonewall Brigade, Age 67
Canty, Sam	D	16 SC		A-12	May be Ganty, S.
Clark, G. M.	F	5 FL		A-C2	
Clayton, R. E.	Capt. F	2 MS		A-H6	
Clymer, Daniel	D	12 VA Cav.	1-30,64	B	Laurel Brigade, Age 35
Connell, R. P.	I	50 GA		A-H7	

Name	Rank/Co.	Regiment	Death Date	Grave No.	Comments
Cook, W. A.	G	31 GA		A-M3	
Cotton, R. W.	Capt.	1 TX Vol.	10-30-62	B	
Crim, T.J.		1 SC		A-K5	May be Grim, T. J.
Dandridge, Adam Steven			1923	D	
Daniels, William B.	C	55 NC		A-J2	
Davenport, Charles S.	Lt.			A-K4	From Charleston, SC
Deakins, J.				A-010	From Union District, SC
Douglas, Henry Kyd	General	VA	1904	E	Staff Officer of Stonewall Jackson
Durank, E.D.B.		26 GA Vol.		A-L2	May be Burbank, E. D.
Eason, C.	E	33 NC		A-H4	
Eason, William	D	2 NC		A-N11	
Edwards, J. K.	H	2 NC		A-M7	
Elliott, J. M.				A-G5	From Huntsville, AL
Entler, John Phil	B	2 VA Inf.	12-30-1909	D	Stonewall Brigade
Farham, N. L.	D	5 FL		A-E1	
Feamster, J. B.		11 MS		A-I1	
Ferrell, Charles F.	B	2 VA Inf.	5-28-1908	B	Stonewall Brigade, Born August 23, 1843
Ferrell, Charles F.		GA		A-J10	
Fountain, M. J.	Corp.	13 GA Vol.		A-K1	
Fraley, David D.	D	12 VA Cav.	12-2-1906	B	Laurel Brigade, Age 66
Frazier, J. W. B.			12-31-1902	B	Age 62
Gageby, Joseph E. N.		1 VA Cav.	7-26-70	A-D3	
Ganty, S.					See Canty, Sam
Garvin, T. J.		2 SC Rifles		A-K2	
Gay, John		31 GA		A-H10	
Gordon, John P.	F	48 NC		A-L7	
Grisby, R.	Capt. A	8 LA		A-B6	
Grim, T. J.					See Crim, T. J.
Grove, F. T.				A-A3	1845-1924, Stonewall Brigade
Harlin, J.	Sgt.			A-D2	
Harris, George W.	F	1 VA Cav.		A-F2	From Shepherdstown, WV
Harvey, W. H.	Lt. H.	21 VA		A-16	May be Harvin, W. H.
Harvin, W. H.					See Harvey, W. H.
Hawn, David	F	1 VA Cav.	6-2	D	Born March 22, 1839
Hendricks, Daniel	D	12 VA Cav.	1-15-1910	H	Laurel Brigade, Born July 26, 1838
Hendricks, Jas. M.	D	12 VA Cav.	6-12-1923	G	Stonewall Bridage, CSA Marker
Herr, E. G. W.	Capt. D	12 VA Cav.	3-8-1901	G	Born March 30, 1829
Hessey, Chas. E.	B	2 VA	1-31-62	B	
Hill, George F.	F	1 VA Cav.	12-18-64	D	Died at Harrisonburg, VA
Hill, John P.	F	1 VA Cav.	1909	H	Born 1826
Hoey, Edward P.		LA Guard Art.	9-19-62	A-P4	KIA Shepherdstown, Age 21
Hoffler, G. W.		4 TX		A-F5	
Holliday, E. P.		5 NC		A-G2	
Hood, D. S.		GA		A-L9	
Hood, D. T.		5 AL Art.		A-E3	
Horn, David George	H	2 VA Inf.	11-13-70	G	Stonewall Brigade, Age 44
Hornbuckler, T. W.		13 NC		A-O11	
Hout, David H.	Corp B.	2 VA Inf.	3-11-1905	B	Stonewall Brigade, Born Nov. 24, 1820
Howell, William	K	10 MS		A-N9	
Humrickhouse, S. P.	B	2 VA Inf.		H	Stonewall Brigade
Ireland, William	C	60 GA		A-M6	
Irwin		GA		A-P10	

Name	Rank/Co.	Regiment	Death Date	Grave No.	Comments
James, John	Lt.	17 MS Vol.		A-J11	Died Sharpsburg, MD
Jarbee, William					See Jebbo, William
Jarbo, William					See Jebbo, William
Jebbo, William				A-H5	May be Jarbo or Jarbee
Johnson, J. Newman		1 MD	7-4-64	A-F9	Born Dec. 27-1839; Killed 7-4, 1864
Jones, Issac T.		50 GA		A-F6	
Jones, S.	Sgt.			A-J6	
Kearney, J. Briscoe	F	1 VA Cav.	9-25-62	B	Born August 20-1832
Kepley, Andrew W.	I	14 NC		A-E6	
Kimes, Henry	B	2 VA Inf.		C	Stonewall Brigade
Kirkland, William Wedbee	Brig. Gen	NC	5-12-1915	F	Promoted Brig. Gen 8-29-1863
Knott, Charles H.	D	12 VA Cav.	4-29-98	H	Laurel Brigade, Age 56
Knott, George S.	D.	12 VA Cav.	6-11-1913	H	Laurel Brigade, Born August 31, 1832
Knott, John L.	Maj.	12 VA Cav.	4-6-65	KH	KIA High Bridge, VA, Age 31
Knott, Samuel M.	D	12 VA Cav.	3-5-1907	H	Laurel Brigade, Born March 2, 1830
Koontz, Thornton	Sgt. F	1 VA Cav.	5-12-86	H	Stuart's Brigade, Born Dec.16, 1821
Lee	Capt.	SC		A-P5	
Lee, Edmund			7-14-96	D	Born Oct. 8-1845
Lee, William Fitzhugh	Lt. Col.	33 VA Inf.	7-29-61	G	WIA 1st Manassas, Born April 27, 1833
Lee, J.				A-O4	
Lemen, John L.	F	1 VA Cav.	1-19-71	B	Stuart's Brigade, Born Nov. 19, 1839
Lemen, Thomas T.	F	1 VA Cav.	6-20-63	B	Stuart's Brigade, WIA 6-17
Lemen, Wynkoop N.	Lt. F.	1 VA Cav.	12-22-1915	D	Stuart's Brigage, Born May 19, 1842
Lemon, Alex	B	2 VA Inf.		A-G11	
Leopold, Andrew		MD		A-B8	
Licklider, G. T.	H	2 VA Inf.	4-6-1903	B	Stonewall Brigade, Age 79
Link, Adom Cruzen	H	2 VA Inf.	3-28-62	H	Stonewall Brigade, Born Nov. 30, 1832
Loyns, Henry M.	B	2 VA	1910	D	Stonewall Brigade
Lyon, C.T.	Lt. H.	48 VA			See Lyon, G.F.
Lyon, G.F.	Lt. A	18 VA		A-Q8	May be Lyon, C.T.
Mabin, M.G.		15 GA		A-G10	May be Maybin
Marsh, E.L.	Rev.	31 GA Vol.		A-M2	
Marshall, James Mason	F	1 VA Cav.	10-11-1911	G	Stuart's Brigade, Age 80
Maybin					See Mabin, M.G.
McBride, Wm. H.	C	12 GA		A-G3	
McCleary, John W.	D	12 VA Cav.	1-10-1902	G	Laurel Brigade
McCown, Joses					See McOnon, J.
McKee, John		2 SC		A-N1	
McOnon, J.	C	12 GA		A-J4	May be McOwen, J.M. or McCown, Joses
McOwen, J.					See McOnon, J.
Melvin, Jacob S.	Capt. H.	2 VA Inf.	1-25-1912	G	Born Jan 6, 1830
Melvin, William	H	2 VA Inf.	2-17-1912	G	Born August 27, 1841
Mercer, W. H.		LA Guard Art.		A-N3	May be Merser
Merser					See Mercer, W. H.
Miller, A.	B	52 NC		A-C6	May be Misler
Miller, Collins		White's Batt.	9-3-61	A-F3	KIA near Winchester, VA
Misler					See Miller, A.

Name	Rank/Co.	Regiment	Death Date	Grave No.	Comments
Moler, Jacob Swagler	D	12 VA Cav.	1-3-1914	H	Born Dec. 28, 1843
Moler, Lee H.	Capt. B	2 VA Inf.	10-23-1908	H	Stonewall Brigade, Born March 12, 1837
Moler, Raleigh	D	12 VA Cav.	4-8-66	G	Laurel Brigade, Age 58
Monaghan, William	Col.	1 VA Cav.		A-B5	
Morgan, Daniel H.	D	6 VA Cav.	4-8-65	B	WIA Petersburg, VA; April 1, 1865
Morgan, Wm. A.	Col	1 VA Cav.	2-14-99	G	Born March 30, 1831
Neel, Rev. A. A. P.	Lt.		11-20-1909	G	
Newall, W. J.	K	12 LA		A-L11	
Ogletree, J. A.	I	13 GA		A-19	
Osbourn, James S. Allen	H	2 VA Inf.	9-29-1901	B	Stonewall Brigade, Age 84
Osbourn, Robert L.	D	12 VA Cav.	5-15-1902	H	Born Oct. 17, 1837
Overton, William G.				A-B3	
Parran, William S.	Doctor		9-17-62	A-B4	KIA Sharpsburg, Born July 5, 1835
Patten, W. D.	D	1 NC		A-L6	
Pendleton, Benjamin S.	B	2 VA Inf.	1-19-1931	H	Stonewall Brigade, Born March 28, 1842
Pendleton, J. Albert			8-30-62	H	Son of J.W. & M.C. Pendleton
Perry, Joel W.		GA		A-Q6	
Porter, Eli	Pvt. B	3 NC Cav.	1-10-63	A-B2	WIA Sharpsburg, Age 33
Pratt, J. H.		30 VA		A-F1	
Randal, Jas. F.			1-1-1912	B	Born March 25, 1824
Rattler, A.				A-G6	May be Roller, A.
Ray, John Reason	B	2 VA Inf.	7-22,-94	H	Stonewall Brigade, Born Dec. 4, 1829
Reinhart, Addison	B	20 NC			See Barnhart, Adrian
Rickard, James R.	B	2 VA Inf.	8-26-1909	H	Stonewall Brigade, Born Feb 21, 1828
Riggs, James	F	4 TX		A-L8	
Rinehart, John	B	59 NC		A-J3	
Robinson, Jas B.	H	2 VA Inf.	6-22-85	G	Born March 27, 1837
Robinson, S. J.		Brook Art.		A-P6	
Rodgers, C. R.		SC		A-P3	
Roller, A.					See Rattler, A.
Ross, C. W.			1862	B	Field slab, not a dressed stone
Roup, George L.	C	5 VA Inf.		A-B1	
Ruse, John M.			11-14-1919	D	Born Jan 3-1841
Rutherford, John T.	H	2 VA Inf.	4-20-76	D	Stonewall Brigade, Age 36
Shaner, A. J.	B	2 VA Inf.	9-26-1920	B	Stonewall Brigade
Shepherd, Abraham	G	Laurel Brigade	11-5-1907	F	Sone of Henry & Frances E. Shepherd
Sherman, O. F. H.	F	1 VA Cav.		B	
Slandiffer, W. E.		11 GA		A-G9	May be Standiffer, W. E.
Slaughter, M. B.		11 LA		A-G8	
Smith, Conrad C.	B	2 VA Inf.	3-14-86	B	Born April 5, 1819
Smith, H. J.	Capt. D	Hampton Leg.		A-O8	
Smith, W. T.	I	GA		A-E5	
Snyder, Henry M.	H	2 VA Inf.	11-11-64	H	Stonewall Brigade, Age 28
Snyder, John	G	1 MD Cav.		E	Potomac Home Brigade, Union Army
Snyder, John	B	2 VA Inf.	6-1-64	G	WIA Wilderness, Age 41
Spohr, H.		9 LA Vol.		A-K3	
Standiffer, W. E.					See Slandiffer, W. E.
Stine (Rightstine), Adam	B	2 VA Inf.			

Name	Rank/Co.	Regiment	Death Date	Grave No.	Comments
Stone, J. B.				A-J5	
Stonebraker, Joe M.	F	1 VA Cav.	1-29-94	G	Stuart's Brigade, Born March 22, 1829
Strider, Isaac H.	B	12 VA Cav.	12-25-1915	G	Age 74
Tanner, Isaac S.	2nd Lt. F	1 VA Cav.	4-10-1903	G	Chief Surgeon Hoke's Division
Tanner, Paddy				A-C3	
Taylor, J. W.		Jenkin's Brig.		A-D5	
Taylor, J. Will	B	2 VA Inf.	12-14-1905	G	Born March 31, 1842
Tew, O. C	2 NC			A-O1	
Thompson	Sgt.			A-C8	
Thompson, F. G.					See Thompson, S. J.
Thompson, F. M.		1 GA		A-E2	
Thompson, S. J.		5 NC		A-G4	May be Thompson, F. G.
Thomson, B.		2 NC		A-D8	
Towner, T. H.	1st Sgt. B	2 VA Inf.	5-23-61	B	Killed at Kernstown, VA
Tucker, J.		41 GA		A-K8	
Unseld, Jno. G.	B	2 VA Inf.	1906	E	Stonewall Brigade
Vaughan, W.				A-O3	
Vespot, A. T.				A-O6	
Wallace, D.					See Wallach, D.
Wallach, D	Capt. A	22 GA		A-C7	May be Wallack, D. or Wallace, D.
Wallack, D.					See Wallach, D.
Walters, Jos. W.	B	2 VA Inf.	11-23-68	D	Stonewall Brigade, Age 34
Warburton, G. T.		Parks Art.		A-E4	
Warner, George W.	F	1 VA Cav.	7-5-70	G	Stuart's Brigade, Age 24
Waters, P.	A	8 GA		A-F7	
Williams	Lt.	Black Horse Cav.		A-P1	
Williams, Andrew J.	Lt. K	3 NC Inf.		A-J1	
Williams, John		Rockbridge Art.	8-12-77	A-G1	From Rockbridge Co., VA
Willis				A-L1	From Spottsylvania County, VA
Willis		AL		A-Q5	
Wilson, C. G.	Lt.			A-13	
Witherspoon, T. J.		NC		A-M11	From Rowan Co., NC
Wright, Amassa P.	C	21 VA		A-C4	
Wyson, R. L.	F	1 VA Cav.	8-25-1907	E	Stuart's Brigade, Born June 21, 1838
Yontz, Geo. R.	F	1 VA Cav.	1-1-85	D	
Yontz, Geo. W.	B	2 VA Inf.		A-A2	Stonewall Brigade
Yontz, Jos. E.	B	2 VA Inf.		A-A1	Stonewall Brigade
York, S. M.	K	8 MS		A-D1	

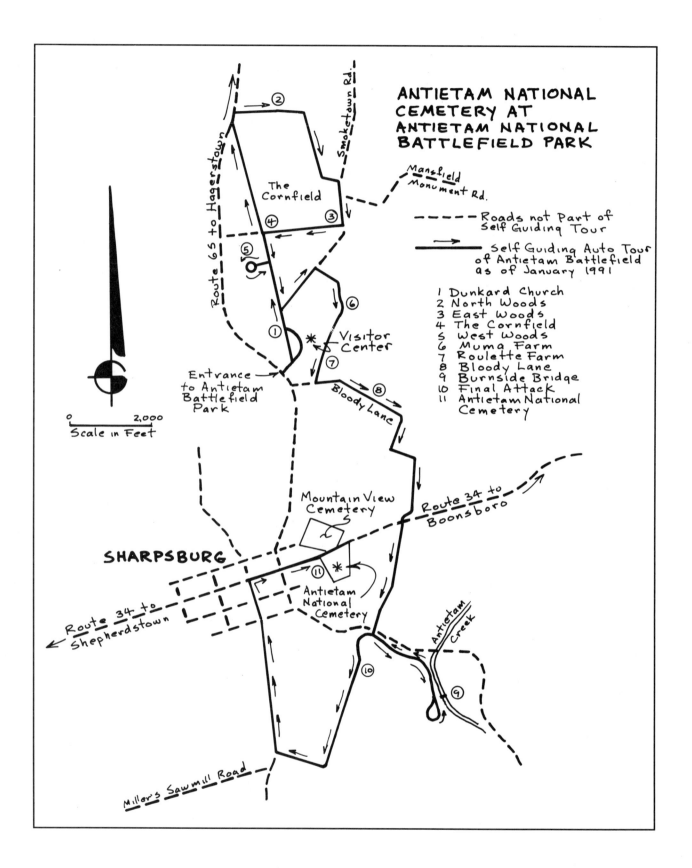

ANTIETAM NATIONAL
CEMETERY AT
ANTIETAM NATIONAL
BATTLEFIELD PARK

Smoketown Rd.

Mansfield
Monument Rd.

The
Cornfield

Route 65 to Hagerstown

Visitor
Center

Entrance
to Antietam
Battlefield
Park

Bloody Lane

Scale in Feet
0   2,000

Mountain View
Cemetery

Route 34 to
Boonsboro

SHARPSBURG

Route 34 to
Shepherdstown

Antietam
National
Cemetery

Antietam Creek

Miller's Sawmill Road

- - - - → Roads not Part of
Self Guiding Tour

————→ Self Guiding Auto Tour
of Antietam Battlefield
as of January 1991

1 Dunkard Church
2 North Woods
3 East Woods
4 The Cornfield
5 West Woods
6 Muma Farm
7 Roulette Farm
8 Bloody Lane
9 Burnside Bridge
10 Final Attack
11 Antietam National
Cemetery

Antietam National Cemetery

Name	Rank/Co.	Reg./State	Death	Grave No.	Removed from/ Comments
Abbott, Abiel J. N.	Pvt. H	4 RI	09-17-1862	2836	Antietam, WIA
Abbott, Charles A.	Pvt. K	6 WI Inf.	09-17-1862	3341	Antietam, KIA
Abbott, David P.	Pvt. F	1 MN Inf.	09-17-1862	3025	Antietam, KIA
Abbott, Levi A.	Corp. A	111 PA Inf.	09-17-1862	3664	Antietam, KIA
Acker, C.					See Ackles, Franklin
Ackerly, Cassander	Pvt. G	8 MI Inf.	12-03-1862	2400	Frederick, WIA Ant.
Ackerson, John	Pvt. D	15 NJ Inf.	07-06-1863	2926	Antietam, age 25
Ackles, Franklin	Pvt. E	9 NY Art.	07-16-1864	63	Fred., WIA Monocacy
Ackley, Wesley	Pvt. E	36 OH Inf.	09-05-1864	1163	Clarysville
Adair, John B.	Corp. B	9 NY Inf.		748	Antietam
Adams		21 MA Inf.		889	Antietam
Adams, Eben	Pvt. C	5 ME Inf.		3177	Antietam
Adams, George	Pvt. B	15 MA Inf.	10-07-1862	1056	Frederick, Antietam
Adams, Joseph	Pvt. I	155 PA Inf.	10-26-1862	3601	Antietam
Adams, William F.	Corp. F	15 MA Inf.	10-10-1862	980	Smoketown
Adamson, Robert	Pvt. I	67 OH Inf.		1241	Cumberland
Addleman, Joseph O.	B 19	IN Inf.	09-17-1862	3451	Antietam
Aderhold, Frederick	Pvt. C	4 PA Res.	11-18-1862	4040	Fred., Ant., Age 27
Adkins, William S.	Pvt. G	13 WV Inf.	09-02-1864	2721	Weverton, Monocacy
Adle, John H.	Pvt. C	34 NY Inf.		826	Antietam
Adler, Ambrose J. S.	Pvt. E	PA Art.	03-04-1862	4196	Fred., Knapp's Bat.
Adsit, James E.	Pvt. F	97 NY Inf.	10-17-1862	590	Smoketown
Aker, William	Pvt. L	14 PA Cav.	01-05-1865	4124	Frederick
Albriz, Fredoline	Pvt. A	15 NY Cav.	07-10-1864	71	Frederick
Alderman, Lafayette F.	Pvt. I	111 PA Inf.	09-17-1862	3661	Antietam, KIA
Aldrich, Henry	Pvt. K	16 CT Inf.	09-17-1862	1085	Antietam, KIA
Alexander, John	Corp. A	6 WI Inf.	09-17-1862	3350	Antietam, KIA
Alexander, William B.		17 IN Art.	04-21-1864	3488	Hagerstown
Algier, G. M.	Pvt E	43 NY Inf.		296	Weverton
Algier, George M.					See Algier, G. M.
Allbaugh, Levi	Pvt. I	54 PA Inf.	09-24-1864	4112	Frederick
Allen, George	Pvt. D	105 NY Inf.	10-08-1862	616	Smoketown
Allen, William	Sgt. G	42 NY Inf.		834	Antietam
Allison, Alexander	Pvt. A	3 WI Inf.	03-14-1862	3212	Frederick, Disease
Allison, James	Pvt. A	12 PA Res.	09-17-1862	3779	Antietam, KIA
Allman, George	Corp. F	19 IN Inf.	10-11-1862	3477	Smoketown
Allton, J. E.	Pvt. D	30 OH Inf.		1379	South Mountain
Allyn, Henry A.	Pvt. H	2 WI Inf.	09-26-1862	3228	Antietam, WIA
Ambrose, Marcus T.		WV		2719	Weverton
Ames, Martin L.	Pvt. A	6 NY Cav.	05-22-1864	137	Frederick

Name	Rank/Co.	Reg./State	Death	Grave No.	Removed from/ Comments
Anders, Ignatius	Pvt. B	2 WI Inf.	09-17-1862	3224	Antietam, KIA
Anderson, Henry A.	Pvt. H	14 NJ Inf.	07-03-1863	2920	Frederick
Anderson, John	Pvt. K	36 OH Inf.	09-14-1862	1428	South Mountain
Anderson, John	Pvt. D	111 PA Inf.	10-14-1862	3716	Smoketown, WIA Ant.
Anderson, John R.	Pvt. C	19 IN Inf.	09-17-1862	3447	Antietam
Anderson, John S.	Pvt A	123 OH Inf.	09-10-1862	1453	Middletown
Anderson, Joseph	Pvt. A	1 US Cav.	09-07-	3507	Weverton, Monocacy
Anderson, Stephen P.	Sgt. D	118 PA Inf.	09-22-1862	3602	Antietam, WIA Ant.
Anderson, William H.	Pvt. M	1 CT Art.	09-04-1862	1196	Age 23 from Bridgeport
Angus, Charles M.	Pvt. A	5 NY Art.	09-16-1864	285	Weverton
Anker, Edwin R.	Pvt. G	193 OH Inf.	03-27-1865	1172	Clarysville
Annis, Myron	Pvt.	1 NY Art.		540	Antietam
Annis, Stelman S.	Pvt. C	2 MA Inf.	11-22-1862	1028	Frederick, Antietam
Anthony, John	Pvt. H	7 PA Res.	10-22-1862	3812	Smoketown, WIA Ant.
Anthony, Lewis	Pvt. A	165 NY Inf.	09-24-1864	303	Weverton, Monocacy
Anton, Levi	Pvt.	19 IN Inf.	09-17-1862	3448	Antietam, KIA
Aplin, John	Pvt.	13 NJ Inf.		2779	Antietam
Applin, Uriah F.	Pvt. D	151 NY Inf.	07-09-1863	184	Frederick
Ardis, Richard	Pvt. F	3 DE Inf.	12-20-1862	3059	Frederick, WIA Ant.
Ardray, M. F.	Pvt. D	24 IA Inf.	01-28-1865	3029	Frederick
Arge, James	Corp. E	1 MI Cav.	09-18-1864	2375	Weverton, Monocacy
Armor, John R.	Pvt. K	111 PA Inf.	09-18-1862	3753	Sharpsburg, WIA Ant.
Armstrong, John G.	Pvt. I	107 PA Inf.	09-17-1862	2054	Antietam, KIA
Armstrong, John W.	Pvt. E	5 OH Inf.	09-17-1862	1345	Antietam
Armstrong, Joshua A.	Sgt. F	23 OH Inf.		1326	Antietam
Arnold, Amassa	Pvt. E	3 MA Cav.	09-17-1864	956	Weverton, Monocacy
Arnold, Charles E.	Pvt. C	96 OH Inf.	04-17-1865	1171	Clarysville
Arrants, William H.	Pvt. G	14 NJ Inf.	12-30-1862	2908	Frederick
Atridge, Richard	Corp. A	6 WI Inf.	01-02-1863	3250	South Mountain, WIA
Atwood, George W.	Pvt. I	6 WI Inf.	09-17-1862	3333	Antietam, KIA
Ault, Henry	Pvt. I	7 WV Inf.		2776	Cumberland
Austin, C. H.	Pvt. F	18 MA	09-24-1862	894	Died Disease, age 26
Austin, Castal	Pvt. B	6 PA Inf.		4033	Middletown
Austin, J. A.	Pvt. F	29 OH Inf.	04-02-1862	1510	Weverton
Austin, Jesse	Pvt H	122 NY Inf.	10-19-1862	396	Hagerstown, Antietam
Averill, Franklin	Corp. H	21 NY Cav.		33	Cumberland
Avery, William	Pvt. G	97 NY Inf.	10-25-1862	505	Smoketown
B., H.	Pvt. C			284	Weverton
Babcock, Charles C.	Pvt. F	6 ME Inf.	07-17-1863	3125	Frederick, Age 20
Bachelle, Von Werner	Capt. F	6 WI Inf.	09-17-1862	858	Antietam, KIA
Bacon, Henry	Pvt. H	7 OH Inf.	09-17-1862	1350	Antietam
Bacon, John	Pvt. K	59 NY Inf.	10-18-1862	501	Smoketown
Baden, Augustus	Pvt.	7 NY Inf.	10-04-1862	145	May be Adolphe Bader
Bader, Adolphe	Pvt. D				See Baden, Augustus
Badger, Oliver	Pvt. A	126 OH Inf.	07-20-1864	1294	Frederick, Monocacy
Bailey, Henry	Pvt. D	34 NY Inf.	09-17-1862	845	Antietam
Bailey, John W.	Pvt. E	8 PA Res.	09-17-1862	3612	Antietam, KIA
Bailey, R. S.	Pvt. F	8 IL Cav.	07-10-1863	3065	Fred., Died of wounds
Bailey, William	Pvt. H	6 WI Inf.	09-17-1862	3347	Antietam, KIA
Baird, James	Pvt. C	45 PA Inf.	09-14-1862	3873	South Mountain, KIA
Baker	Pvt.	MI		2389	Sandy Hook
Baker, Alfred	Pvt. C	13 PA Cav.	08-02-1864	4012	Weverton
Baker, Harris	Pvt. C	78 NY Inf.	09-27-1862	585	Antietam
Baker, J. S.	Pvt. F	4 US Art.	03-12-1862	3580	Frederick
Baker, Jacob	Pvt. K	9 WV Inf.	10-23-1864	2656	Weverton, Age 50
Baker, John	Pvt. E	1 PA Res.	09-17-1862	3733	Antietam, KIA
Baker, John	Pvt. E	11 OH Inf.	09-14-1862	1420	South Mountain
Baker, John T.	Bugler K	8 IL Cav.	07-09-1864	3069	Frederick, Monocacy
Baker, M.	Teamster	46 PA Inf.	12-27-1862	4197	Frederick
Baker, Marion M.	Pvt. G	155 PA Inf.	10-03-1862	3801	Antietam

Name	Rank/Co.	Reg./State	Death	Grave No.	Removed from/ Comments
Baker, Stephen	Pvt. F	116 OH Inf.	04-12-1863	1245	Cumberland
Balcom, Anson F.	Pvt. C	2 CT Art.	10-12-1864	1191	Age 33 from Farrington
Balden, Francis	Pvt. G	4 US Art.	10-23-1862	3540	Frederick, Antietam
Bale, J. G.	Pvt. E	5 US Cav.		3574	Cumberland
Ball, Jabez B.	Pvt. K	11 WV Inf.	08-24-1864	2709	Weverton, Monocacy Age 28
Ball, Joun	Pvt. L	1 OH Art.	09-26-1862	1376	Smoketown
Ballard, Franklin	Pvt. F	67 OH Inf.		1219	Cumberland
Balleony, John	Pvt.	PA Inf.		3865	South Mountain
Bancroft, Andrew J.	Pvt. I	14 PA Cav.	05-11-1864	4093	Frederick
Bane, Stephen J.	Pvt. C	22 PA Cav.	03- -1864	3997	Weverton
Bantas, Gibbon	Pvt.	4 RI Inf.	09-17-1862	2823	Antietam, KIA
Barker, Albert E.	Pvt. D	10 ME Inf.	10-09-1862	3116	Frederick, Antietam
Barker, John D.	Corp. E	3 MD Inf.	07-09-1864	2446	Frederick, Monocacy
Barnard, George M.	Pvt. D	5 CT Inf.	11-21-1862	1137	Antietam
Barnes, David	Pvt. K	1 MD Cav.	09-05-1864	2575	Weverton, Disease
Barnes, Hugh	Pvt. H	14 IN Inf.	10-10-1862	3479	Smoketown
Barnes, John	Pvt. G	37 ME Inf.	09-27-1864	3199	Weverton, Monocacy
Barnes, Joshua L.	Pvt. A	23 OH Inf.	09-14-1862	1402	Middletown, S. MT.
Barnes, Levi	Pvt. B	14 IN Inf.	10-16-1862	3492	Frederick, Antietam
Barnes, Samuel	Pvt. F	9 PA Res.	11-02-1862	3808	Smoketown
Barnes, William H.	Pvt. F	49 NY Inf.	11-10-1862	374	Hagerstown, Antietam
Barnett, John	Pvt. K	9 PA Res.	09-14-1862	3842	South Mountain, KIA
Barnett, Thomas	Pvt. K	10 WV Inf.	11-25-1864	2944	Clarysville
Barns, James A.	Pvt. C	12 PA Res.	09-17-1862	3789	Antietam, KIA
Barons, Henry	Pvt. H	108 NY Inf.	12-22-1862	195	Frederick, Antietam
Barr, Daniel	Pvt. H	8 PA Res.	09-17-1862	3796	Antietam, KIA
Barr, Jacob W.	Pvt. G	137 PA Inf.	10-09-1862	3732	Sharpsburg, Antietam
Barr, Robert L.	Corp. F	1 MD Cav.	09-28-1864	2572	Weverton, Disease
Barrett, J. F.	Pvt. K	75 NY Inf.	09-18-1864	107	Frederick, Monocacy
Barrett, John	Pvt. B	78 NY Inf.		623	
Barrington, Henry	Pvt.	NH	10-12-1862	2820	Antietam, Age 23
Barry, Patrick	Pvt. D	34 MA Inf.	07-30-1864	966	Weverton, Died Wounds
Bartlett, Marcus C.	Pvt. G	10 ME Inf.	11-06-1862	3183	Smoketown
Bartlett, Marston H.	Pvt. D	4 VT Inf.	09-23-1863	2648	Frederick, Age 18
Basler, Jonas	Pvt. F	8 OH Inf.	09-06-1862	1500	Frederick, Antietam
Batchem, Elie D.	Pvt. E	5 WI Inf.	11-11-1864	3210	Clarysville
Bates, Benjamin	Pvt. D	1 WV Cav.	02- -1862	2850	Cumberland
Bates, Benjamin J.	Corp. I	14 NJ Inf.	11-03-1862	2905	Frederick, Antietam
Bates, George F.	Pvt. M	1 VT Art.	08-27-1864	2666	Antietam, (Monocacy ?)
Bates, Smith	Pvt. I	14 NJ Inf.	08-23-1864	2903	Frederick, Monocacy
Battie, David	Pvt. D	55 OH Inf.	07-05-1862	1169	Clarysville
Batty, Davis	Pvt. H	11 CT Inf.	09-17-1862	1127	Antietam, KIA
Bauchman, H. D.	Pvt. F	12 PA Cav.	08-06-1864	4113	Frederick
Baulton, William	Pvt. D	21 NY Cav.	07-16-1864	29	Frederick, Monocacy
Baxter, David	Pvt. D	72 PA Inf.	10-02-1862	4211	Frederick, Antietam
Baxter J. M.	Pvt. F	5 WV Cav.	08-09-1864	2625	Frederick, W/A Winchester, VA
Bayard, Cornelius	Pvt. E	14 NJ Inf.	04-12-1863	2924	Frederick, Age 23
Beach, Benjamin J.	Pvt. E	11 CT Inf.	09-17-1862	1133	Antietam, KIA
Beals, James M.	Pvt.	1 VT Cav.	01-08-1865	2633	Monocacy
Bean, Albert	Pvt. D	2 VT Inf.	10-04-1864	2655	Weverton, Monocacy Age 23
Bean, Charles H.	Pvt. B	1 ME Cav.	09-19-1862	3117	Frederick, Antietam
Bean, Franklin	Pvt. I	5 ME Inf.	07-12-1863	3207	Hagerstown
Bean, Oscar F.	Pvt. D	10 ME Inf.	01-02-1862	3115	Frederick
Beaney, John T.	Pvt. K	14 NJ Inf.	07-09-1864	2927	Frederick, Monocacy
Beardslee, John	Pvt. G	34 NY Inf.	09-17-1862	524	Antietam
Beath, Granville	Pvt I	149 OH Inf.	08-21-1864	1322	Frederick, Monocacy
Beatty, Henry	Pvt E	9 PA Res.	09-17-1862	3757	Antietam, KIA
Beaver, William	Pvt. A	79 NY Inf.	09-17-1862	796	Antietam

Name	Rank/Co.	Reg./State	Death	Grave No.	Removed from/ Comments
Beavers, Norman	Pvt. I	PA Cav		4177	Cumberland
Bechtel, Solomon	Pvt. H	59 NY Inf.	09-17-1862	706	Antietam
Beck, Isaac	Pvt. H	51 PA Inf.	09-17-1862	3620	Antietam, KIA
Beebe, Oliver	Pvt. I	139 PA Inf.	10-16-1862	3948	Hagerstown, Age 22
Beek, Julius	Pvt. A	20 NY Inf.		732	Antietam
Beekman, Franz	Pvt. I	108 NY Inf.		817	Antietam
Beer, Samuel	Pvt. M	14 PA Cav.	08-06-1863	4083	Frederick
Beerman, Daniel	Pvt. F	1 WV Cav.	03-24-1862	2773	Cumberland
Behme, Frederick	Pvt. K	67 OH Inf.		1247	Cumberland
Bell, Robert	Pvt. K	15 WV Inf.	08-26-1864	2622	Frederick, Monocacy
Bellman, Lewis	Pvt. E	55 OH Inf.	07-11-1862	1206	Cumberland
Bemis, Joseph W.	Pvt. C	3 WI Inf.	12-21-1861	3214	Frederick
Bennett, Benjamin	Pvt. I	7 MI	08-09-1863	2556	Frederick, Age 17
Bennett, Charles W.	Pvt. D	116 OH Inf.	12-12-1862	1233	Cumberland
Bennett, George A.	Pvt. H	3 MI Inf.	08-10-1863	2557	Fred., Disease, Age 24
Bennett, James	Pvt. G	50 PA Inf.	09-17-1862	3979	Antietam, KIA
Benson, Aaron	Pvt. H	45 PA Inf.	09-17-1862	3585	Antietam, KIA
Benson, Enoch	Pvt. H	12 PA Res.	11-12-1862	3709	Smoketown, WIA Ant.
Bent, Henry	Pvt. I	2 MA Cav.	06-03-1864	1076	Clarysville, Age 19
Bent, Thomas	Pvt. K	5 PA Res.	09-19-1862	4138	Frederick, WIA S. Mt.
Bentley, Van A.	Pvt. G	2 WI Inf.	09-22-1862	3261	Antietam, WIA
Bently, John	Pvt. F	8 CT Inf.	10-17-1862	1117	Hagerstown, WIA Ant.
Berghauser, August	Pvt. B	4 US Inf.	12-06-1862	3546	Frederick, Antietam
Berry, John S.	Pvt. K	28 PA Inf.	04-07-1862	4193	Frederick, Age 32
Beth, Peter	Pvt. H	160 OH Inf.	08-15-1864	1394	Middletown
Betson, Thomas	Pvt. E	32 NY Inf.	11-27-1862	360	Burkettsville, S. Mt.
Beyers, John	Pvt. C	142 PA Inf.	10-24-1862	3815	Smoketown
Beymier, Frederick	Pvt. L	1 NY Cav	09-16-1863	11	Frederick
Bias, Green	Pvt. H	27 IN Inf.	01-15-1862	3388	Frederick
Bidwell, Hiram	Pvt D	3 PA Inf.	10-20-1862	3932	Frederick
Biegler, John	Pvt. K	192 OH Inf.	03-27-1864	1271	Frederick
Bierwith, Francis V.	Capt. G	69 PA Inf.	09-17-1862	859	Antietam, KIA
Bigelow, Anson D.	Corp. E	60 NY Inf.	10-02-1862	140	Frederick, Antietam
Bingham, Ezra	Pvt. G	151 OH Inf.	07-21-1864	1174	Clarysville
Bingham, James	Pvt. G	3 PA Res.	09-17-1862	3778	Antietam, KIA
Bird, George W.	Pvt. D	14 WV Inf.	12-11-1862	2859	Cumberland
Birdsell, Albert I.	Pvt. G	5 NY Art.	11-21-1864	286	Weverton
Bissell, Henry E.	Pvt.	16 NY Inf.		421	Burkettsville
Black, Hanson	Pvt G	10 WV Inf.	01-27-1863	2772	Cumberland
Black, Mathew	Pvt. D	81 PA Inf.	10-15-1862	3937	Frederick, Antietam
Black, Oscar D.	Pvt. K	9 NY Art.	07-12-1864	70	Monocacy, KIA
Black, William P.	Pvt. A	6 WI Inf.	09-17-1862	3239	Antietam, KIA
Blackhead, Adam	Pvt. L	28 PA Inf.	09-17-1862	3636	Antietam, KIA
Blackwell, Benjamin D.	Pvt. I	14 NJ Inf.	07-23-1864	2932	Frederick, Monocacy
Blades, Major G.	Pvt. D	1 DE Inf.	10-28-1862	3058	Frederick, Age 44
Blahang, William	Pvt. F	42 NY Inf.		833	Antietam
Blair, Edwin B.	Pvt. D	2 PA Art.	04-17-1866	4226	Hagerstown
Blaker, J. H.	Pvt. G	21 NY Inf.		645	Antietam
Blal, John	Pvt. M	2 US Cav.	11-11-1863	3563	Frederick, Age 18
Blanchard, Oliver	Pvt. C	132 PA Inf.	09-24-1862	3740	Antietam, WIA
Blanchard, Simon F.	Pvt. D	17 MI Inf.	11-01-1862	2546	Ant., WIA, from Kalamazoo
Bland, David	Pvt. G	191 OH Inf.	04-14-1865	1160	Clarysville
Blasdel, I. F.	Pvt. G	15 IN Inf.	06-20-1865	3377	Clarysville
Blaurett, George	Pvt.	59 NY Inf.		695	Antietam
Blodgett, Jackson	Pvt. I	11 VT Inf.	12-01-1864	2637	Frederick, Age 29
Bloodkamp, Henry	Pvt. C	152 IN Inf.	04-22-1865	3370	Clarysville
Bloom, Henry E.	Pvt. F	15 NY Cav.	06-15-1864	12	Frederick
Bodecker, Otto	Pvt.	20 NY Inf.		729	Antietam
Bogart, Christopher	Pvt. H	4 PA Res.	11-05-1862	3705	Smoketown
Bogart, Henry L.	Pvt. K	89 NY Inf.	11-03-1862	314	Knoxville, Disease

Name	Rank/Co.	Reg./State	Death	Grave No.	Removed from/ Comments
Boggs, Albert	Pvt. D	1 PA Cav.		4156	Cumberland
Boles, William	Pvt. B	6 US Cav.	11-09-1862	3515	Burkettsville, Antietam
Bollinger, Jacob	Pvt. K	23 OH Inf.	09-25-1862	1405	Antietam
Bolton, Abraham	Pvt. H	24 IA Inf.	09-21-1864	3030	Weverton, Monocacy
Bolyard, Josiah	Pvt. D	6 WV Cav.	06-05-1864	2879	Clarysville
Bolza, Charles E.	2nd Lt.	MI Cav.	07-14-1863	883	Falling Waters, KIA
Bomeling, Thomas	Pvt. C	106 NY Inf.	08-11-1864	102	Died of wounds
Bone, William P.	Pvt. C	1 WV Inf.	07-22-1862	2861	Clarysville
Boner, George W.	Pvt. C	14 IN Inf.	05-11-1863	3420	Frederick
Bonham, Charlton L.	Corp.	6 PA Cav.	07-11-1863	3820	Antietam
Booker, James				2091	Burkettsville, Newton's Brigade
Booles, Amos	Pvt. F	111 PA Inf.	01-22-1863	4064	Frederick, Antietam
Boothe, James S.	Pvt. D	9 WV Inf.	11-08-1864	2734	Weverton
Borchers, Hermanus	Pvt. G	39 IL Inf.	02-14-1862	3076	Cumberland, Disease
Bordin, William	Pvt.	2 NY Inf.		673	Antietam
Boreland, James T.	Pvt. D	137 PA Inf.	11-11-1862	3960	Hagerstown, Age 23
Borg, Peter	Sgt. I	165 OH Inf.	08-18-1864	1167	Clarysville
Bortle, Belden	Pvt. C	108 NY Inf		814	Antietam
Boshler, Thomas	Pvt.	OH		1387	Middletown
Bosley, Thomas	Pvt. B	34 OH Inf.		1209	Cumberland
Boss, John	Pvt. K	11 OH Inf.	09-18-1862	1417	South Mountain
Bosworth, Jodeph T.	Pvt. A	1 RI Art.	09-17-1862	2834	Antietam, KIA
Bouch, Isaac	Pvt. M	14 PA Cav.	09-28-1864	4151	Clarysville
Boughton, Charles W.	Corp. H	8 OH Inf.	09-21-1862	1357	Antietam
Bout, Daniel	Pvt. D	16 CT Inf.	12-12-1862	1140	Antietam
Bowen, A. C.	Pvt.	124 PA Inf.	10-09-1862	3714	Smoketown
Bowers, W. J.	Pvt. F	34 MA Inf.	12-28-1864	1047	Frederick, Disease
Bowman, John W.	Pvt. C	1 MN Bat.	06-22-1865	3021	Frederick
Boyce, George E.	Pvt.	1 MN Inf.		3026	Antietam
Boyd, J. W.	Pvt. H	135 OH Inf.		1391	Middletown
Boyd, James	Corp. H	1 MD Inf.	01-16-1863	2432	Boonsboro, Antietam
Boyle, Bryan	Pvt. D	145 NY Inf.	01-24-1863	187	Frederick, Antietam
Boyle, Thomas	Pvt. K	33 NY Inf.	11-16-1862	375	Hagerstown, Antietam
Boynton, William S.	Pvt. D	21 MA Inf.	09-17-1862	3201	Antietam, KIA
Brackett, Edward E.	Lt. D	10 ME Inf.	09-17-1862	866	Antietam, KIA
Bradburn, P. W.	Pvt. H	9 NY Art.	02-08-1865	131	Frederick
Bradbury, Hugh M.	Pvt. H	10 ME Inf.	09-17-1862	3165	Antietam
Brad ock, Stephen S.	Pvt. G	22 PA Cav.	01-27-1862	1656	Cumberland
Bradford, James	1st Sgt. H	4 NY Inf.	02-04-1863	189	Frederick, Antietam
Bradley, Timothy W.	Pvt. H	22 NY Inf.	10-31-1862	618	S. Mt., Typhoid Fever
Bragg, George E.	Pvt.	7 ME Inf.	10-02-1862	2406	Frederick, Antietam
Brainard, Oliver	Pvt. F	161 OH Inf.	05-28-1864	1199	Cumberland
Braithwaite, Wilson	Pvt. E	5 WI Inf.	10-29-1862	3255	Hagerstown, Died Disease
Bramhall, Sidney	Pvt. M	3 WV Cav.	09-24-1862	2703	Frederick, Antietam
Branc, Oscar	Pvt. H	106 NY Inf.	09-26-1862	38	Cumberland Gap
Brand, David J.	Pvt. K	44 NY Inf.	10-05-1862	328	Weverton, Antietam
Brandage, Levi A.	Pvt. E	35 MA Inf.	09-20-1862	888	Antietam, WIA
Brandt, Charles	Pvt. K	46 PA Inf.	10-04-1862	4146	Frederick, WIA Ant.
Brandt, Ferd(Fred ?)	Pvt. D	7 NY Inf.		818	May be Frank Brather
Brandyberry, Ezra	Pvt. H	147 IN Inf.	05-03-1865	3369	Clarrysville
Brather, Frank					See Brandt, Ferd
Bray, George	Pvt. H	69 NY Inf.	12-02-1862	215	Frederick, Antietam
Brayman, Samuel H.	Pvt. B	61 NY Inf.		819	Antietam
Brazell, Winfield S.	Pvt. C	10 WV Inf.	1862	2747	Cumberland
Breslin, Dennis	Pvt.	59 NY Inf.		697	Antietam
Brewer, Anderson	Pvt. K	20 ME Inf.	10-28-1862	3148	Antietam
Bridge, Wellington	Pvt. E	2 WI Inf.	09-17-1862	3300	Antietam, KIA
Bridges, John C.	Pvt. G	10 ME Inf.	12-01-1862	3196	Weverton, Antietam
Briggs, James	Pvt. E	7 WI Inf.	09-18-1862	3289	Antietam, WIA

Name	Rank/Co.	Reg./State	Death	Grave No.	Removed from/ Comments
Briggs, John	Sgt. D	8 OH Inf.	09-17-1862	1340	Antietam
Briggs, Sylvester F.	Pvt. A	4 VT Inf.	11-13-1862	2677	Hagerstown, Antietam
Brine, William	Pvt. B	10 ME Inf.	09-17-1862	3161	Antietam
Brink, Elias	Corp. B	137 NY Inf.	10-04-1864	334	Weverton, Monocacy
Brinkman, Adolph	Pvt. E	2 DE Inf.	09-17-1862	3049	Antietam, KIA
Brinson, Edward	Pvt. K	78 NY Inf.	10-13-1864	324	Weverton
Britch, George	Pvt. C	55 OH Inf.	07-14-1862	1502	Frederick
Britton, Edward	Sgt. I	69 NY Inf.	10-28-1862	242	Frederick, Antietam
Broadbent, John	Pvt. E	48 PA Inf.		3617	Antietam
Brock, Freeman	Pvt. B	1 ME Cav.	09-21-1862	3119	Frederick
Brogunier, David	Pvt. E	1 MD Inf.	05-21-1862	2585	Point of Rocks
Brommer, Andrew	Pvt. I	102 NY Inf.	10-04-1862	586	Smoketown
Brookman, Charles	Pvt. C	23 OH Inf.	09-22-1862	1404	Middletown, S. Mt.
Brooks, Andrew J.	Pvt. D	13 WV Inf.	04-04-1865	2873	Clarysville
Brooks, George	Pvt. I	9 WV Inf.	09-16-1864	2617	Frederick, Monocacy
Brooks, George W.	Pvt. E	8 PA Res.	09-14-1862	3900	South Mountain, KIA
Brooks, Jonas	Pvt. B	12 OH Inf.	09-14-1862	1416	South Mountain
Brooks, Virgil	Pvt. A	92 OH Inf.	04-18-1865	1155	Clarysville
Brooks, William H.	Pvt. G	30 ME Inf.	01-28-1865	3120	Frederick
Brown, Adam	Pvt. K	130 PA Inf.	09-17-1862	3598	Antietam, KIA
Brown, Amos	Pvt. A	5 NY Cav.	07-25-1864	398	Harpers Ferry
Brown, Charles	Pvt. F	103 NY Inf.	09-17-1862	766	Antietam, KIA
Brown, David L.	Pvt. D	111 PA Inf.	09-17-1862	3653	Antietam, KIA
Brown, Edward	Pvt. C	1 PA Art.	05-02-1865	4018	Burkettsville
Brown, George	Corp. I	1 MD Cav.	08-04-1864	2455	Frederick
Brown, James F.	Pvt. F	6 ME Inf.	10-30-1862	3200	Hagerstown, Antietam
Brown, James R.	Pvt. C	100 PA Inf.	09-20-1862	3919	South Mountain, WIA
Brown, John	Pvt. D	9 WV Inf.	07-29-1864	2864	Clarysville
Brown, John A.	Pvt. D	125 PA Inf.	09-17-1862	3665	Antietam, KIA
Brown, Joseph T.	Pvt. E	1 MN Inf.	04-30-1862	3020	Frederick
Brown, Ralston	Pvt. F	137 PA Inf.		3970	Hagerstown
Brown, S. H.	Pvt. F	35 MA Inf.	10-15-1863	986	Disease
Brown, William	Pvt. A	14 NJ Inf.	07-09-1864	2928	Frederick, Monocacy
Brownell, Jasper	Pvt. F	4 OH Inf.	12-24-1862	1488	Frederick, Antietam
Bruce, Abram	Pvt. H	91 OH Inf.	08-14-1864	1248	Cumberland
Brumage, Allen E.	Pvt. A	1 WV Art.		2710	Weverton
Bruns, Herman	Pvt.	20 NY Inf.		728	Antietam
Brunson, Elie	Pvt. B	7 WI Inf.	09-17-1862	3335	Antietam, KIA
Brunson, W. F.	Pvt.	9 NY Cav.	07-23-1863	174	Frederick, Age 23
Bryan, John L.	Corp. A	4 PA Res.	09-17-1862	3737	Antietam, KIA
Bryant, Daniel W.	Pvt. C	19 MA Inf.	10-15-1862	977	Smoketown
Bryant, Robert	Corp. C	14 IN Inf.		3434	Antietam
Bryeant, James	Pvt. K	8 OH Cav.	09-12-1864	1477	Hagerstown
Bryne, James O.	Corp. K	1 MD Inf.	02-20-1862	2441	Frederick
Bryson, John	Pvt. E	7 PA Res.	09-17-1862	3945	Antietam, WIA
Bub, George	Pvt. E	12 PA Cav.	12-21-1862	3718	Smoketown
Buchanan, Pleasant	Pvt. B	3 IN Cav.	11-01-1862	3495	Frederick, Antietam
Bucher, Henry	Pvt. E	151 PA Inf.	07-14-1863	4089	Frederick
Buck, Luman	Pvt. F.	4 MI Inf.	09-17-1862	2523	Ant., KIA, from Lawrence Co.
Buckley, John	Pvt. C	87 OH Inf.	09-25-1862	1493	Frederick, Antietam
Buffum, George R.	Lt. D	4 RI Inf.	10-19-1862	873	Keedysville, Antietam
Bufler, Edward W.	Pvt. B	1 MD Art.		2450	Williamsport
Bugbee, Henry F.	Pvt. K	51 NY Inf.	10-20-1862	270	Frederick, Antietam
Bullfinch, Byron	Pvt. K	29 OH Inf.	10-28-1862	1479	Frederick, Antietam
Bunce, J. H.	Pvt. H	2 MD Inf.	06-13-1864	2469	Frederick
Burbank, Dewitt C.	Pvt. G	6 WI Inf.	10-07-1862	3251	South Mountain, WIA
Burd, Samuel	Pvt. G	67 OH Inf.		1229	Cumberland
Burdick, Albert	Pvt. G	111 PA Inf.	02-11-1863	3673	Frederick, Antietam WIA
Burdick, Benjamin F.	Corp. D	4 RI Inf.	09-17-1862	2828	Antietam, KIA

Name	Rank/Co.	Reg./State	Death	Grave No.	Removed from/ Comments
Burdick, Stephen H.	Pvt. B	4 RI Inf.	09-17-1862	2822	Antietam, KIA
Burer, John	Sgt. D	66 NY Inf.	10-02-1862	141	Frederick, Antietam
Burger, Charles	Pvt. F	27 NY Inf.		565	Antietam
Burger, Edward T.	Pvt. E	64 NY Inf.	10-17-1862	230	Frederick, Antietam
Burgess, John	Pvt. A	136 PA Inf.	02-01-1863	4066	Frederick
Burk, Joseph				2169	Antietam
Burk, Joseph	Pvt. G	69 OH Inf.		1211	Cumberland
Burke, Peter	Pvt. K	48 PA Inf.	11-14-1862	4041	Frederick, Antietam
Burke, Simeon	Pvt. H	21 NY Cav.	07-15-1864	69	Frederick, Monocacy
Burke, Walter	Pvt. I	69 NY Inf.	09-27-1862	151	Frederick, Antietam
Burkhamer, George W.	Pvt. G	9 WV Inf.	08-27-1864	2728	Weverton, Monocacy
Burnes, James Jr.	Pvt.	1 VT Cav.	09-30-1864	2634	Monocacy
Burnes, Thomas	Pvt. B	1 DE Inf.	03-11-1863	3065	Frederick
Burns	Pvt.	NY		341	Weverton
Burns, Benjamin	Pvt. E	13 WV Inf.	04-28-1865	2716	Clarysville
Burns, Benjamin	Pvt. E	13 WV Inf.	04-28-1865	2953	Weverton
Burns, M. O.	Pvt. A	15 NY Cav.	07-09-1864	61	Frederick, Monocacy
Burns, Thomas	Pvt. B	59 NY Inf.		689	Antietam
Burr, Aaron	Pvt. H	45 PA Inf.	09-14-1862	3895	South Mountain, KIA
Burr, Francis W.	Pvt. G	16 CT Inf.	10-11-1862	1116	Antietam, WIA
Burrows, David	Pvt. F	13 WV Inf.	08-06-1864	2948	Clarysville
Burton, Jered M.	Corp. A	107 PA Inf.	10-09-1862	4203	Frederick, WIA Manassas
Bushnell, David	Pvt. I	121 NY Inf.	10-08-1862	422	Burkettsville, S. Mt.
Buskirk, Jonathan Van	Corp. C	111 PA Inf.	09-17-1862	3663	Antietam, KIA
Buskirk, William S.	Pvt. E	116 OH Inf.	08-26-1864	1460	Weverton, Monocacy
Bussard, William H.	Pvt. A	150 IN Inf.	04-13-1865	3409	Frederick
Butcher, John	Pvt. B	75 NY Inf.	10-12-1864	118	Frederick
Butler, Albert	Pvt. H	2 MA Inf.	09-14-1864	1046	Frederick, Monocacy
Butler, Henry	Pvt. I	15 MA Inf.	11-19-1862	981	Smoketown
Butler, John	Pvt. C	21 NY Cav.	05-03-1865	14	Frederick
Buxton, George	Pvt. I	3 WI Inf.	10-18-1861	3281	Frederick
Byrne, John	Pvt. B	4 NY Inf.		790	Antietam
C., C.	Corp.	NY		289	Burkettsville
C., John H.	Pvt.	7 ME Art.		3194	Middletown
C., Peter M.	Pvt.	17 MI Inf.		2379	Weverton, Died Disease
Cady, J. D.	Pvt. B	2 MA Inf.	09-25-1862	1060	Frederick, Antietam
Calahan, Patrick	Pvt. D	107 NY Inf.	09-17-1862	634	Antietam, WIA
Caldwell, William P.	Pvt. A	1 MD Inf.	12-20-1863	2584	Point of Rocks
Callahan, Peter	Pvt. K	123 PA Inf.	11-04-1862	3824	Sharpsburg, Wounded S. Mt.
Callighan, Patrick	Pvt. D	104 NY Inf.	10-24-1862	244	Frederick, Antietam
Calvin, Frederick	Pvt. D	2 MA Inf.	05-26-1862	1021	Frederick, Age 19
Cameron, Joseph L.	Corp. I	67 OH Inf.		1230	Cumberland
Campbell, Adna H. R.	Pvt. F	6 ME Inf.	07-20-1863	3126	Frederick, Age 19
Campbell, Edward	Pvt. H	23 NY Inf.	10-11-1862	595	Antietam, WIA
Campbell, Henry	Pvt. D	10 ME Inf.	09-17-1862	3169	Antietam
Campbell, Jacob	Corp. A	45 PA Inf.	09-14-1862	3882	South Mountain, KIA
Campbell, John	Pvt. K	155 PA Inf.	11-09-1862	4045	Frederick
Campbell, John	Pvt. E	33 NY Inf.	09-29-1862	426	Burkettsville, S. Mt.
Campbell, John W.	Pvt. G	49 NY Inf.	11-16-1862	384	Hagerstown, Antietam
Canfield, Frederick	Pvt. C	1 PA Res.		3856	South Mountain
Canterberry, Griffin	Pvt. G	3 WV Cav.	04- -1865	2950	Clarysville
Cantwell, A. L.	Pvt. E	27 IN Inf.		3463	Antietam
Carey, James	Pvt. C	2 MA Inf.	02-14-1862	1067	Frederick
Carey, James	Pvt. G	32 MA Inf.	10-25-1862	892	Antietam
Carey, John	Pvt. K	71 PA Inf.	10-10-1862	3935	Frederick, WIA Antietam
Carl, Martin	Pvt. H	CT Cav.		1125	Weverton
Carlow, Thomas W.	Corp. K	14 IN Inf.	09-17-1862	3438	Antietam
Carmichael, Alfred	Sgt. H	NY Inf.		741	Antietam
Carney, Charles B.	Pvt. C	1 PA Res.	09-14-1862	1698	South Mountain, KIA

Name	Rank/Co.	Reg./State	Death	Grave No.	Removed from/ Comments
Carney, John A.	Pvt. G	96 OH Inf.		1255	Cumberland
Carney, Mason	Pvt. I	17 MI Inf.	09-14-1862	2510	S. Mt., WIA, from Dundee
Carpenter, Albert H.	Pvt. A	156 NY Inf.	10-27-1864	117	Frederick
Carpenter, Cyrus	Pvt. B	121 NY Inf.	11-24-1862	390	Hagerstown, Antietam
Carpenter, George	Pvt. C	170 OH Inf.	08- -1864	1468	Weverton, Monocacy
Carpenter, George W.	Pvt. G	111 PA Inf.	09-17-1862	3672	Antietam, KIA
Carpenter, Octavius	Pvt. F	193 OH Inf.	05-10-1865	1157	Clarysville
Carr, Bernard	Pvt. G	69 PA Inf.	06-29-1862	3662	Antietam
Carr, John	Pvt. K	59 NY Inf.	11-12-1862	605	Smoketown
Carr, Michael	Pvt. B	2 US Cav.	07-06-1863	3559	Frederick
Carrigan, James	Pvt.	14 US Inf.		3516	South Mountain
Carroll, James	Pvt. C	9 NY Art.	07-13-1864	64	Frederick, WIA Monocacy
Carroll, Samuel	Pvt. K	2 NJ Inf.	09-17-1862	2781	Antietam, KIA
Carson, Mathew	Pvt. G	21 NY Inf.		644	Antietam
Carter, James	Pvt. B	67 OH Inf.		1234	Cumberland
Carter, James	Pvt. B	192 OH Inf.	04-19-1865	1274	Frederick
Carter, James B.	Sgt. F	7 OH Inf.	09-17-1862	1349	Antietam
Carter, William M.	1st Lt. B	8 PA Res.	09-14-1862	867	Middletown, KIA S. Mt.
Carton, Peter	Corp. H	125 PA Inf.	09-17-1862	3746	Antietam, KIA
Carty, M.	Pvt. E	1 NY Cav.		44	Cumberland
Carver, Daniel	Pvt. K	14 NJ Inf.	12-07-1862	2909	Frederick, Antietam
Case, Oliver C.	Pvt. B	8 CT Inf.	09-17-1862	1090	Antietam, KIA
Case, Orville J.	Pvt. A	16 CT Inf.	10-22-1862	1118	Antietam, Died Disease
Casey, James	Pvt. B	84 PA Inf.		4158	Clarysville
Casey, Miles	Corp. K	108 NY Inf.		553	Antietam
Casey, Richard	Pvt. G	4 US Inf.	10-23-1862	3538	Frederick, Antietam
Casler, Joseph	Pvt. H	121 NY Inf.	11-12-1862	361	Hagerstown, Antietam
Casporas, William J.	Pvt. B	6 WI Inf.	09-17-1862	3343	Antietam, KIA
Casselman, Albert	Pvt. K	9 NY Art.	07-09-1864	79	Monocacy, KIA
Cassidy, Francis	Pvt. G	19 MA Inf.	09-17-1862	901	Antietam
Caster, James L.	Pvt. E	15 WV Inf.	08- -1864	2725	Weverton, Died at Sandy Hook
Castle, James F.	Pvt. F	13 WV Inf.	08-12-1864	2725	See Caster, James L.
Castle, Morton	Pvt. C	8 CT Inf.	10-17-1862	1126	Hagerstown, Ant., Age 19
Casto, Simeon	Pvt. E	1 WV Art.	07-31-1863	2770	Hancock
Cathis, David M.	Pvt. C	104 NY Inf.	07-20-1863	571	WIA Gettysburg, Jul 1 63
Catlin, George W.	Pvt. C	16 MI Inf.	10-26-1862	2522	Sharpsburg, Typhoid Fever
Cator, George H.	Pvt. I	132 PA Inf.	09-17-1862	3809	Smoketown, WIA Ant.
Caughlin, James	Pvt. D	107 PA Inf.	10-10-1862	3934	Frederick, Antietam
Caushey, Lebons B.	Sgt. C	4 PA Cav.	06-29-1863	4073	Frederick
Cayler, Leonanrd	Pvt. H	10 NY Inf.		327	Weverton
Chadbourn, Edward C.	Sgt. C	5 ME Inf.		3192	Smoketown
Chadwick, G. W.	Pvt. I	20 MA Inf.	01-16-1864	1033	Frederick
Chaffer, Wilbur E.	Pvt. I	17 MI Inf.	10-31-1862	2398	Ant., WIA, from Kalamazoo
Chamberlain, Myron	Pvt. I	51 NY Inf.		776	Antietam
Chamberlain, Napolean	Pvt. D	19 IN Inf.	09-17-1862	3450	Antietam
Chamberlin, L. G.	Pvt. I	6 ME Inf.	10-09-1862	3180	Antietam
Chambers, Henry	Pvt. K	45 PA Inf.	09-14-1862	3888	South Mountain, KIA
Chambers, R.	Pvt.	1 NY Art.		542	Antietam
Chandler, Adoniram	Pvt. D	19 MA Inf.	01-03-1864	1032	Frederick, Died Disease
Chedister, John	Pvt. I	15 WV Inf.	10-04-1864	2711	Weverton, Monocacy
Cheney, James A.	Pvt. E	106 NY Inf.	12-13-1862	34	Cumberland Gap
Cherrington, Spencer	Pvt. K	36 OH Inf.	09-14-1862	1496	Frederick, S. Mt.
Chester, Samuel	Pvt. K	2 PA Art.		4160	Frostburg
Chestnut, Jasper	Sgt. C	6 WI Inf.	01-23-1863	3269	Frederick, Died Disease
Chevalere, Edwin	Pvt. A	5 NY Art.		310	Weverton, Monocacy
Chivens, Hiram W.	Pvt. A	194 OH Inf.	03-30-1865	1270	Frederick
Chranister, John D.	Pvt. E	45 PA Inf.	09-25-1862	3918	Middletown, WIA S. Mt.
Christian, Leon	Pvt. I	1 US Art.	09-07-1863	3566	Frederick, Age 23

Name	Rank/Co.	Reg./State	Death	Grave No.	Removed from/ Comments
Christie, Garn M.	Pvt. F	134 PA Inf.	11-07-1862	4036	Frederick, Age 27
Christy, Andrew	Pvt. D	104 NY Inf.	11-12-1862	609	Smoketown
Church, Harry	Pvt. H	7 PA Inf.	09-22-1862	3721	Antietam
Clafferty, P. M.	Pvt.	51 NY Inf.		5	Antietam
Clark	Pvt.	27 IN Inf.		3474	Antietam
Clark, Alvin	Pvt. G	24 NY Inf.	09-14-1862	485	South Mountain, KIA
Clark, Austin	Pvt. C	3 WI Inf.	11-14-1861	3216	Frederick, Died Disease
Clark, Elwin	Pvt. L	12 PA Cav.	07-30-1863	3611	Antietam
Clark, Enoch	Pvt. A	4 MD Inf.	02-17-1862	2440	Frederick
Clark, George	Pvt. G	6 MI Cav.	03-08-1865	2415	Killed Boonsboro, from Lansing
Clark, George A.	Pvt. H	20 ME Inf.	10-25-1862	3155	Antietam
Clark, I. F.	Pvt. M	12 PA Cav.	05-06-1864	4015	Brownsville
Clark, James A.	Pvt. F	7 WI Inf.	09-14-1862	3242	South Mountain, KIA
Clark, James D.	Pvt. H	134 PA Inf.	11-14-1862	4035	Frederick, Age 35
Clark, John	Pvt. A	72 PA Inf.	10-06-1862	4202	Frederick, Antietam
Clark, John W.	Pvt.	1 MA Art.	10-04-1862	1000	Antietam, Age 42
Clark, John W.	Pvt. I	19 IN Inf.	09-17-1862	3449	Antietam
Clark, Joseph B.	Pvt. G	136 PA Inf.	01-20-1863	3713	Smoketown
Clark, Thomas H.	Pvt. I	125 PA Inf.	09-17-1862	3784	Antietam, KIA
Clark, William	Pvt. K	11 PA Res.	09-17-1862	3691	Antietam, KIA
Clark, William H.	Pvt. A	111 PA Inf.	10-13-1862	3817	Smoketown, WIA Ant.
Clarke, George E.	Pvt.	66 NY Inf.		461	South Mountain
Clay, Thomas	Pvt. F	35 MA Inf.	09-17-1862	893	Antietam
Clayton, Isaac	Pvt. A	14 NJ Inf.	12-29-1862	2896	Frederick, Antietam
Clazey, W.	Pvt. F	MD	04-02-1864	2597	Frederick, Age 32
Clegg, Moses	Corp. E	16 OH Inf.	10-13-1864	1311	Frederick
Clehaner, J.	Private B	11 US Inf.	09-21-1862	3570	Frederick, Antietam
Clement, Henry	Pvt. A	3 WI Inf.	10-16-1861	3283	Frederick, KIA
Clements	Pvt.	MI	- -1862	2486	Middletown
Clements, Aaron	Pvt. H	1 NY Cav.	10-07-1864	18	Clarysville, Monocacy
Clendenan, G. Washington	Corp. D	137 PA Inf.	10-24-1862	3929	Frederick
Cleveland, Peter	Pvt. I	94 NY Inf.	10-23-1862	621	Smoketown
Cline, David	Pvt. H	191 OH Inf.	06-23-1865	1170	Clarysville
Close, Levi	Pvt. D	3 WI Inf.	01-25-1862	3215	Frederick
Clouser, William H.	Pvt. D	47 PA Inf.	09-12-1864	4006	Weverton
Clum, Chauncey J.	Pvt. B	33 NY Inf.	10-01-1862	157	Frederick, WIA Ant.
Clute, John	Pvt. E	36 OH Inf.	12-31-1864	1200	Cumberland
Clyce, Jacob	Pvt. C	8 MI Inf.	09-17-1862	2521	Antietam, WIA, from Cos.
Coates, George	Pvt.	28 NY Inf.		471	South Mountain
Coats, William	Pvt. F	15 WV Inf.		2720	Cumberland
Cobb, James	Pvt. G	9 WV Inf.	09-26-1864	2618	Frederick, Monocacy
Coburn, William T.	Pvt. H	126 OH Inf.	07-16-1864	1291	Frederick, Monocacy
Cochran, James F.	Corp. M	3 WV Cav.	09-19-1864	2943	Clarysville
Cockrille, William A.	Pvt. C	12 OH Inf.	09-14-1862	1413	South Mountain
Coe, Alson	Pvt. G	7 OH Inf.	09-21-1862	1373	Smoketown
Coffer, Michael	Pvt.	20 NY Inf.		842	Antietam
Coffin, C. F.	Pvt. I	2 US Sharp.		837	Antietam
Cohn, Uriah	Pvt. M	12 PA Cav.	07-12-1864	4120	Frederick, WIA
Colby, J.				2123	Middletown
Cole, Campbell	Pvt. H	6 PA Res.	09-17-1862	3676	Antietam, KIA
Cole, Charles S.	Pvt. K	75 NY Inf.	09-12-1864	100	Frederick, Monocacy
Cole, John W.	Pvt. F	8 IL Cav.	07-15-1863	3038	Boonsboro
Cole, Orville B.	Pvt. G	8 OH Inf.	09-17-1862	1332	Antietam
Cole, Rufas	Pvt. B	7 WI Inf.	10-07-1862	3247	Antietam, WIA
Cole, Volney A.	Pvt. B	6 WI Inf.	09-17-1862	3339	Antietam, KIA
Cole, William	Pvt. E	15 NY Cav.	09-29-1864	354	Burkettsville, Monocacy
Cole, William H.	Pvt. B	1 WV Inf.	01-09-1865	2698	Frederick
Coleman, Charles	Pvt. E	1 PA Inf.	09-24-1862	3402	Frederick
Coleman, Henry	Pvt.	2 DE Inf.	10-02-1862	3111	Frederick, Antietam

Name	Rank/Co.	Reg./State	Death	Grave No.	Removed from/ Comments
Coligan, W.	Pvt. C	2 MA Cav.	09-28-1864	1050	Frederick, Monocacy
Coller, Thomas	Pvt. I	27 NY Inf.		566	Antietam
Collier, Darius	Pvt. D	37 MA Inf.	10-21-1862	1016	Hagerstown, Died Disease
Collins, Enos S.	Pvt. B	16 NY Inf.	09-30-1862	431	Middletown, Antietam
Collins, George	Pvt. K	39 IL Inf.	07-14-1862	3075	Fulton Co., PA, Died Disease
Collins, John	2nd Lt.	121 NY Inf.		867	Weverton
Collins, Levi	Pvt. I	9 NY Inf.		750	Antietam
Collins, Samuel	Pvt. A	7 MI Inf.	09-24-1862	2382	Ant., Died Disease, from Savilac
Combs, Robert S.	Pvt. E	10 NJ Inf.	08-19-1864	2797	Weverton, Monocacy
Commerford, Daniel	Pvt. B	62 NY Inf.	10-20-1862	124	Frederick, Antietam
Compton, John	Sgt. I	14 NJ Inf.	07-23-1864	2931	Frederick, Monocacy
Comstock, Josephus	Pvt. G	116 OH Inf.	12-16-1862	1214	Cumberland
Conger, William H. H.	Pvt. H	106 NY Inf.	07-17-1864	77	Frederick, Monocacy
Conklin, H. S.	Pvt. E	3 NY Inf.	11-10-1862	383	Hagerstown, Antietam
Conklin, John	Pvt. E	15 NY Cav.	06-03-1864	169	Frederick
Conklin, John H. H.	Pvt. G	124 NY Inf.	07-14-1863	185	Frederick, Age 22
Conklin, W. H.	Pvt. A	14 NY St.M.		458	Middletown
Connelly, Stephen	Pvt. B	2 DE Inf.	09-17-1862	3053	Antietam, KIA
Connelly, Thomas	Pvt. M	5 US Cav.		3497	Hagerstown
Conner, Timothy	Pvt. E	2 WI Inf.	09-17-1862	3299	Antietam, KIA
Connerty, Thomas	Pvt. E	51 NY Inf.		779	
Connor, John M.	Pvt.	8 OH Inf.		1356	Antietam
Connors, Thomas	Pvt.	42 NY Inf.		712	Antietam
Conrad, John	Pvt.	27 IN Inf.		3462	Antietam
Conrow, Darling	Pvt. K	14 NJ Inf.	12-16-1862	2899	Frederick, Antietam
Conway, James	Pvt.	9 NY Inf.		4	Antietam
Conway, Joseph	Corp. E	7 WV Inf.	11-06-1862	2630	Frederick, Antietam
Cook, Allen C.	Pvt. E	105 NY Inf.	10-24-1862	504	Smoketown
Cook, P. E.	Pvt.	89 NY Inf.		1	Antietam
Cook, Walter	Pvt. K	15 NY Inf.	11-11-1864	28	Clarysville
Cook, William	Pvt. K	156 OH Inf.	08-10-1864	1158	Clarysville, Monocacy
Cooley, George W.	Pvt. F	7 WI Inf.	09-14-1862	3243	South Mountain, KIA
Coon, Benjamin	Pvt. I	12 IN Inf.	08-03-1861	3489	Hagerstown
Cooper, Francis	Pvt. B	122 OH Inf.	06-28-1863	1207	Clarysville
Cooper, J. A.	Pvt.	16 IN Inf.		3385	Frederick
Cooper, Jeremiah	Pvt. K	14 PA Cav.	07-12-1864	4095	Frederick
Cooper, Thomas				1749	
Cooper, William	Pvt. D	2 US Cav.	10-25-1864	3510	Weverton
Copp, Andrew J.	Pvt. C	32 MA Inf.	10-09-1862	1079	Lutheran Cemetery, Ant.
Copp, Joseph	Pvt. B	15 NY Inf.	07-23-1864	93	Frederick, Monocacy
Corbett, Charles P.	Pvt. G	16 ME Inf.	10-24-1862	3189	Smoketown
Cormick, John	Pvt.	9 NY Cav.	04-05-1865	134	Frederick
Corn, Moses	Pvt. G	7 IN Inf.	09-29-1862	3380	Cumberland
Cornman, Oscar L.	Corp. B	1 MN Inf.	09-17-1862	3028	Antietam, KIA
Corpers, P.	Pvt.	2 NY Inf.		681	Antietam
Corrigan, John	Pvt. B	24 NY Inf.		254	Antietam, WIA
Corstiruppleicutt, W.	Pvt.	87 NY Inf.		704	Antietam
Corwin, Squire	Pvt. G	23 IL Inf.	09-29-1864	3105	Clarysville, Monocacy
Costello, Charles	Pvt. P	28 PA Inf.	09-17-1862	3745	Antietam, WIA
Costley, John	Pvt. B	136 PA Inf.	10-18-1862	3944	Frederick, Age 22
Cotter, Henry	Pvt. A	138 PA Inf.	07-14-1864	4099	Frederick, Monocacy, Age 28
Cotton, Elisha	Pvt. I	36 OH Inf.	03-03-1865	1161	Clarysville
Cotton, Joseph L.	Corp. B	76 NY Inf.	09-14-1862	472	South Mountain, KIA
Courteny, Charles J.	Pvt. F	89 NY Inf.	09-29-1862	824	Antietam, WIA
Cowan, John	Pvt. B	5 NY Inf.	04-17-1864	408	Burkettsville
Cowan, William	Pvt. E	16 CT Inf.	10-22-1862	1105	Antietam, WIA
Cowell, John	Pvt. A	14 NJ Inf.	01-05-1863	2919	Frederick, Antietam

Name	Rank/Co.	Reg./State	Death	Grave No.	Removed from/ Comments
Cox, Richard H.	Pvt. E	35 MA Inf.	09-22-1862	987	Antietam, WIA
Cox, William L.	Pvt. E	14 WV Inf.	12-26-1862	2754	Cumberland
Coyle, James	Pvt. F	13 NJ Inf.	01-12-1863	2918	Frederick, Antietam
Cozad, W. H. H.	Corp. I	6 WV Inf.	10-08-1864	2951	Clarysville
Craig, F.	Pvt. I	59 NY Inf.		541	Antietam
Craig, Franklin	Pvt. K	149 OH Inf.	07-09-1864	1298	Frederick, Monocacy
Craig, Wesly	Pvt. F	7 WI Inf.	09-17-1862	3334	Antietam, KIA
Craig, William H.	Pvt. D	14 MA Inf.	11-14-1862	1015	Hagerstown, Antietam
Cram, James	Pvt. E	137 NY Inf.	11-07-1862	226	Frederick
Crane, Newman	Pvt. H17	MI Inf.	10-11-1862	2393	S. Mt., WIA, From Fayette
Crater, Jacob B.	Pvt. H	3 PA. Res.	09-17-1862	3797	Antietam, KIA
Crater, John	Pvt. I	10 NJ Inf.	07-12-1865	2938	Frederick
Crawfoed, M. H.	Sgt.	72 NY Inf.	08-24-1864	105	Frederick, Monocacy
Crawford, Charles N.	Pvt. A	104 NY Inf.	10-02-1862	551	Antietam, WIA
Crawford, Walter	Pvt. E	27 NY Inf.	02-27-1863	613	Died Chronic Diarrhea
Crick, J. W.	Pvt.	28 PA Inf.		3641	Antietam
Cronk, Henry	Pvt. F	5 NY Art.		318	Weverton, Monocacy
Crooks, John W.	Pvt. G	100 PA Inf.	10-04-1862	4208	Frederick, S. Mt.
Cross, Charles J.	Pvt. L	9 NY Mil.	11-03-1862	217	Frederick, Antietam
Cross, Nelson N.	Pvt. C	5 VT. Cav.	07-10-1863	2693	Funkstown, Age 18
Crossan, Alexander	Pvt. E	34 OH Inf.	08-24-1864	1318	Frederick, Monocacy
Crouch, Edwin L.	Pvt. I	34 MA Inf.	05-21-1864	1072	WIA
Crouch, George	Pvt. H	75 OH Inf.	07-28-1862	1264	Frederick
Cullen, Frank	Pvt. H	24 NY Inf.	10-05-1862	163	Frederick, Antietam
Culver, Frederick D.	Pvt. K	11 CT Inf.	10-26-1862	1110	Antietam, WIA
Cummings, David	Pvt. K	6 WI Inf.	09-17-1862	3340	Antietam, KIA
Cummons, William	Pvt. E	2 DE Inf.	09-17-1862	3052	Antietam, KIA
Cumpson, Thomas	Pvt. C	9 WV Inf.	07-10-1864	2602	Weverton
Cunningham, G. N.	Pvt. A	16 NY Inf.		356	Burkettsville
Cunningham, J. Franklin	Pvt. C	3 WV Cav.	08-25-1864	2715	Weverton, Monocacy
Cunningham, John	Pvt. K	14 CT Inf.	12-03-1862	1138	Frederick, Antietam
Cunningham, Robert T.	Pvt. K	5 VT Inf.	10-09-1864	2635	Frederick, Monocacy, Age 32
Cunningham, William A.	Pvt. A	10 WV Inf.	07-06-1864	2955	Weverton, Wounded Harpers Ferry
Curley, John	Sgt. B	69 NY Inf.	10-28-1862	238	Frederick, Antietam
Curley, Thomas					See Connerty, Thomas
Curran, T. A.	Pvt.	21 NY Inf.		648	Antietam
Currey, James E.	Pvt. E	84 NY Inf.		456	Antietam, WIA
Curry, John	Pvt. C	5 NY Art.	01-16-1865	126	Frederick
Curry, Joseph	Corp. M	15 NY Cav.		46	Cumberland
Curry, R. C.	Pvt. K	4 NJ Inf.	09-14-1862	2089	South Mountain
Curtis, Hanford	Pvt. A	14 CT Inf.	12-17-1862	1141	Frederick, Antietam
Curtis, Richard	Pvt. E	20 MI Inf.	11-08-1862	2483	Middletown, Antietam
Curtis, Thomas	Pvt. I	150 IN Inf.	04-11-1865	3411	Frederick
Cushman, Fairfield	Pvt. B	1 ME Cav.	07-14-1862	3114	Frederick
D., David	Pvt.	NY		396	Weverton
D., J. H.	Pvt.	11 OH Inf.		1411	South Mountain
Dagle, George V.	Pvt. K	8 CT Inf.	09-17-1862	1095	Antietam, KIA
Dailey, John	Pvt. G	14 IN Inf.	02-25-1862	3374	Cumberland
Dailey, Myers	Pvt. A	53 PA Inf.	09-17-1862	3592	Antietam
Dakin, William G.	Pvt. C	6 WV Inf.	07-13-1864	2761	Cumberland
Daley, Andrew J.	Pvt. K	36 OH Inf.	09-14-1862	1431	South Mountain
Daley, Timothy	Pvt. A	63 NY Inf.	10-09-1862	52	Antietam, WIA
Dall, Robert E.	Pvt. G	51 NY Inf.		778	Antietam
Damren, Charles M.	Pvt. C	29 ME Inf.	11-23-1864	3123	Frederick
Darcey, Patrick	Pvt. I	42 NY Inf.		711	Antietam
Darling, Ansel J.	Pvt. G	17 MI Inf.	09-17-1862	2384	Antietam, KIA, from Backmer
Darly, Greenleaf S.	Pvt. C	14 NJ Inf.	07-09-1864	2933	Frederick, Monocacy

Name	Rank/Co.	Reg./State	Death	Grave No.	Removed from/ Comments
Darragh, John	Pvt. D	145 NY Inf.	12-20-1862	197	Hagerstown, Antietam
Daunt, William	Pvt. E	4 PA Cav.		3822	Antietam
Davenport, Erasonus	Pvt. G	27 IN Inf.	01-01-1862	3391	Frederick
Davidson, David B.	Corp. I	6 VT Inf.	11-05-1862	2668	Hagerstown, Ant., Age 19
Davidson, James S.	Pvt. F	9 OH Inf.		1222	Cumberland
Davidson, Samuel	Pvt. B	59 NY Inf.		690	Antietam
Davidson, William	Pvt. D	137 PA Inf.	11-04-1862	3969	Hagerstown
Davis, Alfred	Pvt. E	15 MA Inf.	09-22-1862	954	Hagerstown, Ant., from Clappsville
Davis, Ethan	Pvt. E	29 OH Inf.	03-08-1862	1217	Cumberland
Davis, George	Corp. B	22 MA Inf.	10-04-1862	1058	Frederick, WIA Ant., Age 44
Davis, George H.	Pvt. B	23 OH Inf.	09-10-1864	1388	Middletown
Davis, George W.	Sgt. K	21 MA Inf.	09-26-1862	990	Antietam
Davis, J. C.	Sgt.	51 PA Inf.		3616	Antietam
Davis, John C.	Pvt. D	125 PA Inf.	09-17-1862	3667	Antietam, KIA
Davis, John E.	Pvt.	26 NY Inf.		686	Antietam
Davis, Lewis E.	Pvt. I	51 PA Inf.	09-14-1862	3911	South Mountain, KIA
Davis, Mathias	Pvt. A	7 IN Inf.		3371	Cumberland
Davis, Miles	Pvt. H	89 NY Inf.	03-08-1863	180	Frederick, Age 19
Davis, Miles H.	Pvt. C	116 OH Inf.	10-12-1864	1454	Weverton
Davis, Randolph	Pvt. L	1 CT Cav.	01-14-1865	1192	Frederick
Davis, William	Pvt. C	121 NY Inf.	12-09-1862	427	Burkettsville, Antietam
Davis, William E.	Pvt. D	192 NY Inf.	04-21-1864	16	Cumberland
Daw, J.	Pvt. D	111 PA Inf.		3659	Antietam
Dawson, Mathew S.	Pvt. H	107 NY Inf.	09-27-1862	150	Frederick, Antietam
Day, George E.	Pvt. F	6 ME Inf.	03-12-1863	3185	Smoketown
Day, Putnam	2nd Lt.	5 CT Inf.	1861	887	Frederick
Day, William H.	Pvt. H	1 VT Cav.	08-25-1864	2657	Weverton, Monocacy, Age 18
Deagle, Gotlieb	Pvt. A	53 PV Inf.	09-17-1862	3593	Antietam
Dean, Henry W.	Pvt. B	12 PA Res.	09-14-1862	3825	South Mountain, KIA
Dean, Jesse P.	Pvt. B	3 WI Inf.	02-05-1863	3270	Frederick, Died Disease
Dean, Patrick	Pvt.	NY Inf.		272	Antietam
Dean, Simon P.	Pvt. C	6 VT Inf.	08-24-1864	2658	Weaverton, Monocacy, Age 32
Dearborn, Henry C.	Pvt. F.	9 NH Inf.	10-01-1862	2800	Antietam
Dearman, Elliot	Pvt. F	11 WV Inf.	09-05-1863	2769	Cumberland
Dearry, Bernard					See Darcey, Patrick
Debretz, Michael	Corp. K	11 OH Inf.	09-14-1862	1421	South Mountain
Deeker, George	Pvt. L	15 NY Cav.	07-09-1864	60	Hagerstown
Deincher, D. H.	Pvt. A	2 MD Inf.	09-30-1864	2438	Clarysville, Self-inflicted wounds
Delagrange, Omie	Pvt. C	1 WV Cav.	07-17-1862	2704	Hancock
Delahanty, Patrick	Pvt. F	14 VT Inf.	07-17-1863	2652	Frederick, Age 18
Delahunt, William	Pvt. K	27 IN Inf.	10-13-1862	3494	Frederick, Antietam
Delaney, Daniel	Pvt. B	1 MD Cav.	01-05-1865	2437	Clarysville
Delaney, John	Pvt. C	57 NY Inf.	12-26-1862	194	Hagerstown, Antietam
Delano, Macey	Pvt. E	77 NY Inf.	11-20-1862	365	Hagerstown, Antietam
Delavergue, G. A.	Pvt.	9 NY Inf.		742	Antietam
Dellinger, John	Pvt.	4 US Art.		4232	Hagerstown, Removed Dec. 1889
Delorme, Louis	2nd Lt. H	99 NY Inf.	09-17-1862	860	Antietam
Demerest, Martin V. B.	Pvt. K	13 NJ Inf.	10-20-1862	2791	Frederick, Antietam, Age 21
Denfetney, James	Pvt. B	NY Art.	08-04-1864	319	Weverton, Monocacy
Denham, Joseph	Pvt. A	146 IN Inf.	04-15-1865	3366	Clarysville
Denn, Myron H					See Dunn, M. H.
Denney, William	Pvt. I	111 PA Inf.	09-17-1862	3660	Antietam, KIA
Dennis, Richard	Pvt. D	17 MI Inf.	10-02-1862	2484	Weverton, Died Disease
Deputy, Henry	Pvt. E	27 IN Inf.	01-18-1863	3425	Frederick, Antietam

Name	Rank/Co.	Reg./State	Death	Grave No.	Removed from/ Comments
Deputy, William	Pvt.	27 IN Inf.		3452	Antietam
DeShetler, Basil L.					See Deshleter, Basil L.
Deshields, William	Corp. K	1 MD Cav.	08-06-1864	2563	Keedysville, KIA
Deshleter, Basil L.	Pvt. D	7 MI Inf.	10-09-1862	2516	Antietam, WIA, from Monroe
Detrick, George	Pvt. F	23 OH Inf.		1409	South Mountain
Devlin, John	Pvt.	9 NY Inf.		755	Antietam
Dewey, Daniel D.	Pvt. E	196 OH Inf.	04-22-1865	1152	Clarysville
Dexter, Samuel	2nd Lt. B	42 NY Inf.	09-17-1862	854	Antietam
Dey, Austin A.	Pvt. K	14 NJ Inf.	11-16-1862	2914	Frederick, Antietam
Deyarman, John	Pvt. F	7 WV Inf.	02-12-1862	2849	Cumberland
Dickers, Charles	Pvt. E	116 OH Inf.	09-25-1864	1465	Weverton, Monocacy
Dickinson, Thomas	Pvt. E	6 MI Cav.	03-08-1865	2402	Frederick, Died Disease, from Bashnell
Dickson, John E.	Corp. G	24 MA Inf.	06-15-1864	1077	Clarysville
Dickson, William S.	Pvt. K	9 PA Res.	12-05-1862	4049	Frederick, WIA Ant.
Diekey, Orrin	Pvt. D	30 ME Inf.	02-17-1865	3122	Frederick
Diendonnie, M.	Pvt. E	1 NY Inf.	11-24-1862	211	Hagerstown, Antietam
Dierfield, James H.	Pvt. H	125 PA Inf.	09-17-1862	3610	Antietam, KIA
Dimock, Franklin	Pvt. F	29 OH Inf.	02-28-1862	1235	Cumberland
Dix, Hosea	Pvt. H	2 USSS	10-18-1862	268	Frederick, Antietam
Dixon, Robert A.	Pvt. I	23 OH Inf.	09-15-1862	1434	South Mountain
Dobbins, Thomas	Pvt. E	42 NY Inf.		835	Antietam
Dodds, William	Sgt. F	1 MI Cav.	02-07-1862	2409	Frederick, Died Disease, from Lapeer
Dodge, Henry C.	Pvt. H	8 CT Inf.	11-16-1862	1107	Antietam, WIA
Dodson, Charles G.	Pvt. C	13 WV Inf.	08-31-1864	2620	Frederick, Monocacy
Dolan, Pat					See Dooling, Patrick, 108 NY
Dolson, Frank	Pvt.	15 NY Inf.	05-15-1864	26	Clarysville
Donavan, William	Pvt. K	126 OH Inf.	09-15-1864	1469	Weverton, Monocacy
Donelson, Walter	Pvt. I	NY Art.		399	Weverton
Donley, Edward	Pvt. C	55 NY Inf.	11-07-1862	225	Hagerstown, Antietam
Donohoe, Francis	Pvt. H	9 NY Inf.		759	Antietam
Donohoe, James	Pvt. A	34 NY Inf.	09-17-1862	832	Antietam
Donohoe, Thomas					See Donohoe, Francis
Donoley, Michael	Pvt. B	105 NY Inf.		683	Antietam
Dooling, James	Corp. D	1 CT Cav.	07-08-1862	1188	Frederick
Dooling, Patrick	Pvt. I	59 NY Inf.	10-03-1862	255	Hagerstown, Antietam
Dooling, Patrick	Pvt. K	108 NY Inf.	10-10-1862	144	Frederick, Antietam
Dorlan, George	Pvt. F	10 NY Inf.		309	Weverton
Dorsey, Daniel	Pvt. K	1 MD Inf.	03-08-1864	2578	Weverton
Dose	Pvt.	NY		477	South Mountain
Doty, Nathaniel	Pvt. E	102 PA Inf.	11-07-1864	4128	Frederick, Age 35
Dougherty, Hugh	Pvt. F	81 PA Inf.	10-17-1862	3811	Smoketown
Douglass, Andrew J.	Pvt. B	14 WV Inf.	08-27-1864	2726	Weverton, Monocacy
Douglass, Edmund	Pvt.	72 PA Inf.		3643	Antietam
Douglass, George	Pvt. I	6 WI Inf.	09-17-1862	3349	Antietam, KIA
Dove, Henry	Pvt. B	7 MD Inf.	01-23-1863	2451	Hagerstown, Age 26
Dowd, Thomas	Pvt. D	106 PA Inf.	09-17-1862	3786	Antietam, KIA
Dowda, Robert O.	Pvt. N	28 PA Inf.	09-17-1862	3639	Antietam, KIA
Dowling, James	Corp. G	51 PA Inf.	09-17-1862	3583	Antietam, KIA
Downey, Henry	Pvt. K	91 OH Inf.	11-01-1864	1309	Frederick
Dows, James G.	Pvt. H	77 NY Inf.	11-25-1862	229	Hagerstown, Antietam
Drake, Francis E.	Pvt. C	1 ME Cav.	10-24-1862	3140	Frederick, Antietam
Drake, George C.	Pvt. A	1 WI Inf.	07-02-1861	3259	Falling Waters VA, KIA
Drake, Guy F.	Pvt. G	3 WV Cav.	03-21-1865	2700	Frederick
Dreber, William	Pvt. H	50 PA Inf.	11-04-1862	4005	Weverton, Antietam
Drinkwater, George	Pvt. E	12 US Inf.	11-02-1862	3548	Frederick, Antietam
Ducia, Anthony	Pvt. C	196 OH Inf.	05-24-1865	1154	Clarysville
Dudeck, Alexander	Pvt. B	7 NY Inf.	11-03-1862	222	Hagerstown

Name	Rank/Co.	Reg./State	Death	Grave No.	Removed from/ Comments
Dudley, Charles E.	Pvt. I	29 OH Inf.	04-01-1862	1251	Cumberland
Dudman, Charles	Pvt.	7 NY Inf.		550	Antietam
Duffee, D.	Pvt. C	1 DE Inf.	10-03-1862	3112	Frederick, Antietam
Dufford, Chronce	Pvt. D	137 PA Inf.	10-18-1862	3989	Hagerstown
Duffy, James	Pvt. K	27 IN Inf.	11-06-1862	3428	Frederick, Antietam
Duffy, John	Pvt. A	42 NY Inf.		714	Antietam
Duffy, John R.	Pvt. L	14 PA Cav.	06-10-1864	4092	Frederick
Dunham, Hiram G.	Pvt. G	39 IL Cav.	02-23-1862	3074	Cumberland
Dunham, John R.	Pvt. B	24 NY Cav.	07-30-1864	397	Weverton, Monocacy
Dunlap, William	Pvt. B	170 OH N.G.	07-28-1864	1300	Frederick, Monocacy
Dunn, Calvin	Pvt. D	123 OH Inf.	09-22-1864	1466	Weverton, Monocacy
Dunn, John	Pvt. A	23 OH Inf.	09-14-1862	1437	South Mountain, WIA
Dunn, M. H.	Corp. H	168 NY Inf.	08-30-1863	172	Hagerstown, Age 18
Durbin, David H.	Pvt. F	7 WV Inf.	05-20-1862	2881	Clarysville
Dusang, Samuel G.	Pvt. E	19 IN Inf.	09-29-1862	3480	Antietam
Dusold, J. G.	Pvt. D	8 IL Cav.	07-10-1863	3040	Boonsboro
Dutton, Johnathan R.	Pvt. G	49 NY Inf.	09-17-1862	734	Antietam, KIA
Dye, James	Pvt. I	194 OH Inf.	03-30-1865	1273	Frederick
Dye, John W.	Pvt. D	14 WV Inf.	12-07-1862	2854	Cumberland
Dyer, Nathaniel	Pvt. A	12 MA Inf.	09-17-1862	1876	Antietam
Eagon, James	Pvt. G	42 NY Inf.		668	Antietam
Eagon, John	Pvt. D	6 WI Inf.	10-10-1862	3264	Frederick, WIA Ant.
Eastman, Dunbar	Pvt. I	2 MA Inf.	02-22-1862	1063	Frederick
Eastman, Israel C.	Pvt. D	19 ME Inf.	10-23-1862	3933	Frederick
Easty, George W.	Pvt. D	10 ME Inf.	10-23-1862	3141	Frederick, Antietam
Eaton, Hiram A.	Corp. G	2 MA Inf.	07-20-1862	1066	Frederick
Eaton, James D.	Pvt. K	10 ME Inf.	09-17-1862	3159	Antietam
Ebert, Augustus	Pvt. F	103 NY Inf.	09-17-1862	498	Antietam, KIA
Ebert, John	Pvt. A	4 MI Inf.	11-30-1862	2401	Frederick, Died Disease, from Adrian
Edens, John	Pvt. A	13 WV Inf.	05-08-1865	2874	Clarysville
Edgerly, Amos	Pvt. D	135 OH N.G.	07-07-1864	1395	Middletown
Edmunson, Theodore	Pvt. C	36 OH Inf.	09-14-1862	1430	South Mountain, KIA
Edwards, Hamilton	Pvt. G	10 WV Inf.	04-23-1862	2852	Cumberland
Edwards, James	Pvt. F	69 PA Inf.	09-29-1862	4207	Frederick, Antietam
Edwards, William	Pvt. F	23 OH Inf.	09-14-1862	1401	Middletown, WIA S. Mt.
Eichendine, A.	Pvt. C	51 NY Inf.		780	Antietam
Eimer, Frederick	Pvt. H	15 WV Inf.	11-19-1862	2863	Clarysville, Antietam
Eister, Louis	Pvt. D	4 NY Inf.		537	Antietam
Elderkin, Jackson	Pvt. G	2 WV Cav.	11-09-1864	2615	Frederick
Eldridge, James V.	Pvt. D	23 OH Inf.	10-05-1862	1360	Antietam
Eldridge, M. D.	Pvt. L	22 NY Cav.	10-07-1864	298	Weverton, Monocacy
Elliott, Baker	Pvt. G	13 IN Inf.		3376	Cumberland
Elliott, John	Pvt. C	21 NY Inf.	11-30-1862	503	Smoketown
Ellis, J. H.	Pvt. F	7 WI Inf.	04-07-1862	3272	Frederick, Age 21, Died Disease
Ellison	Lt.	18 MA Inf.		861	Antietam
Ellsworth, Orrison	Pvt. A	9 NY Cav.	09-22-1864	312	Age 54
Elsey, Joshua	Pvt. A	7 WV Inf.	11-09-1862	2629	Frederick, Antietam
Elterman, Gustave	Pvt. G	2 WI Inf.	09-17-1862	3303	Antietam, KIA
Elwood, George	Pvt. D	26 NJ Inf.	11-06-1862	2798	Hagerstown, Antietam
Emery, Adam	Pvt. B	134 PA Inf.	11-12-1862	4034	Frederick
Emery, Frederick V.	Pvt. E	14 NY Inf.	10-13-1862	264	Frederick, Antietam
Emery, Jonas	Pvt. D	14 IN Inf.	10-27-1862	3470	Antietam
Emily, Alonzo	Pvt. G	14 NJ Inf.	12-07-1862	2911	Frederick, Antietam
Emly, Thomas	Pvt. G	15 NY Cav.	07-12-1864	32	Cumberland
Emrick, Henry	Pvt. B	24 NY Inf.	10-24-1862	243	Frederick, Antietam
English, George	Pvt. I	45 PA Inf.	09-14-1862	3890	South Mountain, KIA
Eno, Cleophas	Pvt. B	91 OH Inf.	08-09-1864	1258	Clarysville
Eoff, Leander	Pvt. E	116 NY Cav.	07-28-1864	1150	Clarysville

Name	Rank/Co.	Reg./State	Death	Grave No.	Removed from/ Comments
Erhart, Nicholas	Pvt. C	29 PA Inf.	03-10-1862	4187	Frederick, Age 41
Erichsen, Peter	Pvt. F	14 US Inf.	12-08-1862	3545	Frederick, Antietam
Erskine, Lewis	Pvt D	23 OH Inf.	03-13-1865	1162	Clarysville
Erskine, Theodore	Pvt. G	59 NY Inf.		694	Antietam
Estes, Samuel S.	Pvt. M	2 MA Cav.	06-15-1865	1073	Clarysville
Evans, Henry D.	Corp. I	16 CT Inf.	09-17-1862	1084	Antietam, KIA
Evans, James	Sgt. K	22 NY Inf.	09-14-1862	489	South Mountain, KIA
Evans, Joseph	Pvt. K	27 IN Inf.	01-20-1862	3393	Frederick
Evans, Leverett F.	Pvt. A	8 CT Inf.	11-15-1862	1139	Frederick, Antietam
Evans, William	Pvt.	26 NY Inf.		687	Antietam
Everest, George W.	Sgt. E	1 VT Cav.	07-14-1863	2671	Williamsport, Age 18
Everitt, David	Pvt. E	7 OH Inf.	10-06-1862	1375	Smoketown
Ewers, Edmund Jr.	Pvt. D	30 OH Inf.	09-21-1862	1364	Antietam
Eyre, Alfred	Pvt. E	4 NY Cav.	07-08-1862	50	Frederick
Eyton, Henry	Pvt.	5 OH Inf.		1342	Antietam
F., L.				2025	Antietam
Fably, Dennis	Pvt. B	66 NY Inf.	10-12-1862	262	Frederick, Antietam
Facenbaker, William	Pvt. G	2 MD Inf.	08-15-1862	2429	Cumberland
Fadden, Charles	Pvt. F	1 PA Res.		3853	South Mountain
Faehndrich, Julius	Pvt. G	103 NY Inf.	11-07-1862	223	Frederick, Antietam
Faidley, John	Sgt. I	13 WV Inf.	11-25-1862	2860	Clarysville
Fair, Chambers	Pvt. B	139 PA Inf.	11-13-1862	3968	Hagerstown, Age 20
Fairly, Samuel	Pvt. G	123 PA	11-14-1862	4039	Frederick, Age 19
Fales, Albert E.	Pvt. K	3 VT Inf.	09-21-1864	2661	Weverton, MOnocacy, Age 43
Fales, Anthony	Pvt. E	9 NY Art.	07-13-186 4	74	Frederick, WIA Monocacy, Age 23
Fanning, Henry C.	Pvt. D	8 CT Inf.	10-28-1862	1106	Antietam, WIA
Farlin, Burwell	Pvt. E	13 WV Inf.	03-10-1865	2877	Clarysville
Farmer, Thomas	Pvt. I	15 WV Inf.	01-29-1865	2886	Clarysville
Farmer, W.	Corp. D	8 CT Inf.		1112	Antietam
Farrell, Isaac	Pvt. H	4 WV Inf.	12-26-1864	2741	Clarysville
Fastnought, W. H.	Corp. K	142 PA Inf.	10-28-1862	3924	Frederick
Fawvor, James H.	Pvt. A	49 PA Inf.	11-16-1862	3957	Frederick
Fay, Emerson C.	Pvt. D	10 VT Inf.	09-24-1864	2660	Weaverton, Monocacy, Age 19
Fay, Michael	Pvt. A	2 RI Inf.		2840	Antietam, Age 38
Fee, Samuel	Pvt. F	3 PA Inf.	10-16-1862	3938	Frederick, Age 23
Felix, Warner	Pvt. H	9 WV Inf.	09-04-1864	2621	Frederick, Monocacy
Fenton, Henry	Corp. G	45 PA Inf.	09-14-1862	3879	South Mountain, KIA
Ferguson, James	Pvt. B	122 OH Inf.	07-15-1863	1471	Weverton
Ferguson, Scott M.	Pvt. E	11 PA Res.	09-14-1862	3847	South Mountain, KIA
Ferry, Amos	Pvt. E	11 OH Inf.	09-17-1862	1366	Antietam
Fesler, Samuel	Pvt. H	107 PA Inf.	09-17-1862	3736	Antietam, KIA
Fessington, Clinton	Pvt. E	11 CT Inf.	09-21-1862	1097	Antietam, WIA
Fessmeyer, Joseph	Pvt. K	6 MD Inf.	07-08-1863	2594	Frederick, Age 40
Fiddler, Joseph	Pvt.	27 IN Inf.		3458	Antietam
Fiddler, William	Pvt. D	27 IN Inf.	10-06-1862	3469	Antietam
Field, Benjamin F.	Corp. C	6 WV Cav.	07-17-1864	2952	Clarysville
Fields, James B.	Pvt. C	45 PA Inf.	03-19-1863	4079	Fred., WIA S. Mt., Age 19
Fields, John S.	Pvt. F	8 OH Inf.	09-17-1862	1334	Antietam
Fields, Myron H.	Pvt. A	21 NY Inf.	11-30-1862	620	Smoketown
Filkins, Anthony	Pvt. E	14 US Inf.	01-01-1863	3556	Frederick, Antietam
Finch, James	Pvt. M	5 IN Cav.	03-18-1865	3368	Clarysville
Finch, Richard G.	Sgt. D	1 MI Cav.	04-13-1862	2412	Frederick, Typhoid Fever, From Duplain
Finken, Henry	Pvt. K	8 CT Inf.	09-17-1862	1094	Antietam, KIA
Finly, William	Sgt. M	2 US Art.	09-17-1862	3519	Antietam
Finn, Michael	Pvt. A	88 NY Inf.	10-09-1862	162	Frederick, Antietam
Finney, Ira J.	Pvt. C	1 ME	08-21-1862	3197	Weverton

Name	Rank/Co.	Reg./State	Death	Grave No.	Removed from/ Comments
Finns, Dennis	Sgt. H	51 NY Inf.		768	Antietam
Fish, Harry	Pvt. D	105 NY Inf.	10-01-1862	142	Frederick, Antietam
Fish, Henry	Pvt. G	4 RI Inf.	09-17-1862	2824	Antietam, KIA
Fisher, Adolphus	Pvt. H	4 NY Cav.	07-18-1862	138	Frederick
Fisher, Albert H.	Pvt. H	7 MI Cav.	08-21-1864	2481	Frederick, Died Disease, From Barry
Fisher, Ezra R.	Pvt. I	4 ME Inf.	11-27-1862	3133	Frederick, Antietam
Fitz, James	Pvt. G	12 MA Inf.	11-06-1862	976	Smoketown
Fitzgerald, John	Pvt. E	13 NJ Inf.	12-01-1862	2778	Antietam, Died at Sharpsburg
Fitzgibbons, Patrick	Corp. I	5 OH Inf.	10-01-1862	1341	Antietam
Fitzpatrick, John	Pvt.			1260	Clarysville
Fitzpatrick, Michael	Pvt. I	139 PA Inf.	11-16-1862	3951	Hagerstown, Age 18
Fitzroy, Reginald	Pvt. E	21 NY Cav.	07-01-1864	65	Frederick
Flanagan, Vincent	Pvt. E	2 WI Inf.	09-17-1862	3296	Antietam, KIA
Fleak, William	Pvt. I	112 OH Inf.	08-12-1864	1450	Middletown
Fleming, Lewis G.	Pvt. C	11 WV Inf.	08-22-1864	2857	Clarysville
Fleming, Thomas	Pvt. I	28 MA Inf.	09-17-1862	951	Hagerstown, Antietam
Flemmer, Thomas	Pvt. A	12 PA Cav.	08-03-1864	4107	Frederick, Age 24
Flenner, L. G.	Pvt. I	161 OH Inf.	08-08-1864	1316	Frederick, Monocacy
Fletcher, Oliver	Pvt. I	5 ME Inf.		3191	Smoketown
Fletcher, Theodore	Pvt. G	2 WI Inf.	09-26-1862	3230	Antietam, WIA
Fliege, Henry	Pvt. F	7 MI Inf.	10-19-1862	2394	Antietam, WIA, From Haughton
Flinn, Michael	Pvt. L	21 NY Cav.	08-18-1864	101	Frederick, Monocacy
Flintham, George L.	Sgt. A	5 MD Inf.	10-24-1862	2591	Frederick, WIA Ant.
Floid, J. N.	Pvt. H.	15 NY Cav.	07-08-1864	73	Frederick
Flood, Edward	Pvt. P	28 PA Inf.	09-17-1862	3626	Antietam, KIA
Floyd, Benjamin	Pvt. B	5 NY Inf.	02-09-1863	591	Smoketown
Fluck, Peter L.	Pvt. K	138 PA Inf.	08-06-1864	4106	Frederick, WIA Monocacy
Fogg, Hosea	Pvt. A	14 PA Cav.	08-12-1864	4116	Frederick
Foley, Cornelius	Sgt.	2 NY Inf.		678	Antietam
Foley, Morgan	Pvt. H	14 US Inf.	11-29-1862	3551	Frederick, Antietam
Folfey, M.	Pvt. H	14 NJ Inf.	11-28-1862	2910	Frederick, Antietam
Folger, Augustus	Pvt. F	1 PA Res.		3904	Middletown
Folts, Richard D.	Pvt. I	3 WI Inf.	09-17-1862	3285	Frederick, Died Disease
Ford, Charles	Pvt. D	3 VT Inf.	12-22-1862	2669	Hagerstown, Died in Court-house, Ant.
Ford, D. W.			12-11-1862	1720	Frederick, Antietam
Ford, George	Lt. C	17 MI Inf.		879	Keedysville, From Cold Water
Ford, James	Pvt. C	12 US Inf.	12-24-1862	3552	Frederick, Antietam
Ford, John	Pvt. I	1 CT Cav.	10-17-1864	1120	Antietam, WIA Harpers Ferry
Ford, Robert T.				4230	Frederick
Forrest, William E.	Pvt. A	9 PA Res.	09-19-1862	3909	Middletown, WIA S. Mt.
Forrester, Archibald B.	Pvt. M	11 PA Cav.	11-23-1864	4011	Weverton
Forst, John	Pvt. C	191 OH Inf.	04-19-1865	1168	Clarysville
Foss, Nathan A.	Pvt.	4 ME Art.	06-03-1863	3131	Frederick
Fossett, Robert M.	Pvt. C	16 ME Inf.	10-25-1862	3190	Smoketown
Foster, Jacob C.	Pvt. D	15 NY Cav.	11-12-1864	30	Clarysville
Foster, Norman O.	Pvt. C	64 NY Inf.		792	Antietam
Foster, Phillip H.	Pvt. B	16 CT Inf.	09-17-1862	1101	Antietam, KIA
Fowler, Mead	Pvt. I	67 OH Inf.		1213	Cumberland
Fowles, Erred	Pvt. G	155 PA Inf.	10-06-1862	3724	Antietam
Fox, Aaron	Pvt. B	32 NY Inf.	11-25-1862	388	Hagerstown, Antietam
Fox, William	Pvt. D	10 WV Inf.	04-29-1862	2707	Frederick
Fox, William	Pvt. H	2 PA Res.	09-23-1862	4141	Frederick
Fox, William	Sgt. I	6 WI Inf.	09-24-1862	3235	Smoketown, WIA Antietam
Fox, William	Pvt. M	15 NY Cav.		42	Cumberland

Name	Rank/Co.	Reg./State	Death	Grave No.	Removed from/ Comments
Francis, Joseph	Pvt.	4 NY		789	Antietam
Frazee, Johnathan T.	Pvt. I	2 MD Inf.	07-30-1862	2427	Cumberland
Fredenburgh, William	Pvt. D	111 PA Inf.	11-08-1862	3707	Smoketown, WIA Antietam
Frederick, John	Pvt. B	129 PA Inf.	12-02-1862	4048	Frederick
Freeman, Alonzo	Pvt. H	61 NY Inf.	11-29-1862	212	Frederick
Freeman, George W.	Pvt. D	1 PA Art.	03-19-1865	4172	Clarysville
Fremas, William	Pvt.	7 OH Inf.		1166	Cumberland
French, C. R.	Pvt. K	1 US Art.	07-13-1863	3560	Frederick, Age 19
French, David J.	Pvt. H	152 IN Inf.	03-27-1865	3362	Antietam
French, John H.	Pvt. A	107 NY Inf.	09-19-1862	637	Antietam, WIA
French, Joseph S.	Pvt. D	1 RI Art.	10-24-1862	2838	Smoketown
Fresler, George C.	Sgt. B	107 PA Inf.	09-17-1862	3761	Antietam
Frey, Frederick	Corp. D	103 NY Inf.	09-17-1862	846	Antietam
Friend, Elijah	Pvt. A	MD	08-24-1864	2436	Clarysville
Friend, Francis A.	Pvt. D	3 MD Inf.	12-23-1862	2592	Frederick, Antietam
Fries, Daniel D.	Pvt. G	87 PA Inf.	08-12-1863	3622	Antietam
Frodine, John W.	Pvt. G	6 WI Inf.	10-15-1862	3263	Frederick, WIA Antietam
Frost, George	Pvt. M	12 NY Art.	05-22-1862	389	Hagerstown
Fry, Isaak	Pvt. I	53 PA Inf.	11-27-1862	4046	Frederick, Antietam
Fuller, George J.	Pvt. H	10 ME Inf.	09-17-1862	3164	Antietam
Fullers, William	Pvt. C	64 NY Inf.		791	Antietam
Fullerton, James Jr.	Pvt. I	12 NH Inf.		2818	Antietam
Fulp, Emanuel	Pvt. E	27 IN Inf.	11-17-1862	3431	Frederick, Antietam
Funk, William	Pvt. E	4 US Art.		3503	Sandy Hook, Age 22
Furlong, Patrick	Pvt. E	4 NY Inf.	10-01-1862	152	Frederick, Antietam
Furr, Abraham	Pvt. H	10 WV Inf.	03-22-1865	2699	Frederick
G., P.	Pvt.	OH Inf.		1156	Oakland
Gallagher, Frank H.	Pvt. M	12 PA Cav.	07-10-1864	4103	Frederick
Gallagher, Hugh	Pvt. B	61 NY Inf.		804	Antietam
Gallaher, Crawford	Pvt. H	11 WV Inf.	12-23-1864	2614	Frederick
Gallop, Henry	Pvt. F	3 WI Inf.	02-16-1862	3221	Frederick, Died Disease
Galusha, Truman	Corp. C	111 PA Inf.	09-21-1862	3720	Smoketown, WIA Antietam
Gammell, Robert	Pvt. K	13 NJ Inf.	12-11-1862	2900	Frederick, Antietam
Gandall, George	Corp. B	51 NY Inf.	11-04-1862	218	Frederick, Antietam
Gant, John F.	Pvt. F	1 MD Cav.	02- -1862	2443	Frederick
Gardner, John	Pvt. C	27 IN Inf.		3454	Antietam
Garland, John W.	Pvt. H	9 NH Inf.	11-26-1862	2811	Weverton, Died at Knoxville
Garrett, Andrew	Pvt. E	160 OH N.G.	08-19-1864	1392	Middletown
Garrison, Joseph	Pvt. C	27 IN Inf.	06-29-1862	3397	Frederick
Garrity, William	Pvt.	2 NY Inf.		657	Antietam, WIA
Garvin, Milton	Pvt. C	134 PA Inf.	10-27-1862	3618	Sharpsburg, Antietam
Gass, Philip					See Glaser, Philip
Gaston, John T.	Corp. F	3 WI Inf.	11-30-1861	3278	Frederick, Died Disease
Gates, James	Pvt. F	8 PA Res.	09-17-1862	3717	Smoketown, WIA Antietam
Gates, Lorenzo	Pvt. K	7 MI Cav.	10-20-1862	2396	Frederick
Gavey, Anson	Pvt. D	97 NY Inf.	10-02-1862	155	Frederick, Antietam
Gaylord, Albert H.	Pvt. D	34 MA Inf.	07-30-1864	965	Weverton, Died Disease
Geary, Francis	Pvt. D	6 WI Inf.	09-17-1862	3351	Antietam, KIA
Gee, J. W.	Pvt. K	3 WI Inf.	10-28-1862	3266	Antietam
Gehr, Lewis D.	Pvt. E	111 PA Inf.	08-15-1862	4136	Frederick, Age 20
Geiner, Frederick	Pvt. D	35 NY Inf.	9-26-1862	130	Frederick, Antietam
Geisel, Edward	Pvt. C	5 WI Inf.	12-07-1862	3258	Hagerstown, Died Disease
Geisler, Francis	Corp.	59 NY Inf.		693	Antietam
Gentholz, Gotlieb	Pvt. F	2 DE Inf.	10-21-1862	3042	Smoketown
Gentle, George W.	Pvt. E	5 OH Inf.	09-17-1862	1480	Frederick, Antietam
Gentz, Christian	Pvt. H	20 NY Inf.	11-20-1862	387	Hagerstown, Antietam
George, William	Pvt. G	134 PA Inf.	11-18-1862	4038	Frederick, Age 35
Geraty, Martin	Corp.	2 NY Inf.		672	Antietam

Name	Rank/Co.	Reg./State	Death	Grave No.	Removed from/ Comments
Gerlough, Franklin	Pvt. A	6 WI Inf.	09-17-1862	3238	Antietam, KIA
Gestbent, Nicholas	Pvt. A	103 NY Inf.		495	Antietam
Getchell, H. D.	Pvt. C	15 MA Inf.	10-14-1862	982	Smoketown
Gibberd, John	Pvt. H	6 PA Res.	09-17-1862	3674	Antietam, KIA
Gibbons, Henry J.	Pvt. G	36 OH Inf.	09-14-1862	1432	South Mountain
Gibbony, James H.	Corp. G	125 PA Inf.	09-17-1862	3644	Antietam, KIA
Gibbs, Mason	Corp. F	54 PA Inf.		4183	Cumberland
Gibbs, William	Pvt. I	97 NY Inf.	12-07-1862	204	Frederick, Antietam
Gibson, Isaac H.	Pvt. A	14 NJ Inf.	07-17-1864	2934	Frederick, Monocacy
Gibson, Israel	Sgt. K	111 PA Inf.	07-16-1862	4188	Frederick
Gibson, Thomas			09-05-1863	1712	Frederick, Forage Mast'r
Gift, Martin Van Buren	Pvt. A	1 MD Inf.	01-06-1864	2459	Antietam
Giggly, Rudolph	Pvt. F	49 NY Inf.	11-15-1862	227	Frederick, Antietam
Gilbert, C. S.	Pvt. C	8 IL Cav.	07-12-1864	3067	Frederick, Monocacy
Gilbert, David	Pvt. I	172 PA Inf.	07-26-1863	4081	Frederick, Age 18
Gilbert, E. J.				2482	
Gilbert, George	Pvt. I	2 WI Inf.	09-14-1862	3275	South Mountain, KIA
Gillen, James S.	Sgt.	NY Inf.		455	Antietam
Gillespie, Theophilus	Pvt. A	13 WV Inf.	02-08-1865	2736	Clarysville
Gillett, George M.	Pvt. B	1 MI Cav.	07-31-1863	2392	Hagerstown, From Margette
Gilligan, Thomas B.		2 NY Inf.		676	Antietam, WIA
Gilliland, John	Pvt. C	Engineer	06-03-1865	4130	Frederick, PA Section
Gilman, Henry	Pvt. A	34 NY Inf.	09-17-1862	831	Antietam
Gilvoy, James	Pvt. E	103 NY Inf.		497	Smoketown
Ginter, Peter	Pvt. F	17 PA Cav.	12-09-1864	4127	Frederick
Gitney, Thomas	Pvt. G	69 NY Inf.	12-24-1862	198	Frederick, Antietam
Gladding, Timothy	Pvt. G	16 CT Inf.	09-17-1862	1088	Antietam, KIA
Glaser, Philip	Pvt. E	9 NY Inf.		754	Antietam
Glass, James	Pvt. F	5 WV Cav.	03-18-1864	2628	Frederick
Glass, John	Pvt.	3 NY Art.		348	Weverton
Glass, William H.	Pvt. K	1 MD Inf.	01-21-1862	2442	Frederick
Glasur, Frederick	1st Sgt. A	3 WI Inf.	10-26-1862	3316	Antietam, WIA
Glenn, James H.	Corp. A	45 PA Inf.	09-14-1862	3881	South Mountain, KIA
Glessner, Philip	Pvt.	12 US Inf.		3525	Antietam
Gluth, Frederick	Pvt. B	6 WI Inf.	09-17-1862	3344	Antietam, KIA
Godfrey, William C.	Pvt.	PA		3959	Hagerstown
Goings, George W.	Pvt. F	27 IN Inf.	02-25-1862	3398	Frederick
Golden, William H.	Pvt. C	20 PA Res.	03-13-1865	4238	Boonsboro
Golder, Joseph	Pvt.	NY	10-19-1862	278	Hagerstown, Antietam
Goldsmith, William R.	Pvt. B	9 WV Inf.	09-28-1864	2612	Frederick, Monocacy
Good, Christian	Pvt. K	130 PA Inf.	09-17-1862	3599	Antietam, KIA
Good, Robert	Corp. I	27 IN Inf.		3453	Antietam
Goodall, Asaph	Pvt. H	33 NY Inf.	02-10-1863	612	Smoketowm
Goodbrane, Alfred	Pvt. D	161 OH Inf.	07-06-1864	1286	Frederick
Goodloe, Virian	Corp. C	12 OH Inf.	09-17-1862	1327	Antietam
Goodman, Charles B.	Pvt. C	45 PA Inf.	09-14-1862	3855	South Mountain, KIA
Goodman, Mabury	Pvt. E	23 OH Inf.	09-17-1862	1324	Antietam
Goodnough, Johnathan	Pvt.	59 NY Inf.		701	Antietam, WIA
Goodrich, Allen	Pvt. F	18 NY Inf.	12-11-1862	214	Frederick, WIA Antietam
Goodsell, Edward W.	Corp. C	7 OH Inf.	09-19-1862	1374	Smoketown
Goodwin, Arthur	Pvt. G	16 ME Inf.	10-27-1862	3187	Smoketown
Goodwine, William	Pvt. G	150 IN Inf.	03-03-1865	3412	Frederick
Gordon, Samuel	Pvt. F	21 NY Cav.	08-00-1864	287	Middletown
Gorman, William	Corp. I	3 DE Inf.	10-14-1862	3056	Frederick, Antietam
Gosnell, Moses A.	Pvt. C	1 MD PHB	07-12-1864	2468	Frederick, WIA Monocacy
Gosser, Franz					See Groser, Franz
Gould, Henry	Pvt. F	7 WV Inf.	03-11-1862	2746	Cumberland
Goundry, John E.	Pvt. B	1 MN Inf.	09-17-1862	3023	Antietam, KIA
Graf, John	Pvt. D	7 NY Inf.		816	Antietam
Graham, John	Pvt.	4 PA Cav.	10-04-1861	3962	Hagerstown, 3 months service

Name	Rank/Co.	Reg./State	Death	Grave No.	Removed from/ Comments
Graham, Robert M.	Pvt. F	111 PA Inf.	09-17-1862	3671	Antietam, KIA
Grambling, Solomon	Pvt. I	54 PA Inf.	06-01-1864	4157	Clarysville
Gramlich, Martin	Pvt.	20 NY Inf.		821	Antietam
Grant, Alexander	Pvt. I	19 MA Inf.	09-17-1862	900	Antietam
Gravie, Ferdinand	Pvt. F	42 NY Inf.	10-10-1862	587	Smoketown
Gray, Alvah M.	Corp. D	6 VT Inf.	09-17-1862	2640	Frederick, Antietam, Age 32
Gray, Jeduthan	Pvt. B	19 IN Inf.	10-12-1862	3476	Smoketown
Gray, John N.	Pvt. I	184 OH Inf.		1205	Cumberland
Gray, Richard G.	Pvt. F	89 NY Inf.	09-22-1862	849	Antietam, WIA
Gray, William	Sgt. K	29 OH Inf.	12-10-1862	1489	Frederick, Antietam
Grayham, Seymour	Pvt. K	152 IN Inf.	04-04-1865	3406	Frederick
Greathouse, Richard	Pvt. B	9 WV Inf.	08-01-1864	2947	Clarysville
Greegin, James	Pvt. I	16 CT Inf.	09-17-1862	1082	Antietam, KIA
Green, Alonzo	Pvt. C	35 NY Inf.		544	Antietam, WIA
Green, John	Pvt. A	13 WV Inf.	02-10-1865	2887	Clarysville
Green, John C.	Pvt. A	14 PA Cav.	08-12-1864	4115	Frederick
Green, Scott W.	Pvt. B	12 PA Cav.		4028	Burkettsville
Green, T. W.	Pvt. F	151 NY Inf.	07-16-1864	81	Frederick, Monocacy
Greenlaw, Theophilus	Pvt. F	26 MA Inf.	10-27-1862	961	Weverton
Greenville, Charles	Pvt. K	8 IL Cav.	07-09-1864	3068	Weverton, KIA Monocacy
Gregory, James W.	Pvt. K	7 WV Inf.	09-17-1862	2604	Smoketown
Gregory, Philip	Pvt. H	1 DE Inf.		3057	Frederick, Antietam
Griffin, Timothy	Pvt. G	5 US Cav.		3518	South Mountain
Griffis, Hoy. O.	Pvt. F	8 NY Inf.	11-21-1862	228	Frederick, Antietam
Griffith, Henry P.	Pvt. A	35 MA Inf.	10-13-1863	960	Weverton, Died Disease, Age 28
Griffith, John	Pvt. M	12 PA Cav.	07-10-1864	4097	Frederick
Griffith, Wesley	Pvt. D	142 PA Inf.	12-16-1862	3706	Smoketown
Grim, Adam W.	Pvt. K	14 PA Cav.	11-13-1864	4173	Clarysville
Grimes, Micah M.	Sgt. M	1 MI Cav.	09-03-1864	2373	Died of Wounds, From Niles
Grissman, Michael	Sgt. E	9 NY Inf.		581	Antietam, WIA
Grog, Joseph	Pvt. G	10 WV Inf.	01-15-1863	2853	Cumberland
Grogen, T. R.	Pvt. I	9 NY Inf.		775	Antietam
Groser, Franz	Pvt. C	9 NY Inf.		753	Antietam
Grosvenor, Joseph A.	Pvt. B	16 CT Inf.	09-17-1862	1093	Antietam, KIA
Grove, George W.	Pvt. D	7 WV Inf.	09-17-1862	2609	Antietam
Grove, William P.	1st Lt. A	45 PA Inf.	09-22-1862	4140	Frederick, WIA S. Mt.
Grover, Samuel	Pvt. F	14 NJ Inf.	11-07-1862	2913	Frederick, Antietam
Gunther, William	Pvt. F	9 NY Inf.		749	Antietam
Gusten, Harrison C.	Pvt. H	6 PA Res.	10-03-1862	4210	Frderick, WIA Antietam
Gutemuth, Frederick	Pvt. B	20 MA Inf.	09-17-1862	936	Antietam
Gutzler, Jacob	Pvt. A	5 OH Inf.	09-17-1862	1348	Antietam
H., Peter	Pvt. A	1 MI Cav.	08-02-1864	2374	Weverton, Monocacy
Haas, Edward	Pvt. G	1 NY Inf.	07-28-1864	92	Frederick, Monocacy
Hackenburg, J. W.	Sgt. D	131 PA Inf.	11-04-1862	4052	Frederick
Hacker, Charles E.	Pvt.	2 NY Inf.		664	Antietam
Hadley, Issac N.	Pvt. I	12 IN Inf.	10-28-1861	3443	Antietam, Age 20
Hahn, Sidney	Pvt. A	47 PA Inf.	08-08-1864	4117	Frederick
Hailton, William	Pvt. D	23 OH Inf.	09-13-1864	1464	Weverton, Monocacy
Haines, Sylvester L.	Pvt. G	49 NY Inf.	12-01-1862	377	Hagerstown, Antietam
Hair, Daniel B.	Pvt. C	16 NY Inf.	10-12-1862	588	Bakersville
Halbert, George F.	Corp. F	7 WI Inf.	09-20-1862	3248	Middletown, WIA S. Mt. Smoketown
Hale, George C.	Pvt. G	35 NY Inf.		344	Hagerstown
Hale, James P.	Pvt. B	9 NH Inf.	10-01-1863	2891	Frederick, Died Disease
Hall, A. P.	Pvt. K	13 MA Inf.	09-17-62	1001	Antietam, KIA, Age 25
Hall, Albert	Pvt. M	5 NY Art.	07-31-1864	409	Maryland Heights
Hall, Jared	Pvt. B	5 US Art.	01-15-1864	3567	Frederick
Hall, Theodore H.	Pvt. E	4 VT Inf.	08-12-1864	2638	Fred., Monocacy, Age 23

Name	Rank/Co.	Reg./State	Death	Grave No.	Removed from/ Comments
Hall, Volney F.	Pvt. D	14 PA Inf.	06-11-1865	4129	Frederick
Hallan, William	Pvt. A	15 NY Cav.	02-09-1864	297	Weverton
Halloway, George W.	Corp. C	2 WI Inf.	09-17-1862	3301	Antietam, KIA
Hallowell, John	Pvt. C	51 PA Inf.	09-17-62	3723	Antietam
Halpin, William P.	Pvt. G	192 OH Inf.	04-25-1865	1220	Clarysville
Ham, J. W.	Corp. I	11 IN Inf.		3486	Hagerstown
Haman	Pvt. A	PA		3731	Antietam
Hamblin, Elijah	Pvt. D	106 NY Inf.	11-23-1862	39	Cumberland
Hamilton, Arthur T.	Corp. H	2 WI Inf.	09-17-1862	3288	Antietam, KIA
Hamilton, Benjamin	Corp. C	9 WV Inf.	08-03-1864	2742	Clarysville
Hamilton, Hancey	Pvt. B	16 CT Inf.	09-17-1862	1092	Antietam, KIA
Hamilton, James	Pvt. N	28 PA Inf.	09-17-1862	3752	Antietam, KIA
Hamman, John	Pvt. A	11 OH Inf.		1328	Antietam
Hammil, Bernard	Pvt. B	108 NY Inf.		813	Antietam
Hammock, Martin V. B.	Pvt. I	11 WV Inf.	07-23-1864	2738	Clarysville
Hancock, Edwin R.	Corp. B	7 WI Inf.	09-20-1862	3253	Middletown
Hancock, J. O.	Pvt. A	9 MN Inf.		3019	Westernport
Hand, John	Pvt. K	69 PA Inf.	09-17-1862	3657	Antietam, KIA
Hanghliter, C. M.	Pvt.	72 PA Inf.		3682	Antietam
Hankins, George W.	Pvt. H	132 PA Inf.	10-04-1862	3700	Smoketown, WIA Antietam
Hanlin, James	Pvt. B	195 NY Inf.	08-26-1864	283	Weverton, Monocacy
Hann, John H.	Pvt. G	7 IN Inf.	10-04-1862	3400	Frederick, Antietam
Hanna, William	Pvt. B	3 IN Cav.	09-30-1862	3399	Frederick, Antietam
Hannan, Patrick	Pvt. F	59 NY Inf.		661	Antietam
Hannay, Theron	Pvt. F	146 NY Inf.	07-02-1863	183	Frederick
Hannon, John M.	Pvt. F	7 WV Inf.	11-29-1862	2631	Frederick, Antietam
Hansell, John W.	Pvt. A	27 IN Inf.	09-17-1862	4217	Bakersville, Antietam
Hanson, Edward	Sgt.	2 MD		2573	Weverton, From Eastern Shore
Hanton, John	Pvt. I	5 NY Art.	07-01-1864	337	Weverton
Harbin, John W.	Pvt. C	116 OH Inf.	08-06-1863	1343	Antietam
Harding, John	Pvt. I	6 WI Inf.	11-18-1862	3245	Boonsboro, WIA S. Mt.
Hardy, Abraham	Pvt. H	1 MD Inf.	04-29-1864	2445	Frederick, Died Disease
Hardy, John	Pvt. D	4 RI Inf.	09-17-1862	2827	Antietam, KIA
Harland, John	Pvt. C	1 PA Art.	08-20-1863	4019	Burkettsville
Harley, W.	Pvt. B	149 OH Inf.	07-23-1864	1292	Frederick, Monocacy
Harman, Henry	Pvt. F	1 WV Cav.	03-15-1862	2764	Cumberland
Harman, Henry	Pvt. G	12 PA Res.	10-03-1862	4145	Frederick, Antietam
Harmison, John F.	Pvt. E	1 MD Inf.	09-06-1864	2465	Frederick, Monocacy
Harnot, Julius	Pvt.	16 NY Inf.		441	Middletown
Harold, John L.	Pvt. G	2 MI Cav.	03-09-1865	2420	Frederick
Harper, Wilson B.	Pvt. H	23 OH Inf.	09-17-1862	1400	Middletown, WIA S. Mt.
Harrall, William	Pvt. G	121 NY Inf.	11-21-62	394	Hagerstown, Antietam
Harrington, Joseph				2042	Weverton
Harrington, Morey	Pvt. B	1 MI Cav.	01-12-1865	2476	Frederick, From Dexter
Harris, George	Pvt. C	79 NY Inf.	09-17-1862	848	Antietam, KIA
Harris, James	Pvt. B	12 US Inf.	12-24-1862	3555	Frederick, Antietam
Harris, James C.	Pvt. A	94 NY Inf.	09-14-1862	488	South Mountain, KIA
Harris, Robert	Pvt. B	128 PA Inf.	10-12-1862	3821	Antietam, WIA
Harrison, J. F.	Pvt. I	115 PA Inf.	06-29-1863	4076	Frederick
Harrison, William P.	Pvt. K	6 WI Inf.	09-17-1862	3236	Antietam, KIA
Harsh, Andrew	Pvt. K	14 IN Inf.	09-17-1862	3436	Antietam
Hart, Thomas	Pvt. P	28 PA Inf.	09-17-1862	3627	Antietam, KIA
Hartman, William H.	Pvt.	39 IL Inf.		3107	Cumberland
Hartsell, George	Pvt. M	12 PA Cav.	09-10-1864	4108	Frederick, Sandy Hook
Harvey, James	Pvt. K	26 MA Inf.	09-16-1864	1043	Frederick, Monocacy
Harvey, Samuel	Corp. B	4 RI Inf.	06-11-1863	2842	Frederick, Age 30
Harvey, William F. L.	Corp. H	12 WV Inf.	09-04-1864	2600	Weverton, Monocacy
Harwood, E. O.	Pvt. E	20 MA Inf.	09-17-1862	904	Antietam
Hascall, Arther Foote	Sgt. C	61 NY Inf.	11-11-1862	614	Smoketown

Name	Rank/Co.	Reg./State	Death	Grave No.	Removed from/ Comments
Haselton, Enoch E.	Pvt. D	9 NH Inf.	10-17-1862	2809	Middletown, Died Wounds
Hasper, Peter W.	Pvt. A	10 WV Inf.	12-17-1864	2880	Clarysville
Hatfield	Pvt. D	OH Inf.	04-07-1864	1456	Weverton
Hathaway, Calvin	Pvt. A	2 VT Inf.	11-23-1862	2679	Hagerstown, Ant., Age 18
Hathaway, Charles	Pvt. G	23 NY Inf.	11-28-1862	506	Smoketown, WIA Antietam
Hathaway, Jesse	Pvt. K	137 PA Inf.	10-21-1862	3991	Hagerstown
Hathfen, W. S.	Pvt. G	1 PA Inf.	08-08-1863	4166	Oldtown
Havens, Edward	Pvt. D	14 NJ Inf.	07-15-1864	2897	Frederick, Monocacy
Haverty, Daniel	Pvt. H	5 CT Inf.	01-20-1862	1183	Antietam, From Manchester
Haviland, Charles H.	Pvt. F	14 NJ Inf.	07-15-1864	2930	Frederick, Monocacy
Hawkey, George	Pvt.	2 NY Inf.		655	Antietam
Hawkinberry, Chandler	Pvt. G	15 WV Inf.	08-05-1864	2626	Frederick, Monocacy
Hawkins, J. W.	Pvt. D	7 MI Inf.	07-20-1863	2554	Frederick, Age 22
Hawkins, Joseph	Pvt. E	27 IN Inf.	12-22-1862	3423	Frderick, Antietam
Hawks, James T.	Pvt. E	15 NY Cav.		43	Cumberland
Hawksby, George		42 NY Inf.		713	Antietam
Hawse, William N.	Pvt. C	20 PA Cav.	09-23-1864	4155	Clarysville
Hay, Henry C.	Pvt.	1 MA Inf.		957	Weverton
Hayden, Frank L.	Pvt. H	15 MA Inf.	09-27-1862	1055	Frederick, Antietam
Hayes, William B.	Pvt. K	155 PA Inf.	11-19-1862	4037	Frederick, Age 20
Hayes, William M.	Pvt. C	1 ME Cav.	11-10-1862	3137	Frederick, Antietam
Hayne, Mathew	Pvt. E	2 MD		2580	Weverton
Hays, Abraham	Pvt. E	14 WV Inf.	12-29-1862	2757	Cumberland
Hays, Raswell F.	Pvt. C	35 NY Inf.	11-13-62	606	Smoketown
Hazeltine, Moses	Pvt. C	12 MA Inf.	10-16-1862	1022	Frederick, Antietam
Hazen, Jacob F.	Pvt. C	19 MA Inf.	09-17-1862	983	Smoketown
Heard, Thomas	Pvt. I	51 PA Inf.	10-19-1862	3942	Frederick, Age 42
Heatherton		NY Art.		414	Burkettsville
Heaton, Daniel	Pvt. H	3 NJ Inf.		2940	Cumberland
Heavener, Robert	Pvt. I	3 MD Inf.	09-11-1864	2464	Frederick, Died Disease
Hebler, Paul	Pvt. H	106 NY Inf.	07-29-1864	96	Frederick, Monocacy
Heeley, Thomas	Pvt. I	2 NY Inf.	09-09-1864	109	Frederick, Monocacy
Heether, James	Pvt.	118 PA Inf.		3589	Antietam
Heise, Frederick	Pvt. H	2 WI Inf.	10-26-1862	3298	Antietam, WIA
Helm, Willis N.	Pvt. G	39 IL Inf.	08-10-1862	3073	Cumberland, Died Disease
Hemberger, Andrew W.	Pvt. K	2 NJ Inf.	09-14-1862	2784	Burkettsville, KIA
Hemmerich, Christian	Pvt. B	145 NY Inf.	01-05-1863	199	Frederick, Antietam
Hemming, Henry	Pvt. I	54 PA Inf.	04-22-1864	4153	Clarysville
Henderson, Lyman M.	Pvt. B	1 MI Eng.	04-04-1865	2419	Clarysville
Henderson, Thomas	Pvt. C	PA Art.	11-18-1862	3711	Smoketown, WIA Antietam
Hennen, Joseph W.	Pvt. E	100 PA Inf.	09-16-1861	3917	Middletown
Hennessey, Jere	Pvt. H	2 MA Inf.	03-11-1863	1035	Frederick
Henry, Lewis	Pvt. A	108 NY Inf.	12-05-1862	206	Frederick, Antietam
Henry, Robert	Corp. I	42 NY Inf.		717	Antietam
Hensler, Peter	Pvt.	20 PA Cav.	06-09-1864	4094	Frederick
Hensley, W. J.	Pvt. G	27 IN Inf.	09-17-1862	3460	Antietam
Hensley, William	Corp. G	1 WV Inf.	07-27-1865	2777	Clarysville
Herger, Michael	Pvt. D	129 PA Inf.	11-17-1862	4058	Frederick, Age 28
Hess, Samuel	Pvt. H	125 PA Inf.	09-17-1862	3609	Antietam, KIA
Hess, William	Pvt. F	30 OH Inf.	09-30-1864	1494	Frederick, Monocacy
Hetrick, James	Pvt.	72 PA Inf.		3765	Antietam
Hewins, Henry	Pvt. D	2 MA Inf.	11-29-1862	984	Smoketown
Heythorn, Maurice E.	Pvt. C	18 NY Inf.		429	Burkettsville
Hickey, Peter	Pvt.	2 US Inf.		3504	Antietam
Hickman, George W.	Pvt. C	14 NY Inf.	09-18-1862	567	Antietam, WIA, Age 38
Hickman, Jacob					See Hickman, George W.
Higgins, Henry	Pvt. G	8 MI Inf.	10-11-1862	2395	Fred., WIA, From Lenawee
Higgins, James	Pvt. H	51 NY Inf.		783	Antietam
Hill, Charles L.	Pvt. K	7 MI Inf.	10-17-1862	2550	Antietam, WIA, From Burr Oak

Name	Rank/Co.	Reg./State	Death	Grave No.	Removed from/ Comments
Hill, Church			09-24-1862	1707	Frederick
Hill, Elisha M.	Pvt. B	5 NH Inf.	10-08-1863	2890	Frederick, Died Disease
Hill, Ely J.	Pvt.A	116 OH Inf.	08-31-1864	1317	Frederick, Monocacy
Hill, Henry	Pvt. E	9 WV Inf.	12-14-1862	2848	Cumberland
Hill, John O.	Pvt. E	7 MA	09-21-62	1017	Hagerstown, Antietam
Hill, Thomas	Pvt.	5 PA Res.		3903	South Mountain
Hills, Percival S.	Pvt. B	5 CT Inf.	08-23-1862	1187	Fred., Age 40, From Bristol
Himes, James	Pvt. I	16 CT Inf.	09-25-1862	1091	Antietam, WIA
Himes, Stephen	Pvt. I	16 CT Inf.	09-17-1862	1081	Antietam, KIA
Himes, William W.	Pvt. M	22 PA Cav.	06-03-1864	4154	Clarysville, Cumberland
Hinman, Wait	Pvt. L	6 NY Art.	10-16-1864	336	Weverton, Age 38
Hipper, John	Pvt. B	3 MD Inf.	09-21-1862	2562	Antietam
Hires, Josiah	Pvt. G	14 NJ Inf.	12-11-1862	2907	Frederick, Antietam
Hitchcock, Alfred	Pvt. D	37 MA Inf.	08-07-1864	1041	Frederick, Died Wounds
Hitchins, Charles	Pvt. C	2 MD		2430	Cumberland
Hoage, Lewis S.	Pvt. I	3 WI Inf.	01-12-1862	3218	Frederick, Accidental Death
Hobbs, Benjamin	Pvt. I	106 NY Inf.	11-13-1862	37	Cumberland
Hodde, John H.	Pvt. E	28 MA Inf.		967	Middletown
Hoederson, George	Pvt. G	3 MD	02-28-1863	2595	Frederick, Age 32
Hoesch, George	Pvt. E	110 OH Inf.	08-08-1864	1315	Frederick, Monocacy
Hoffacker, John	Corp. E	18 PA Cav.	07-13-1863	4002	Weverton, From Hanover
Hoffman, David	Pvt. F	NY Art.		305	Weverton, Monocacy
Hoffman, Gustavus A.	Pvt. P	28 PA Inf.	09-17-1862	3628	Antietam, KIA
Hogg, John	Pvt.	2 MA Inf.	03-13-1864	959	Weverton, Age 24
Holbert, James	Pvt. G	10 WV Inf.	07-07-1864	2603	Antietam
Holden, Hollis	Pvt. K	13 MA Inf.	09-17-1862	1007	Antietam, KIA
Holden, Nicholas	Pvt.	8 PA Res.	10-05-1862	4201	Frederick, Antietam
Holland, Patrick	Sgt. G	9 NY Inf.		752	See Holland, Patrick
Holliday, Milton G.	Corp. H	45 PA Inf.	09-14-1862	3887	South Mountain, KIA
Hollingsworth, George	Corp. B	4 PA Res.	09-17-1862	3722	Antietam, WIA
Hollingsworth, John	Pvt. I	72 PA Inf.	10-22-1862	3928	Frederick, WIA Antietam
Hollister, Bridgeman J.	Pvt. H	16 CT Inf.	09-25-1862	1104	Antietam, WIA
Holloran, Michael	Pvt. K	96 PA Inf.	09-26-1862	3976	Hagerstown, WIA Crampton's Gap
Holloway, Samuel	Pvt. G	14 NJ Inf.	03-18-1863	2925	Frederick
Holman, Peter	Pvt. H	123 OH Inf.	09-10-1864	1452	Middletown
Holmes, Lyman B.	Pvt. K	3 VT Inf.	11-01-1862	2647	Frederick, Ant. Age 20
Holt, Abbott D.	Pvt. G	9 NH Inf.	10-4-1862	2816	Antietam, Died Disease
Holt. J. N.	Pvt. H	15 NY Cav.	07-18-1864	62	Frederick
Holtz, A.	Pvt. I	85 NY Inf.		463	South Mountain
Holtzman, William	Pvt. K	41 NY Inf.	07-15-1863	176	Frederick
Honke, Nathan	Pvt. K	1 NY Art.	07-19-1862	129	Frederick
Hooker, Frederick	Pvt. L	2 CT Art.	12-01-1864	1190	Frederick, Age 19
Hoose, Sylvester J.	Pvt. K	3 VT Inf.	11-24-1862	2674	Hagerstown, Ant., Age 22
Hoover, John W.	Pvt. K	36 OH Inf.	09-14-1862	1497	Frederick, South Mountain
Hopkins, George	Pvt. F	NY		329	Weverton
Hopkins, Patrick	Pvt. C	10 VT Inf.	08-07-1864	2641	Frederick, Monocacy
Hopkins, Thomas C.	Pvt. G	11 PA Inf.	09-17-1862	3735	Antietam, KIA
Hopkins, William H.	Pvt. A	109 PA Inf.	07-05-1862	4192	Frederick
Hopper, B. C.	Pvt.	NJ Inf.		2041	Unknown
Hopper, Joseph	Pvt. I	5 CT Inf.	06-24-1862	1184	Fred., From Salisbury
Horan, Michael B.	Pvt. I	63 NY Inf.	10-16-1862	271	Frederick, WIA Antietam
Horner, Albert N.	Pvt. I	6 VT Inf.	11-19-1862	2676	Hagerstown, Ant., Age 31
Horner, John	Pvt. F	3 MD Inf.	01-22-1862	2447	Frederick
Horsefall, G.	Pvt. K	151 NY Inf.	07-16-1864	80	Frederick, Monocacy
Horton, George	Pvt. F	8 PA Res.	09-17-1862	3768	Antietam, WIA
Horton, James H.	Pvt. G	11 WV Inf.	11-21-1864	2883	Clarysville
Hostetler, John J.	Pvt. E	107 PA Inf.	10-24-1862	3927	Frederick, Antietam
Hostutler, Mark	Pvt. A	9 WV Inf.	08-02-1864	2712	Weverton, Monocacy
Hotchkiss, John M.	Pvt. H	45 PA Inf.	09-14-1862	3877	South Mountain, KIA

Name	Rank/Co.	Reg./State	Death	Grave No.	Removed from/ Comments
Houghtaling, A.	Pvt. M	5 NY Art.	07-30-1864	94	Frederick, Monocacy
Houlihan, John	Pvt. K	23 IL Inf.	02-07-1864	3104	Westernport, WIA
Hovey, Spencer H.	Pvt. D	17 MI Inf.	09-14-1862	2513	S. Mt., KIA, From Augusta
Howard, David H.	Pvt. B	12 NY Inf.	10-20-1862	740	Antietam
Howard, George	Pvt. B	5 OH Inf.	09-09-1862	1369	Smoketown
Howe, John	Sgt. H	9 NH Inf.	10-10-1862	2804	Antietam, Died Big Spring
Howe, Nicholas	Pvt. B	6 NY Art.		670	Antietam
Howell, James	Sgt. E	110 OH Inf.	07-11-1864	1290	Frederick, Monocacy
Howell, Tappan	Pvt. C	76 NY Inf.	09-28-1862	460	South Mountain
Howley, Edmund Burke	Pvt. A	18 NY Inf.	09-14-1862	439	Crampton's Gap, KIA S. Mt.
Hoye. Patrick	Pvt. G.	4 NY Inf.	11-05-1862	221	Frederick, Antietam
Hoyt, Jesse	Pvt. A	27 NY Inf.		345	Hagerstown
Hubbard, Howard A.	Pvt. A	5 WI Inf.	11-04-1862	3267	Frederick, Died Disease
Huber, Edward	Corp. I	72 PA Inf.	09-17-1862	3683	Antietam, KIA
Huck, William	Pvt. H	6 PA Res.	09-17-1862	3677	Antietam, KIA
Huggins, James E.	Pvt. K	1 MD Inf.	09-13-1862	2569	Boonsboro, KIA
Hughes, George	Pvt. N	28 PA Inf.	09-17-1862	3640	Antietam, KIA
Hughes, John	Pvt. M	1 NY Cav.	7-16-1864	76	Frederick, Monocacy
Hughes, Thomas	Pvt. I	59 NY Inf.	10-09-1862	53	Frederick, Antietam
Hull, Herman D.	Sgt. B	15 NY Inf.		304	Weverton
Hull, Michael	Pvt. I	7 MD Inf.	10-03-1863	4233	Hagerstown, Died Disease
Hull, Richard L.	Corp. I	14 CT Inf.	09-17-1862	1098	Antietam, KIA
Hull, Samuel H.	Pvt. H	116 OH Inf.	08-04-1864	1513	Weverton, Monocacy
Hunn, Horace	Pvt. B	16 CT Inf.	10-12-1862	1113	Frederick, Died Big Spring
Hunt, George	Pvt. A	142 PV Inf.	10-25-1862	3810	Smoketown
Hunter, William	Pvt. D	45 PA Inf.	09-14-1862	3871	South Mountain, KIA
Huntington, George	Pvt.	77 NY Inf.		722	Antietam
Hurd, Hiram A.	Pvt. F	12 MA Inf.	09-17-1862	938	Antietam, KIA
Hurd, James	Pvt. F	45 PA Inf.	09-14-1862	3878	South Mountain
Hurley, Luke	Pvt. G	30 MA Inf.	08-30-1864	1042	Frederick, Monocacy
Hurst, Amer	Pvt. D	16 IN Inf.	12-29-61	3382	Frederick
Hurst, William J.	Corp. G	50 PA Inf.	09-17-1862	3586	Antietam, KIA
Hussey, George Jr.	Pvt.	16 ME Inf.	10-18-1862	3193	Smoketown
Hutchings, F. M.	Pvt. C	US Art.	08-31-64	3508	Weverton, Monocacy
Hutchings, George H.	Pvt. B	106 NY Inf.	11-21-1862	40	Cumberland Gap
Ingalls, M. M.	Pvt. H	22 MA Inf.	10-24-1862	972	Antietam
Inman, J. R.	Teamster	OH	03-23-1862	1511	Frederick
Ira, A. J.	Pvt. C	NY		301	Frederick
Ireland, Rinaldo	Pvt. F	20 ME Inf.	10-21-1862	3147	Antietam
Irwin, David	Pvt. K	36 OH Inf.	07-24-1864	1175	Clarysville
Irwin, Robert C.	Pvt. E	17 MI Inf.	09-17-1862	2501	Antietam, KIA, From Brooklyn
Isams, Charles	Pvt. C	1 DE Inf.	10-03-1862	3113	Frederick, Antietam
Isdell				1898	Antietam
Islep, George	Corp. F	6 WI Inf.	09-17-1862	3345	Antietam, KIA
Itle, John	Pvt. M	12 PA Cav.	09-03-1864	3995	Weverton, Sandy Hook
Ives, William C.	Pvt. A	29 OH Inf.	03-05-1862	1212	Cumberland
J., F. W.				1751	Antietam, Could be W., J. F.
J., R.				1878	Antietam
J., W.	Pvt.	17 NY Inf.		350	Antietam
Jackson, Henry	Pvt. D	5 NY Art.	08-01-1864	99	Frederick, Monocacy
Jackson, John	Pvt. A	14 PA Cav.	05-10-1864	4016	Brownsville
Jackson, Thomas	Pvt. M	18 PA Cav.	07-14-1863	3961	Hagerstown, Died Wounds
Jacquith, James	Corp. F	19 ME Inf.	11-27-1862	3132	Frederick, Antietam
Jadwin, Isaac	Pvt. D	30 OH Inf.	09-14-1862	1412	South Mountain
Jam, A.	2nd Lt.	20 NY		857	Antietam
James, George	Pvt. I	96 PA Inf.	09-14-1862	4027	Burkettsville, KIA Crampton's Gap
James, Thomas	Pvt. G	11 PA Res.	09-14-1862	3845	South Mountain, KIA
Jameson, John E.	Pvt. C	2 NY Inf.	10-03-1862	154	Frederick, Antietam

Name	Rank/Co.	Reg./State	Death	Grave No.	Removed from/ Comments
Jansen, Herman	Pvt. E	2 NJ Inf.	10-01-1862	2788	Weverton
Jarvis, Alfred	Corp.	106 NY Inf.		35	Cumberland
Jeffries, Henry	Pvt. I	53 PA Inf.	02-28-1863	4077	Frederick, Age 24
Jenkins				2367	Antietam
Jenkins, David	Pvt.	3 MD Inf.	03-18-1863	2448	Frederick
Jewell, Zenas	Sgt. G	18 PA Cav.	07-06-1863	3981	Hagerstown, Killed
Jobenour, L.	Pvt.	5 OH Inf.		1397	Middletown
John, S.	Teamster		10-02-1864	1713	Frederick
Johns, Joshua P.	Pvt. H	3 WI Inf.	09-17-1862	3327	Antietam, KIA
Johnson, Abram S.	Pvt. A	23 OH Inf.	10-19-1864	1307	Frederick
Johnson, C. E.	Pvt. B	21 NY Inf.		543	Antietam
Johnson, David	Pvt. H	9 NY Inf.	09-17-1862	758	Antietam
Johnson, E. W.	Pvt. A	151 NY Inf.	08-20-1864	85	Frederick, Monocacy
Johnson, Emmet J.	Corp. K	3 WI Inf.	09-17-1862	3324	Antietam, KIA
Johnson, Henry H.	Pvt. I	19 IN Inf.	11-15-1862	3430	Frederick, Antietam
Johnson, Horace	Pvt. A	9 NY Art.	07-28-1864	88	Fred., WIA Monocacy, Age 18
Johnson, Ira	Pvt. B	67 OH Inf.		1224	Cumberland
Johnson, James	Pvt. G	7 ME Inf.	09-17-1862	3171	Antietam
Johnson, John	Pvt. B	15 NJ Inf.	10-16-1864	114	Frederick, WIA Monocacy
Johnson, John Chris.	Pvt. K	3 WI Inf.	04-25-1862	3211	Frederick
Johnson, John F.	Pvt. H	9 NY Inf.	09-27-1862	774	Antietam
Johnson, Phineas E.	Sgt. F	10 NY Inf.		235	Frederick
Johnson, Thomas	Pvt. K	170 OH Inf.	08-11-1864	1462	Weverton, Monocacy
Johnson, William	Pvt. E	29 OH Inf.	04-10-1862	1252	Cumberland
Johnson, William	Pvt. B	20 PA Cav.		4171	Cumberland
Jolly, Peter	Pvt. D	34 NY Inf.	10-09-1862	593	Smoketown
Jones, Calvin	Pvt.	11 US Inf.		3531	Antietam, Age 25
Jones, Edward	Pvt. G	2 MA Inf.	11-17-1862	891	Antietam
Jones, George	Pvt. B	12 PA Cav.	08-23-1864	4118	Frederick
Jones, John	Pvt. F	7 WV Inf.	02-28-1863	2752	Cumberland
Jones, John	Pvt. I	191 OH Inf.	04-04-1865	1269	Frederick
Jones, Joshua	Pvt. E	19 IN Inf.	10-29-1862	3473	Antietam
Jones, Moses W.	Pvt. K	3 WI Inf.	09-17-1862	3256	Antietam, KIA
Jones, S. S.	Pvt. A	3 DE Inf.	03-01-1863	3064	Frederick
Jones, Samuel	Pvt. A	13 WV Inf.	05-12-1865	2758	Cumberland
Jones, Waldo B.	Pvt. C	20 ME Inf.	10-27-1862	3179	Antietam
Jones, William D.	Pvt. I	130 PA Inf.	12-14-1862	4062	Frederick, Antietam
Jones, William H.	Pvt. L	6 NY Cav.	05-11-1865	19	Clarysville
Jones, William M.	Pvt. D	13 MA Inf.	08-26-1862	1054	Frederick, Died Disease
Jordan, James E.	Pvt. B	10 ME Inf.	09-18-1862	3174	Antietam
Jordan, Martin	Pvt. M	100 PA Inf.		3885	South Mountain
Jott, Harrison	Pvt. I	1 MI Cav.	08-31-1864	2377	Weverton, From Aurelius
Judge, James				2177	Antietam
Judge, Michael	Pvt.	59 NY Inf.		698	Antietam
Kaercher, James	Pvt. G	96 PA Inf.	02-08-1863	4067	Frederick, WIA S. Mt.
Kaiser, Charles	Pvt. C	8 NY Inf.	01-29-1862	51	Frederick
Kanas, James P.	Pvt.	7 OH Inf.		1244	Cumberland
Kane, Andrew	Pvt. K	Long Is.	09-20-1862	376	Hagerstown, Antietam
Kane, George W.	Pvt. G	27 IN Inf.	12-26-1861	3390	Frederick
Kane, William	Pvt. F	66 NY Inf.		809	Antietam
Kaufman, John	Pvt. B	20 NY Inf.		823	Antietam
Kaump, Henry A.	Pvt. F	7 WI Inf.	09-14-1862	3240	South Mountain, KIA
Kayser, Jacob	Pvt. A	20 NY Inf.		839	Antietam
Keefe, John O.	Pvt. F	63 NY Inf.	10-20-1862	248	Frederick, Antietam
Keefe, Michael	Pvt. I	51 NY Inf.		786	Antietam
Keefe, Michael	Pvt. E	1 MD Cav.	10-24-1862	2586	Point of Rocks
Keeler, Amos D.	Pvt. D	6 WI Inf.	10-07-1862	3233	Smoketown, WIA Ant.
Keenan, Patrick	Pvt. F	66 NY Inf.		808	Antietam
Keep, Alsinus	Corp. E	111 PA Inf.	09-17-1862	3666	Antietam, KIA
Keeran, John	Pvt. G	8 OH Inf.	09-17-1862	1333	Antietam

Name	Rank/Co.	Reg./State	Death	Grave No.	Removed from/ Comments
Kehoe, Thomas	Pvt. C	107 PA Inf.	09-29-1862	3696	Smoketown, WIA Ant.
Kehr, George W.	Pvt. K	20 MA Inf.	09-17-1862	903	Antietam
Keibler, Henry	Pvt. E.	2 MD Inf.	1862	2579	Weverton
Keilt, John	Pvt. C	69 NY Inf.	10-26-1862	239	Frederick, Antietam
Keis, John	Pvt. E	5 MI Cav.	05-12-1865	2422	Clarysville
Keister, Alfred L.	Pvt. F	28 PA Inf.	11-28-1862	4047	Frederick, Antietam
Keith, Friend H.	Sgt. H	20 MA Inf.	09-17-1862	934	Antietam
Keller, Fidelle	Pvt. A	87 PA Inf.	10-10-1864	4126	Frederick, Monocacy
Kells, James	Pvt. B	137 NY Inf.	11-23-1862	201	Frederick, Antitam
Kelly, Amer	Pvt. D	102 PA Inf.	10-23-1862	3949	Hag., Clear Spring, Age 44
Kelly, Isaac	Pvt. H	160 OH Inf.	08-17-1864	1393	Middletown
Kelly, James	Pvrt.	2 NY Inf.		663	Antietam
Kelly, James	Pvt. B	9 US Cav.	10-22-1862	3542	Frederick, Antietam
Kelly, Jeremiah	Pvt.	2 NY Inf.		682	Antietam
Kelly, John	Pvt.	2 NY Inf.		630	Antietam
Kelly, Levi	Pvt. D	6 US Cav.	09-01-1863	3565	Frederick, Age 22
Kelly, Michael J.	Pvt. D	1 US Cav.	03-22-1865	3568	Frederick
Kelly, Patrick	Pvt. E	90 PA Inf.	09-17-1862	3648	Antietam, KIA
Kelly, Patrick	Pvt. H	14 NJ Inf.	04-13-1863	2922	Frederick
Kelly, Shelden	Pvt. D	160 NY Inf.	08-29-1864	299	Sandy Hook, Age 30
Kelly, William	Pvt.	2 MD		2458	Antietam
Kelsey, C. J.	Pvt. B	37 MA Inf.	08-17-1864	955	Weverton, Monocacy
Kelsh, Jacob	Pvt. B	20 NY Inf.		349	Hagerstown
Kelso, R. N.	Pvt. G	14 IN Inf.	09-17-1862	3435	Antietam
Kemp, Charles	Pvt. E	192 OH Inf.	04-19-1865	1280	Frederick
Kendall, Lorenzo	Pvt. K	5 OH Inf.	09-17-1862	1352	Antietam
Kennedy, Ira	Pvt.	1 OH Art.	10-06-1862	1472	Hagerstown, Antietam
Kennedy, James	Pvt.	3 MD		2424	Cumberland
Kennedy, Partial	Pvt. K	50 PA Inf.	10-18-1862	3941	Frederick, WIA S. Mt.
Kennedy, W. O.	Corp. F	3 IN Inf.	08-15-1863	3418	Frederick, Age 29
Kenney, George W.	Pvt. G	12 PA Res.	10-01-1862	3743	Antietam, WIA
Kennicott, Walter J.	Pvt. F	8 IL Cav.	07-15-1863	3041	Boonsboro
Kenny, Peter B.	Pvt. I	9 NY Mil.	01-02-1863	191	Frederick, Antietam
Kenouse, L. J.	Pvt. F	2 US Cav.	03-19-1865	3498	Hagerstown
Kensing, Charles	Pvt.	20 NY Inf.		731	Antietam
Kent, C. B.	Sgt. C	2 RI Inf.	07-25-1863	2889	Frederick
Kent, George W.	Corp. F	7 WV Inf.	11-17-1862	3606	Smoketown
Kent, John S.	Pvt. G	16 CT Inf.	09-17-1862	1087	Antietam, KIA
Keplar, Jacob	Pvt. K	45 PA Inf.	09-14-1862	3893	South Mountain, KIA
Kepner, Daniel S.	Pvt. A	14 IN Inf.	09-17-1862	3441	Antietam
Kermie, J. D.	Pvt.	59 NY Inf.		702	Antietam
Kerns, John J.	Sgt. B	1 MD Cav.	01-10-1864	2590	Clear Spring, KIA, Age 32
Kerr, Robert	Pvt. C	45 PA Inf.	09-14-1862	3872	South Mountain, KIA
Kidder, Ellis	Pvt. C	4 NY Inf.	09-22-1862	570	South Mountain
Kiger, Elias D.	Pvt. H	150 IN Inf.	04-10-1865	3410	Frederick
Kiger, John	Pvt. H	15 WV Inf.	12-20-1862	2856	Cumberland
Kiles, Charles	Pvt. B	1 PA Inf.	12-01-1862	4059	Frederick
Kilgore, James A.	Pvt. D	150 IN Inf.	05-03-1865	3364	Frederick
Kimball, Andrew J.	Pvt. F	8 CT Inf.	11-19-1862	1111	Keedysville, Died Disease
Kimball, George H.	Pvt.	1 VT Inf.		2672	Williamsport
Kimball, William	Pvt. K	12 NH Inf.	11-15-1862	2893	Frederick, Died Disease
Kimbell, Henry	Pvt. A	171 PA Inf.	07-20-1863	4090	Frederick, Age 23
Kimberlin, John G.	Pvt. B	11 PA Res.	09-18-1862	3898	Middletown, WIA S. Mt.
Kimble, Andrew J.	Pvt. F	8 CT Inf.	11-19-1862	1111	Keedysville, Died Disease
Kimble, D.				2071	Weverton
Kimpland, Charles B.	Pvt. D	111 NY Inf.	08-02-1863	171	Frederick, Age 34
King J. A.	Pvt. F	7 WV Inf.	04-23-1862	2851	Cumberland
King, Cyrel	Pvt.	1 NY Inf.		294	Weverton
King, Stephen	Pvt. D	136 PA Inf.	12-06-1862	4055	Frederick, Age 20
King, Warren H.	Pvt. G	2 MA Inf.	09-27-1862	1068	Frederick, Antietam

Name	Rank/Co.	Reg./State	Death	Grave No.	Removed from/ Comments
Kingsland, J. W.	Pvt. K	9 NY Inf.	10-02-1862	160	Frederick, Antietam
Kingston, Judkins	Pvt.	NY Inf.		452	Middletown
Kinkle, George H.	Pvt. E	14 IN Inf.	10-04-1862	3437	Smoketown
Kinniston, W. W.	Pvt. K	36 OH Inf.	09-14-1862	1447	South Mountain
Kinter, Montgomery	Pvt. C	111 PA Inf.	07-10-1862	4190	Frederick, Age 25
Kirby, Patrick	Pvt.	5 PA Art.		3975	Hagerstown
Kirby, Patrick E.	Pvt. E	9 NY Art.	07-21-1864	89	Frederick, WIA Monocacy
Kirk, George M.	Pvt. B	17 MI Inf.	09-14-1862	2405	S. Mt., KIA, From Pipestone
Kirkman, Madison	Pvt.	16 IN Inf.		3387	Frederick
Kirkpatrick, James E.	Corp. K	22 PA Cav.	08-04-1864	4003	Weverton, Sandy Hook
Kirkpatrick, John	Pvt. D	137 PA Inf.	10-02-1862	3967	Hagerstown, Age 18
Kitchen, Stephen	Pvt. I	176 NY Inf.	12-21-1864	123	Frederick
Klein, Adam	Pvt.	2 NY Inf.		666	Antietam
Klein, Constantine	Corp. H	20 NY Inf.	10-21-62	277	Hagerstown, Ant., Age 23
Kline, William	Pvt. I	49 NY Inf.	12-16-1862	347	Hagerstown, Antietam
Kline, William	Pvt. A	6 WI Inf.	09-29-1862	3229	Keedysville, WIA Ant.
Knapp, Benjamin P.	Pvt. H	77 NY Inf.	10-10-1862	598	Smoketown
Knapp, Brundage	Pvt. E	55 OH Inf.	08-12-1862	1267	Frederick
Knight, Christopher L.	Pvt. K	89 NY Inf.	09-14-1862	470	South Mountain
Knights, W. S.	Pvt. F	9 NH Inf.	11-30-1862	2810	Frederick, Antietam
Knipp, Philip	Pvt. H	28 PA Inf.	07-01-1862	4194	Frederick, Age 21
Knoppenberger, Charles	Pvt. N	28 PA Inf.	12-01-1862	4050	Frederick, WIA Ant.
Knotson, Thomas	Corp. H	2 WI Inf.	09-17-1862	3295	Antietam, KIA
Knowlton, Chauncey	Pvt. P	22 MA Inf.	10-13-1862	890	Antietam, WIA, Age 21
Knutsen, Isaac	Pvt. H	2 WI Inf.	10-10-1862	3231	Smoketown, Died Disease
Koch, Lewis	Pvt. E	5 NY Art.		306	Weverton, Monocacy
Koffler, Joseph	Pvt. H	6 WI Inf.	09-17-1862	3346	Antietam, KIA
Kohler, John J.	Pvt. I	66 OH Inf.	10-14-1862	1372	Smoketown
Kolhman, Charles	Corp. H	5 MD Inf.	10-01-1862	2461	Frederick, WIA Antietam
Koons, John	Pvt. G	110 OH Inf.	03-01-1863	1227	Cumberland
Kop, Peter	Capt. E	27 IN Inf.	09-17-1862	875	Keedysville, From Bloomington
Kosier, Jesse	Pvt. D	47 PA Inf.	10-31-1864	3996	Weverton
Kregen, Frank	Pvt. H	110 OH Inf.	07-09-1864	1283	Frederick, Monocacy
Kreuson, Luther	Pvt. E	3 PA Res.	09-17-1862	3742	Antietam, WIA
Krobb, John	Pvt. C	3 MD Inf.	12-31-1862	2593	Frederick, Died Disease
Kronmuller, Philip	Pvt. H	97 NY Inf.	10-07-1862	166	Frederick, WIA Antietam
Krum, William F.	Pvt. G	132 PA Inf.		3741	Smoketown, WIA Antietam
Kugler, Samuel D.	Pvt. F	49 PA Inf.	08-06-1864	4105	Frederick
Kuhnel, George	Pvt. F	7 MI Inf.	10-10-1862	2551	Ant., WIA, From Haughton
Kunkle, Andrew	Pvt. A	28 PA Inf.	09-17-1862	3631	Antietam, KIA
Kuntz, Lewis	Pvt. F	7 WI Inf.	09-17-1862	3336	Antietam
Kurtz, Jacob	Pvt.	20 NY Inf.		841	Antietam
L.	Pvt.	2 MA Inf.		958	Hagerstown
La Count, Zacharia				1800	Berlin(Brunswick)
Labrie, Octave	Pvt. H	126 OH Inf.	07-23-1864	1301	Frederick, Monocacy
Lackie, Marvin H.	Pvt. K	6 VT Inf.	10-24-1863	2651	Frederick, Age 18
Lacky, Oliver L.	Pvt. B	22 NY Inf.	09-14-1862	486	South Mountain, KIA
Laclause, Gustavus	Pvt. D	7 MI Inf.	10-30-1862	2399	Frederick, Antietam
Lacy, Louis	Pvt. D	19 IN Inf.	09-14-1862	3482	Middletown, South Mountain
Ladam, Peter	Pvt. A	5 VT Inf.	08-22-1864	2663	Weaverton, Monocacy, Age 18
Ladd, Albert	Pvt. D	15 NY Cav.	05-24-1864	22	Clarysville
Laird, Samuel	Pvt. G	1 MN Inf.	08-22-1862	3022	Antietam, KIA
Lakin, John	Pvt. D	5 OH Inf.	02-13-1862	1232	Cumberland
Lambert, John	Pvt. K	1 WV Inf.	03-25-1865	2942	Clarysville
Lambert, Joseph	Corp. F	91 OH Inf.	09-16-1864	1470	Weverton, Monocacy
Lambright, Isaac	Pvt. F	55 OH Inf.	03-03-1862	1266	Frederick
Lamphear, Eli	Pvt. A	193 NY Inf.	10-1865	45	Cumberland Gap

Name	Rank/Co.	Reg./State	Death	Grave No.	Removed from/ Comments
Lampman, Augustus	Pvt. B	5 NY Art.		313	Weverton
Lampson, V. R.	Pvt. E	7 MI Inf.	09-20-1862	2404	Frederick, Antietam
Lancaster, William R.	Pvt. H	10 NJ Inf.	09-15-1864	2936	Frederick, Monocacy
Lane, Horace E. L.	Pvt. B	5 CT Inf.	02-23-1862	1182	Fulton Co. Pa.
Lane, Noah L.	Pvt. D	4 VT Inf.	11-14-1862	2675	Hagerstown, Antietam
Lane, Stanton	Pvt. I	102 NY Inf.	09-17-1862	709	Antietam, KIA
Lang, Joseph	Pvt. G.	18 NY Inf.	05-05-1863	178	Frederick, Age 19
Lank, M.	Pvt. C	3 DE Inf.	12-26-1862	3063	Frederick, Antietam
Lanning, George	Sgt. H	OH N.G.	09-01-1864	1461	Weverton, Monocacy
Lantry, John	2nd Lt. B	8 OH Inf.	09-17-1862	852	Antietam
Lapham, Amza	Pvt. G	55 OH Inf.	08-06-1862	1268	Frederick
Lapine, Mathew	Pvt.	16 NY Inf.		424	South Mountain
Laquie, Abraham	Pvt. D	2 MD Inf.		2431	Bloomington
Largee, Benjamin F.	Pvt. D	126 OH Inf.	07-21-1863	1282	Frederick, Age 18
Last, Ferdinand	Pvt. D	3 WI Inf.	09-17-1862	3329	Antietam, KIA
Late, David	Pvt. K	1 VT Cav.	01-02-1865	2636	Frederick, Age 19
Laughery, William	Pvt. B	11 PA Res.	09-14-1862	3837	South Mountain, KIA
Lavers, Richard	Pvt. E	27 NY Inf.		346	Weverton
Law, James	Pvt. C	2 USSS	10-15-1862	4148	Frederick, Antietam
Lawber, Frederick T.	Pvt. E	20 ME Inf.	10-30-1862	3151	Antietam
Lawick, Benjamin	Pvt. H	116 OH Inf.	10-02-1864	1308	Frederick, Monocacy
Lawrence, John H.	Pvt. A	1 RI Art.	09-17-1862	2835	Antietam
Lawrence, Samuel B.	Pvt.	9 NY Inf.		744	Antietam
Lay, Horace	Pvt. I	16 CT Inf.	09-17-1862	1100	Antietam, WIA
Layman, Ephraim	Corp. I	118 PA Inf.	09-20-1862	3605	Ant., WIA Shepherdstown
Layman, John J.	Pvt. F	12 WV Inf.	09-15-1864	2723	Weverton, Monocacy
Layman, Martin	Pvt. C	27 IN Inf.		3455	Antietam
Layman, William	Pvt. H	19 IN Inf.	10-11-1862	3483	Middletown
Leach, Edward	Sgt. I	19 MA Inf.	09-17-1862	899	Antietam
Leach, J. R.	Sgt. A	59 NY Inf.		696	Antietam
Leach, Peter	Pvt.	20 NY Inf.		822	Antietam, May be Lenz
Leach, William	Pvt. D	16 NY Inf.	11-23-1862	391	Hagerstown
Lebkuchler, Ferd.	Pvt. D	7 NY Inf.	12-06-1862	202	Frederick, WIA Antietam
Lee, Andrew J.	Sgt. D	16 NY Inf.	09-15-1862	423	Burkettsville
Lee, Bristol A.	Pvt. C	24 MI Inf.	08-02-1862	2555	Fred., Disease, From Plymouth
Lee, Jacob A.	1st Lt. C	27 IN Inf.	10-24-1862	876	Keedysville, Antietam
Lee, William	Pvt.	42 NY Inf.		716	Antietam
Leeper, Archibald	Pvt. K	170 OH N.G.		1458	Weverton
Leese, James	Pvt. F	3 PA Res.	09-17-1862	3776	Antietam, KIA
Leggett, Elijah	Pvt. E	5 CT Inf.	02-14-1862	1181	Antietam, From Bristol
Legrass, T. J. P.	Pvt. E	30 MA Inf.	04-19-1865	1075	Clarysville
Lemming, Samuel S.	Pvt.	IN		3468	Antietam
Lemon, Levi				1665	Cumberland
Lenz, Peter	Pvt. H	20 NY Inf.		822	Antietam, May be Leach
Leonanrd, J. W.	Sgt.	5 VT Cav.	07-1863	2692	Funkstown
Leonard, Charles	Pvt. I	21 MA Inf.	10-18-1862	1023	Frederick, Antietam
Leonard, William N.	Pvt. K	106 NY Inf.	07-04-1863	372	Hagerstown, Age 30
Lerch, John	Pvt. B	9 PA Res.	10-22-1862	3926	Frederick, WIA S. Mt.
Lesher, William	Pvt. C	14 NJ Inf.	11-18-1862	2912	Frederick, Antietam
Lester, John F.	Pvt. G	27 IN Inf.	01-04-1862	3394	Frederick
Leutz, John H.	Sgt. K	126 OH Inf.	02-18-1863	1238	Cumberland
Levick, Casper	Pvt. B	49 NY Inf.	01-16-1863	600	Smoketown
Lewis, Daniel S.	Pvt. I	7 MI Inf.	12-02-1862	2407	Fred., Disease, From Kalamazoo
Lewis, Edward	Pvt. D	87 PA Inf	10-10-1864	3999	Weverton, Monocacy
Lewis, Ennis	Pvt. F	89 NY Inf.	09-17-1862	738	Antietam, KIA
Lewis, James	Pvt.	20 MA Inf.		895	Antietam
Lewis, Joseph	Sgt. E	3 IN Cav.		3485	Middletown
Lewis, W. H.	Pvt.	34 NY Inf.		844	Antietam

Name	Rank/Co.	Reg./State	Death	Grave No.	Removed from/Comments
Lewis, William C.	Corp. K	194 OH Inf.	04-09-1865	1272	Frederick
Leyden, Michael	Pvt. K	63 NY Inf.	10-23-1862	253	Antietam, WIA
Libbey, John	Pvt. D	69 NY Inf.	12-11 1862	205	Fred., Ant., May be Lilly
Lichtenheld, Edward	Pvt.	20 NY Inf		720	Antietam
Liebe, Joseph	Pvt. D	123 OH Inf.	07-16-1864	1257	Clarysville
Liebencutt, Gotlieb	Corp. D	4 NY Cav.	09-08-1864	291	Weverton, Monocacy, Age 31
Lier, John	Pvt. E.	125 PA Inf.	09-17-1862	3634	Antietam, KIA
Light, Henry C.	Pvt. I	12 OH Inf.		1399	Middletown
Light, Mathias	Pvt. F	116 OH Inf.	07-08-1864	1164	Clarysville
Lightner, David	Pvt. E	45 PA Inf.	09-25-1862	4032	Middletown, WIA S. Mt.
Lilly, David V.	Pvt. I	17 MI Inf.	09-14-1862	2509	From Leighton
Lilly, J.					See Libbey, John
Limbark, Jacob	Pvt. D	49 NY Inf.	01-03-1863	192	Frederick, Antietam
Limkins, Jas. A.	Pvt. F	7 WI Inf.	10-09-1862	3223	Frederick, Antietam
Lindley, John H.	Sgt. D	23 OH Inf.	10-03-1862	1406	South Mountain
Lindsley, Abraham S.	Pvt. E	15 NY Cav.	09-15-1864	13	Clarysville
Link, David H.	Pvt. C	7 WI Inf.	10-28-1862	3234	Smoketown, Died Disease
Linn, Henry	Pvt. A	6 PA Res.	03-31-1863	4078	Frederick, WIA Ant., Age 25
Little, Augustus	Pvt. G	12 PA Cav.	10-18-1864	4007	weverton, Sandy Hook
Littlefield, Charles H.	Pvt.	5 ME Art.	04-25-1865	3121	Frederick
Littlefield, Moses	Pvt. I	20 ME Inf.	10-30-1862	3150	Antietam
Livermore, Henry W.	Pvt. G	106 NY Inf.	07-26-1864	87	Frederick, Monocacy
Livingston, Alexander	Pvt. A	2 US Inf.	11-25-1862	594	Smoketown
Livsey, John	Pvt. A	1 DE Inf.	09-17-1862	3045	Antietam, KIA
Livsley, John	1 DE Inf.				See Livsey, John
Loafman, William	Corp. K	8 PA Res.	09-25-1862	4143	Frederick, WIA S. Mt.
Locklin, Dennis	Pvt. C	10 VT Inf.	07-12-1864	2645	Frederick, Monocacy, Age 33
Lockmiller, James	Pvt. IOH			1218	Cumberland
Lockwood, J. C. F.	Pvt.	9 NY Inf.		787	Antietam
Loetze, Hugo	1st Lt. I	7 NY Inf.	09-17-1862	870	Keedysville, Antietam
Lofland, Joshua	Pvt. H	3 DE Inf.	01-12-1863	3060	Frederick, Antietam
Logan, George E.	Pvt. I	8 CT Inf.	11-15-1862	1123	Weverton, Died Disease
Logan, James	Pvt. H	139 PA Inf.	10-13-1862	3965	Hag., Downsville, Age 27
Logan, James M.	Corp. K	10 ME Inf.	08-01-1862	3118	Frederick
Logan, Nathan	Pvt. E	27 IN Inf.		3467	Antietam
Lone, Thomas	Pvt. K	89 NY Inf.	11-14-1862	331	Weverton, Died Disease
Long, August	Pvt. D	20 NY Inf.	10-21-1862	276	Hagerstown, Age 18
Long, Charles M.	Corp. E	23 OH Inf.	09-17-1862	1344	Antietam
Long, Daniel	Pvt. F	23 OH Inf.	08-26-1864	1313	Frederick, Monocacy
Lonsdale, Thomas	Pvt. C	14 IN Inf.	10-28-1862	3433	Frederick, Antietam
Looker, Thomas J.	Corp. C	14 NJ Inf.	09-26-1864	2937	Frederick, Monocacy
Loomis, Chamberlin	Pvt. E	134 PA Inf.	12-23-1862	4069	Frederick, Age 21
Loomis, Joseph	Pvt. G	29 OH Inf.	02-26-1862	1242	Cumberland
Lord, Benjamin	Pvt. K	137 PA Inf.	10-31-1862	3984	Hagerstown
Lord, D. R.	Pvt.	PA		3738	Antietam
Lore, James	Corp. H	126 OH Inf.	09-03-1864	1323	Frederick, Monocacy
Loud, Benjamin	Pvt. E	2 MA Cav.	04-27-1865	1078	Clarysville, Age 18
Loud, George W.	Corp. C	51 NY Inf.		788	Antietam
Love, James	Pvt. E	19 IN Inf.		2568	Boonsboro
Loveland, John	Pvt. C	16 CT Inf.	11-18-1862	1099	Antietam, WIA
Lovett, Olivar W.	Pvt. A	6 NH Inf.	09-29-1862	2801	Antietam
Lowe, Isaac N.	Pvt. M	1 MI Cav.	01-05-1862	2408	Fred., Disease, From Waterszeit
Lowrey, Thomas	Pvt. H	19 IN Inf.	10-17-1864	3471	Antietam
Lucas, Benjamin	Pvt. I	73 PA Inf.	06-17-1862	4133	Oldtown
Lucas, Elisha	Pvt. B	4 OH Inf.	12-04-1862	1482	Frederick, Antietam
Lucast, Christian	Pvt. A	2 MD Inf.	09-17-1862	2456	Antietam, KIA
Luders, Ludwig	Pvt. A	9 MD Inf.	05-03-1864	2472	Frederick
Lutz, Frederick	Pvt. K	1 MD Inf.	06-22-1864	2467	Frederick
Lydick, Daniel	Pvt. GPA			4167	Oldtown

Name	Rank/Co.	Reg./State	Death	Grave No.	Removed from/ Comments
Lynch, J. R.	Sgt. G	2 MA Inf.	05-29-1862	1020	Hagerstown
Lynch, J. W.	Pvt. E	23 OH Inf.	09-26-1864	1304	Frederick, Monocacy
Lynch, John	Pvt. I	87 PA Inf.	02-15-1865	4131	Frederick
Lynch, Patrick	Pvt. E	108 NY Inf.	10-18-1862	502	Smoketown
Lyndon, James P.	Pvt. C	2 NJ Inf.	09-14-1862	2787	Burkettsville, KIA S. Mt.
Lyons, John	Pvt. K	104 NY Inf.	09-20-1862	642	Antietam, WIA
Lyons, Lewis	Pvt.	OH Inf.		1243	Cumberland
Lyons, William	Pvt. B	34 OH Inf.	08-26-1864	1149	Clarysville
Mackaboy, E.	Pvt. C	20 NY Inf.		547	Antietam
Mackaboy, George					See Mackaboy, E.
Mackling, R.				2120	Middletown
Madden, James	Pvt. K	28 PA Inf.	09-17-1862	3750	Antietam, KIA
Madden, William	Pvt. A	61 NY Inf.	12-07-1862	203	Frederick, Antietam
Maddrel, James	Pvt. D	2 NY Cav.	09-18-1864	111	Frederick
Magee, J. V.	Pvt. A	14 NJ Inf.	07-25-1864	2929	Frederick, Monocacy
Magloskey, Frederick	Pvt. B	3 WI Imf.	09-20-1862	3319	Antietam, WIA
Magnet, Edward	Pvt. I	69 NY Inf.	10-30-1862	240	Frederick, Antietam
Maguire, John	Pvt. B	43 NY Inf.	01-1863	326	Weverton
Mahaffey, Robert	Sgt. C	9 PA Res.	09-17-1862	3758	Antietam, KIA
Mahan, Walter	Pvt. E	34 MA Inf.	08-24-1864	1070	Clarysville
Maier, John	Pvt. B	3 US Art.	08-13-1865	3576	Clarysville
Maining, Edward C.	Pvt. E	10 NY Art.	10-18-1864	322	Weverton
Mallow, Isaac	Corp. I	7 WV Inf.	09-22-1862	2706	Frederick, Antietam
Malloy, William	Pvt. L	2 CT Cav.		1121	Weverton
Malone, William	Pvt. F	8 PA Res.	11-20-1862	3814	Smoketown
Maloney, Joseph	Pvt. K	1 MD Inf.	11-27-1864	2581	Antietam
Maloney, Michael	Pvt. H	3 VT Inf.	11-21-1862	2673	Hagerstown, Ant., Age 21
Maloney, Thomas	Pvt. K	63 NY Inf.	10-05-1862	161	Frederick, WIA Antietam
Mammoth	Sgt.	PA Res.		3690	Antietam
Managan, W.	Pvt.	59 NY Inf.		699	Antietam
Manchester, Thomas	Pvt. F	4 RI Inf.	11-23-1862	2839	Smoketown
Mandigo, Henry H.	Corp. I	2 VT Inf.	10-15-1862	2689	Hagerstown, Ant., Age 27
Mangold, Peter	Pvt. F	1 PA Res.	10-16-1862	3940	Frederick, WIA S. Mt.
Manley, M.	Pvt. K	1 MD Cav.	05-03-1864	2473	Frederick
Mann, Albert	Pvt. B	20 NY Inf.		730	Antietam
Mann, George	Pvt. K	9 NY Art.	07-27-1864	86	Fred., WIA Monocacy, Age 41
Mann, William R.	Pvt. H	8 OH Inf.	11-30-1862	1483	Frederick, Antietam
Manning, Abraham	Pvt. D	4 WV Inf.	03-17-1865	2774	Clarysville
Manning, Albert	Pvt. F	7 MI Inf.	11-08-1862	2552	Antietam, WIA, From Haughton
Mapes, Seymour B.	1st Sgt. D	102 NY Inf.	07-16-1862	48	Frederick
Mapp, James F.	Pvt. K	129 PA Inf.	10-23-1862	3619	Sharpsburg, Antietam
Marchand, Nicholas	Pvt. A	155 PA Inf.	11-19-1862	3921	Frederick, Age 18
Marks, John L.	Pvt. F	7 WI Inf.	09-14-1862	3244	Ant., KIA South Mountain
Marks, Joseph H.	Pvt. G	6 PA Cav.	01-06-1863	4065	Frederick
Marsh, Albert N.	Pvt. G	17 US Inf.	12-01-1862	3549	Frederick, Antietam
Marsh, Benson B.	Corp. E	106 NY Inf.	12-08-1862	36	Cumberland Gap
Marsh, J. W.	Pvt. C	2 PA Art.	09-30-1863	4170	Oldtown
Marsh, Moses	Pvt. D	14 WV Inf.	01-22-1863	2744	Cumberland
Marsh, Thaddius	Pvt. H	29 OH Inf.		1228	Cumberland
Marshall, James	Pvt. E	PA Art.	09-17-1862	3615	Antietam
Marshall, John	Pvt. L	28 PA Inf.	09-17-1862	3600	Antietam
Marson, Joseph	Pvt. H	4 VT Inf.	09-15-1864	2643	Frederick, Monocacy
Martin, Austin	Pvt.	8 IL Cav.	10-15-1862	3031	Frederick, Antietam
Martin, Henry	Pvt. E	142 PA Inf.	11-24-1862	3697	Smoketown
Martin, William H.	Pvt. I	137 PA Inf.	11-05-1862	3704	Smoketown
Mason, Christian				1849	Antietam
Mason, Theodore	Pvt. E	90 PA Inf.	09-17-1862	3649	Antietam, KIA
Mason, Vicent H.	Pvt. G	10 ME Inf.	09-17-1862	3166	Antietam
Mason, W. W.	Pvt. A	151 NY Inf.	07-23-1863	173	Frederick, Age 22

Name	Rank/Co.	Reg./State	Death	Grave No.	Removed from/ Comments
Mass, Jacob	Pvt. A	20 NY Inf.	10-22-1862	245	Frederick, Antietam
Massie, Harvey	Pvt. H	9 WV Inf.	08-20-1864	2946	Calarysville
Massy, A.	Pvt.	104 NY Inf.		539	Antietam
Mathews, Charles	Pvt. H	107 NY Inf.	09-13-1862	633	Harpers Ferry
Mathis, Albert	Pvt. A	174 OH Inf.	02-27-1865	1246	Clarysville
Matte, Charles	Pvt. E	3 WI Inf.	07-06-1862	3213	Fred., WIA Winchester VA
Maxfield, David E.	Sgt. E	97 NY Inf.	10-27-1862	237	Frederick, Antietam
Maxson, William M.	Pvt. I	1 PA Res.	09-14-1862	3851	South Mountain, KIA
Mayley, Spencer	Pvt. G	14 WV Inf.	09-04-1863	2745	Cumberland
Mc.	Pvt.	PA		3973	Hagerstown
McAffeny, Charles	Pvt. I	6 US Inf.	09-17-1862	3522	Antietam
McAllister, Daniel	Pvt. G	3 MD	07-12-1864	2470	Frederick, Monocacy
McArthur, Robert	Pvt.	8 IL Cav.		3036	South Mountain
McArthur, Thomas	Pvt. P	28 PA Inf.	02-28-1862	4195	Frederick
McCallen, Charles	Pvt. K	12 PA Cav.	06-17-1864	3998	Weverton, Sandy Hook
McCallins, John	Pvt. A	2 PA Res.	10-08-1862	3698	Smoketown
McCann, James	Pvt. K	45 PA Inf.	09-14-1862	3892	South Mountain, KIA
McCann, Samuel	Pvt. F	1 US Cav.	08-10-1863	3524	Frederick, Age 24
McCann, William J.	Pvt. F	4 US Art.	03-15-1862	3581	Frederick
McCarl, Edward	Pvt. E	84 PA Inf.	07-17-1863	3613	Antietam
McCarthy, Jeremiah	Pvt. F	5 NY Art.		316	Weverton, Monocacy
McCarthy, John	Pvt.	ME Vol.		3156	Antietam
McCarthy, John	Corp. K	2 MA Inf.	12-28-1862	1031	Frederick, Antietam
McCarty, John	Pvt. A	173 NY Inf.	10-07-1864	311	Weverton, Monocacy
McCarty, Timothy	Pvt. I	60 NY Inf.	08-24-1862	128	Frederick
McCawdron, Martin	Pvt. B	6 WI Inf.	09-17-1862	3348	Antietam, KIA
McClara, James	Pvt. C	11 OH Inf.	09-14-1862	1414	South Mountain
McClarren, George	Pvt. F	100 PA Inf.	09-14-1862	3889	South Mountain, KIA
McClary, William	Pvt. A	15 WV Inf.	09-16-1864	2619	Frederick, Monocacy
McClinchy, John	Pvt.	5 NY Art.	04-15-1864	405	Burkettsville
McCloskey, Thomas M.	Sgt. F	28 PA Inf.	09-17-1862	3637	Antietam, KIA
McConnell, James	Corp. G	2 WV Cav.	08-25-1864	2868	Clarysville
McConnell, William	Pvt. F	5 US Art.		3505	Hagerstown
McConnolley, William	Pvt. D	12 WV Inf.		2763	Cumberland
McCorkle, J. H.	Pvt.	2 NY Inf.		677	Antietam
McCormick, David B.	Pvt. F	9 PA Res.	10-09-1862	3699	Smoketown
McCormie, Patrick	Pvt. C	4 NY Inf.	09-30-1862	153	Frederick, Antietam
McCoy, Jesse C.	Pvt. A	27 IN Inf.	03-12-1862	3392	Frederick
McCoy, John	Pvt. A	61 NY Inf.	10-16-1862	267	Frederick, Antietam
McCracken, Alexander	Pvt. G	145 PA Inf.	12-13-1862	4063	Frederick, Age 30
McCracken, Joseph	Pvt. F	125 PA Inf.	09-17-1862	3608	Antietam, KIA
McCullen, Charles H.	Pvt. G	7 MI Inf.	10-10-1862	2518	Hook
McCully, Samuel	Pvt. D	4 NJ Inf.	11-09-1864	2796	Sandy Hook
McCune, Edward B.	Pvt. B	36 OH Inf.	10-13-1862	1473	Antietam
McCurdy, James	Pvt. M	28 PA Inf.	09-24-1862	4144	Frederick, WIA Ant.
McDaniel, Joseph	Pvt. B	14 PA Cav.	07-11-1864	4104	Frederick
McDaniel, Milton	Sgt. K	3 WV Cav.	03-15-1865	2702	Frederick
McDermott, James	Pvt. F	4 US Art.	04-10-1862	3579	Frederick
McDermott, Thomas J.	Pvt. I	118 PA Inf.	09-24-1862	3603	Shepherdstown, Ant.
McDevitt, Hugh	Pvt. C	69 PA Inf.	12-10-1862	4056	Fred., WIA Ant., Age 30
McDonough, John	Pvt. F	20 MA Inf.	09-17-1862	905	Antietam
McDougall, John	Pvt. H	11 NJ Inf.	10-28-1862	2916	Frederick, Antietam
McEwen, John	Sgt. A	1 MN Inf.	09-17-1862	3027	Antietam, KIA
McFadden, John	Sgt. I	7 OH Inf.	10-30-1862	1481	Frederick, Antietam
McFall, Robert	Pvt. B	29 OH Inf.	06-27-1862	1506	Frederick
McFarland, Archibald	Pvt. H	110 OH Inf.	01-18-1863	1203	Cumberland
McFarlane, Johnson	Pvt. C	1 WV Inf.	05-14-1862	2708	Frederick
McGee, John	Pvt. G	110 OH Inf.	12-10-1862	1225	Cumberland
McGee, Robert	Pvt. E	102 NY Inf.	09-21-1862	601	Antietam, KIA
McGill, William	Pvt. H	5 NY Art.	08-29-1864	108	Frederick, Monocacy

Name	Rank/Co.	Reg./State	Death	Grave No.	Removed from/Comments
McGinty, John	Pvt. B	10 ME Inf.	09-17-1862	3162	Antietam
McGlann, Daniel	Pvt. C	50 PA Inf.	09-17-1862	3978	Antietam, KIA
McGowan, William	Pvt. C	4 RI Inf.	09-17-1862	2831	Antietam, KIA
McGowen, Michael	Pvt. A	154 IN Inf.	06-07-1865	3378	Frederick
McGrath, James	Pvt. E	16 CT Inf.	09-17-1862	1080	Antietam, KIA
McGuigan, John M.	Pvt. C	PA	09-16-1864	4186	Frederick
McGuin, Hugh	Pvt. F	162 NY Inf.	08-05-1864	95	Frederick, Monocacy
McGuire, M. C.	Pvt. H	128 PA Inf.	11-18-1862	4042	Frederick, Antietam
McGuire, Samuel	Pvt. C	4 US Inf.	09-30-1862	3571	Frederick, Antietam
McGuoy	Pvt.	MD		2583	Berlin(Brunswick)
McHardy, Horman	Pvt. B	2 WI Inf.	03-30-1863	3273	Ant. died Diseasae, Age 32
McIlvan, William	Pvt. G.	35 NY Inf.	10-07-1862	164	Frederick, Antietam
McIntosh, Lachlin L.	Pvt. E	2 WI Inf.	09-17-1862	3317	Antietam, KIA
McIvery, George	Corp. K	14 IN Inf.	12-02-1862	3427	Frederick, Antietam
McKay, William	Sgt. B	67 OH Inf.		1198	Cumberland
McKechner, William	Pvt. E	2 PA Res.	09-17-1862	3791	Antietam, KIA
McKeever, John	Pvt. D	14 PA Cav.	05-07-1864	4014	Brownsville
McKeldin, Edward	Pvt. I	11 MD Inf.	07-09-1864	2439	Frederick, Monocacy
McKellar, Charles	Pvt.	PA Res.		3862	South Mountain
McKenzie, James T.	1st Sgt. G	116 OH Inf.	08-24-1864	1455	Weverton, Monocacy
McKenzie, John	Pvt. K	108 NY Inf.		561	Antietam
McKenzie, R. Harrison	Pvt. C	2 WI Inf.	09-26-1862	3297	Antietam, WIA
McKibbins, Thomas	Pvt. F	108 NY Inf.		810	Antietam
McKinney, W. M.	Pvt. F	2 NY Inf.	09-28-1862	494	Antietam
McKinney, William G.	Pvt. C	7 WI Inf.	09-23-1862	3227	Antietam, WIA
McKinster, Alexander	Pvt. E	17 MI Inf.	09-14-1862	2502	S. MT., KIA, From Sheboygan
McKirtrick, William	Pvt. K	30 OH Inf.	09-14-1862	1439	South Mountain
McLauchlin, Patrick	Pvt.	2 NY Inf.		679	Antietam
McLaughlin, J.	Pvt. M	4 PA Cav.		3823	Antietam
McLaughlin, James	Pvt. K	9 MA Inf.	11-12-1863	1040	Frederick, Died of Wounds
McLaughlin, John	Pvt.	23 IL Inf.	12-15-1864	3071	Frederick, Died of Wounds
McLaughlin, John H.	Pvt. D	6 PA Res.	09-14-1862	3920	Middletown, KIA S. Mt.
McLaughlin, Robert	Pvt.	27 IN Inf.		3459	Antietam
McLay, James	Pvt. C	2 MA Inf.	10-05-1862	1061	Frederick, Antietam
McMahan, Patrick	Pvt. G	59 NY Inf.		691	Antietam
McMahon, John	Pvt. G	61 NY Inf.	10-18-1862	273	Frederick, Antietam
McMartin, Daniel E.	Pvt. D	17 MI Inf.	09-14-1862	2507	S. Mt., KIA, From Kalamazoo
McMasters, George	Pvt. K	14 WV Inf.	08-24-1864	2724	Weverton, Monocacy
McMillan, Archibald	Pvt. B	155 PA Inf.	11-07-1862	3621	Sharpsburg, Antietam
McMonigle, John	Pvt. C	2 NJ Inf.	09-17-1862	2780	Antietam, KIA
McMullen, Alexander J.	Pvt. F	28 PA Inf.	09-17-1862	3747	Antietam, KIA
McNally, Robert	Sgt. E	28 MA Inf.	09-24-1862	988	Antietam
McNaughton, Abraham W.	Pvt. A	29 OH Inf.	01-28-1862	1590	Frederick
McNeal, Patrick	Pvt. B	4 RI Inf.	09-17-1862	2832	Antietam, KIA
McNight, James	1st Sgt. C	1 PA Art.	11-07-1862	3950	Hagerstown, Antietam
McNight, John	Pvt. E	73 PA Inf.	07-26-1862	4189	Frederick, Age 34
McPherson, Charles	Capt. C	42 NY Inf.	09-17-1862	855	Antietam
McPherson, Finley	Pvt. F	6 MI Cav.	05-05-1865	2421	Clarysville, Disease, From Ada.
McPheters, Warren A.	Pvt. C	7 ME Inf.	09-17-1862	3170	Antietam
McQuade, Thomas	Pvt. B	69 NY Inf.	09-24-1862	139	Frederick, Antietam
McQueen, James	Pvt. K	69 NY Inf.	10-18-1862	266	Frederick, Antietam
McQuestion, Clinton	Pvt. D	20 MA Inf.	09-17-1862	898	Antietam
McTague, Patrick	Pvt. I	6 PA Res.	09-27-1862	4205	Frederick, Antietam
McVety, William	Pvt. F	108 NY Inf.	12-13-1862	210	Frederick, Antietam
McVey, John	Pvt. K	106 PA Inf.	10-17-1862	3695	Smoketown, WIA Antietam
Meachem, Eldridge F.	Pvt. B	7 OH Inf.	09-17-1862	1351	Antietam

Name	Rank/Co.	Reg./State	Death	Grave No.	Removed from/ Comments
Mead, Edward	Pvt. C	3 NY Cav.	05-25-1865	10	Cumberland
Meadows, John A.	Pvt. F	10 WV Inf.	12-14-1862	2762	Cumberland
Means, Henry W.	Pvt. G	2 PA Res.	11-28-1862	3719	Smoketown
Means, James H.	Pvt. D	12 MA Inf.	02-19-1862	1069	Frederick
Means, John	Pvt. C	3 MD Inf.		2561	Antietam
Meckbach, George	Pvt. I	20 NY Inf.		650	Antietam
Meckback	2nd Lt.	20 NY Inf.		856	Antietam
Mellen, Sidney F.	Pvt.	8 MA Art.	10-11-1862	969	Middletown, Antietam
Melman, Charles	Pvt. B	1 NJ Inf.	10-31-1862	2904	Frederick, Antietam
Melott, Frederick	Pvt. C	12 PA Res.	09-14-1862	3913	South Mountain, KIA
Melton, William H.	Pvt. K	144 IN Inf.	04-05-1865	3373	Cumberland
Mentzer, Thomas	Pvt. L	1 MD Cav.	07-05-1864	2471	Frederick
Mercer, George	Pvt. C	51 PA Inf.	10-20-1862	3943	Frederick, Antietam
Mercer, Levi J.	Pvt. C	2 WV Inf.	04-09-1865	2701	Frederick
Mereer, William H. H.	Pvt. F	170 OH N.G.		1457	Weverton
Merling, George	Pvt. G	9 MD Inf.	09-20-1862	2462	Frederick, Antietam
Merrill, G. C.	Pvt. B	13 NY Inf.	11-04-1862	366	Hagerstown, Antietam
Merritt, Richard D.	Pvt. D	35 NY Inf.	09-14-1862	473	South Mountain, KIA
Messie, Levi S.	Pvt. G	3 NJ Cav.	08-02-1864	330	Weverton, Monocacy
Metzinger, Charles	Pvt.	2 NY Inf.		667	Antietam
Metzker, Samuel	Pvt. G	8 OH Inf.	03-01-1862	1239	Cumberland
Meurer, John	Pvt.	77 NY Inf.		735	Antietam
Meyer, Adolph	Sgt. B	1 US Cav.	07-11-1863	3520	Antietam
Meyers, Charles	Pvt. L	5 NY Art.	08-13-1864	403	Sandy Hook, Age 21
Meyers, John	Pvt. D	3 WI Inf.	11-17-1861	3220	Frederick, Died Disease
Meyres, Antonio De	Pvt. L	5 NY Art.	07-27-1864	400	Sandy Hook
Mibbon, Daniel	Pvt. G	13 NY Inf.	10-03-1862	159	Frederick, Antietam
Miles, Lyman S.	Pvt. K	89 NY Inf.	09-17-1862	763	Antietam, KIA
Miles, Thomas J.	Pvt. G	49 NY Inf.	09-17-1862	736	Antietam
Miller, Aaron	Pvt. H	96 PA Inf.	09-30-1862	4031	Burkettsville, WIA S. Mt.
Miller, Alexander	Pvt. A	106 NY Inf.	07-16-1864	78	Frederick, Monocacy
Miller, Carl	Pvt. D	3 NJ Cav.	08-22-1864	2795	Weverton, Monocacy
Miller, Daniel P.	Sgt. A	145 NY Inf.	10-24-1862	236	Frederick, Antietam
Miller, Edward	Corp.	51 NY Inf.		782	Antietam
Miller, Edward F.	Pvt. H	99 NY Inf.	10-07-1862	165	Frederick, Antietam
Miller, George	Pvt. E	1 PA Res.	09-14-1862	3861	South Mountain, KIA
Miller, Jacob N.	Pvt. E	111 PA Inf.	09-17-1862	3668	Antietam, KIA
Miller, James H.	Pvt. C	51 NY Inf.		777	Antietam
Miller, Jeremiah	Pvt. H	96 PA Inf.	01-03-1863	4070	Frederick, WIA S. Mt.
Miller, John	Pvt. F	18 NY Inf.	11-17-1862	231	Frederick, WIA Ant.
Miller, John	Pvt. F	5 OH Inf.	09-17-1862	1354	Antietam
Miller, John C.	Pvt. C	100 PA Inf.	09-14-1862	3884	South Mountain, KIA
Miller, John R.	Corp. D	87 OH Inf.	09-19-1862	1263	Frederick, Antietam
Miller, Meeker				2078	Weverton
Miller, Samuel	Pvt. D	104 PA Inf.	02-27-1865	4132	Frederick
Miller, Samuel	Pvt.	59 NY Inf.		707	Antietam
Miller, William	Pvt. E	6 WV Inf.	09-20-1864	2866	Clarysville
Miller, William H.	Pvt. B	172 PA Inf.	07-21-1863	4084	Frederick, Age 33
Millhoff, Charles	Pvt. A	88 PA Inf.	09-17-1862	3655	Antietam, KIA
Milligan, Jephtha	Pvt. K	132 PA Inf.	09-17-1862	3594	Antietam
Milliken, M. B.	Pvt. F	1 MN Inf.	09-17-1862	3024	Antietam, KIA
Mills, Thomas B.	Pvt. E	6 US Inf.	01-05-1863	3554	Frederick, Antietam
Miricle, Henry	Pvt. I	22 PA Cav.	07-23-1864	4109	Frederick
Mitchell, Joseph	Pvt. C	16 ME Inf.	11-06-1862	3181	Smoketown
Mitchell, Samuel	Pvt.	12 US Inf.	10-06-1862	3572	Frederick, Antietam
Mitchell, Samuel	Pvt.	90 PA Inf.	09-17-1862	3651	Antietam, KIA
Mix, Joel	Pvt. E	76 NY Inf.	11-14-1862	607	Smoketown
Moaghan, Michael	Pvt. L	22 PA Cav.		4182	Cumberland
Molkte, Magness	1st Lt.	5 MD Inf.	09-17-1862	871	Antietam, KIA
Monaghan, Hamilton	Pvt. F	124 PA Inf.	09-23-1862	4135	Frederick, WIA Ant.

Name	Rank/Co.	Reg./State	Death	Grave No.	Removed from/ Comments
Monett, T. T. B.	Pvt. E	66 OH Inf.	04-15-1862	1507	Frederick
Monroe, James L.	Pvt. B	108 NY Inf.		815	Antietam
Monser, Casper	Pvt. G	66 OH Inf.	10-10-1862	1371	Smoketown
Monsun, C. L.	Pvt. K	147 IN Inf.	04-03-1865	3408	Frederick
Montgomery, Benjamin F.	Musician	14 NJ Inf.	11-22-1862	2902	Frederick, Antietam
Montgomery, F.	Pvt.	2 NY Inf.		675	Antietam
Montgomery, John H.	Pvt. D	29 OH Inf.	01-04-1862	1504	Frederick
Montgomery, Thomas	Pvt.	2 NY Inf.		656	Antietam
Moon, Josiah	Pvt. B	4 RI Inf.	09-17-1862	2829	Antietam, KIA
Moore, Francis	Pvt. H	1 NY Cav.	11-22-1864	116	Frederick
Moore, Franklin	Pvt. I	15 WV Inf.	02-20-1863	2846	Cumberland
Moore, Henry C.	Pvt. E	51 PA Inf.		3584	Antietam
Moore, Isaac L.	Pvt. K	155 PA Inf.	11-15-1862	4044	Frederick, Age 20
Moore, John	Pvt. H	92 OH Inf.	05-15-1865	1148	Clarysville
Moore, Joseph	Pvt. G	28 PA Inf.	03-14-1862	4198	Frederick, Age 21
Moore, Joseph M.	Corp. G	6 WI Inf.	10-19-1862	3237	Boonsboro, Antietam
Moore, Richard	Pvt. C	82 NY Inf.	11-10-1862	603	Smoketown
Moore, T. S.	Pvt.	1 PA Res.		3730	Antietam
Moore, William	Pvt. K	14 WV Inf.	08-04-1864	2767	Cumberland
Moore, William H.	Pvt. L	4 PA Cav.	08-24-1864	4119	Frederick
Moran, George	Pvt. I	34 MA Inf.	07-30-1864	971	Antietam, Sunstroke
Moran, John	Pvt. F	63 NY Inf.	11-06-1862	224	Frederick, Antietam
Morehead, Robert	Pvt.	59 NY Inf.		688	Antietam
Moreland, Alex	Pvt.	51 NY Inf.			Antietam
Mores, Robert R.	Pvt. C	15 MA Inf.	10-05-1862	973	Smoketown
Morgan, David B.	Pvt. A	193 OH Inf.	05-23-1865	1151	Clarysville
Morgan, Dorr	Pvt. B	1 MD Cav.	01-30-1862	2410	Frederick
Morgan, Robert P.	Pvt. E	16 CT Inf.	09-24-1862	1102	Antietam, WIA
Morley, John	Pvt. C	6 NY Inf.	09-28-1862	158	Frederick, Antietam
Morris, John V.	Capt. M	8 IL Cav.	07-09-1864	886	Frederick, Monocacy
Morris, William Edward	Pvt. I	66 OH Inf.	09-17-1962	1368	Smoketown
Morrow, William T.	Corp. F	1 WV Cav.		2870	Clarysville
Morse, D. E.	Pvt. G	89 NY Inf.	09-14-1862	468	South Mountain, KIA
Morse, David	Pvt. A	11 PA Inf.	01-03-1863	4071	Frederick, Antietam
Morse, Isaac E.	Pvt.	3 VT		2665	Antietam
Morse, Joel F.	Pvt. D	56 PA Inf.	06-02-1863	4075	Frederick
Morton, James					See Murphy, James
Morton, Noah C.	Pvt. I	45 PA Inf.	09-27-1862	4142	Frederick, WIA S. Mt.
Mosier, S. E.	Pvt. C	3 WI Inf.	10-16-1861	3284	Frederick, KIA
Moss, Charles	Pvt. E	8 PA Res.	09-14-1862	3858	South Mountain, KIA
Moss, James	Pvt. C	69 PA Inf.	09-17-1862	3787	Antietam, KIA
Mossgrove, George V.	Sgt. L	1 WV Cav.	07-23-1864	2867	Clarysville
Mott, Charles	Pvt. L	16 NY Cav.	09-12-1864	321	Weverton, Monocacy
Mott, George H.	Pvt.	39 IL Inf.		3109	Cumberland
Mott, J. Milton	Capt. K	5 WI Inf.	07-26-1863	885	Frederick, Age 45
Mower, Jacob	Pvt. C	131 PA Inf.	10-16-1862	3799	Sharpsburg, Accidental Death
Mowser, Irvin	Pvt. G	66 OH Inf.	02-23-1862	1210	Cumberland
Mullen, Emile	Pvt. I	46 NY Inf.	10-21-1862	251	Frederick
Mullen, J. B.	Pvt. G	13 IN Inf.	08-14-1862	3403	Frederick
Mullen, Robert M.	Pvt. P	28 PA Inf.	09-17-1862	3625	Antietam, KIA
Mullender, William	Pvt. F	2 NJ Inf.		2785	Burkettsville
Mumford, Samuel	Pvt. E	2 DE Inf.	10-18-1862	3054	Smoketown
Mundle, John	Pvt. B	8 MI Inf.	11-21-1862	2381	Sandy Hook, From Dallas
Mundoff, John P.	Pvt. C	83 PA Inf.	10-28-1862	3925	Frederick
Munsick, David	Pvt. C	51 PA Inf.		4001	Weverton
Muntz, John	Pvt. B	10 VT Inf.	02-23-1862	2697	Cumberland
Murg, Joseph	Sgt. B	103 NY Inf.	10-02-1862	772	Antietam, KIA
Murphy, Bernard	Pvt. G	6 PA Res.	09-17-1862	3715	Smoketown, KIA Ant.
Murphy, James	Pvt. I	9 NY Mlt.		635	Antietam

Name	Rank/Co.	Reg./State	Death	Grave No.	Removed from/ Comments
Murphy, James B.	Pvt. E	12 MA Inf.	10-25-1862	1025	Frederick, Antietam
Murphy, John	Pvt. B	1 NH Cav.	09-08-1864	2812	Weverton, Sandy Hook
Murphy, Michael	Pvt. G	1 NY Cav.	10-26-1864	17	Clarysville
Murphy, Patrick	Pvt. A	2 MD Inf.	10-18-1864	2425	Clarysville, Died Disease
Murphy, Thomas	Pvt. C	33 NY Inf.	11-01-1862	279	Hagerstown, Antietam
Murray, James	Pvt. I	15 NY Cav.	09-17-1864	288	Weverton, Monocacy
Murray, Michael				1807	Burkettsville
Murray, Michael	Pvt. B	69 NY Inf.	09-30-1862	156	Frederick, Antietam
Murray, William F.	Pvt. K	32 MA Inf.		964	Weverton
Murry, Melvin	Pvt. E	4 WV Inf.	12-24-1864	2755	Cumberland
Murry, Otto C.	Pvt. H	1 MD Inf.	05-29-1864	2596	
Mushgrove, Thomas	Pvt. I	77 NY Inf.	10-19-1862	280	Hagerstown, Antietam
Musk, Edward	Pvt. K	10 VT Inf.	10-02-1864	2680	Fred., Monocacy, Age 24
Myers, John M.	Pvt. B	7 WV Inf.	02-05-1862	2610	Antietam
Nace, Josiah	Pvt. D	90 PA Inf.	09-17-1862	3645	Antietam, KIA
Nagle, George	Pvt. C	2 WV		2844	Cumberland
Nash, Francis J.	Pvt. B	35 MA Inf.	12-15-1862	1030	Disease, Age 38
Nason, Christian					See Mason, Christian
Neal, John B.	Pvt. B	91 OH Inf.	09-21-1864	1314	Frederick, Monocacy
Nearon, Jacob	Pvt. A	14 IN Inf.	09-17-1862	3440	Antietam
Neason, John	Pvt. G	22 NY Inf.	09-14-1862	487	South, Mountain
Neaville, Henry B.	Pvt. C	2 WI Inf.	09-17-1862	3313	Antietam, KIA
Nedren, Jacob	Pvt. D	22 PA Cav.	10-17-1864	4161	Clarysville
Negus, Alexander	Pvt. G	9 NY Inf.		745	Antietam
Neibergall, Lewis W.	Pvt. K	1 MD Inf.	01-07-1862	2444	Frederick
Nelson, William A.	Corp. I	2 WI Inf.	10-16-1862	3222	South Mountain, WIA
Nesbit, James	Pvt. E	110 PA Inf.		4178	Cumberland
Ness, Robert	Pvt. H	9 PA Res.	10-26-1862	3930	Frederick, WIA South Mountain
Nevin, Thomas	Pvt. F	63 NY Inf.	10-25-1862	241	Frederick, Antietam
Newbert, Neville A.	Pvt. I	20 ME Inf.	10-29-1862	3149	Antietam
Newbury, Lewis	Pvt.	20 NY Inf.		726	Antietam
Newcomb, W. B.	Pvt. C	7 WI Inf.	03-05-1863	3271	Frederick, Age 23
Newell, D. D.	Pvt. K	8 OH Inf.	09-27-1862	1495	Frederick, Antietam
Newell, L. D.	Pvt. B	14 NY Inf.	09-27-1864	295	Weverton, Monocacy
Newell, Thomas J.	Sgt. K	194 OH Inf.	04-23-1865	1153	Clarysville
Newman, Francis	Pvt. A	18 NY Inf.	08-08-1863	175	Frederick, Age 24
Newpher, James	Pvt. I	1 PA Res.	10-06-1862	4200	Frederick, WIA South Mountain
Newton, George H.	Pvt. K	105 NY Inf.	10-15-1862	263	Frederick, Antietam
Newton, Thomas K.	Pvt. E	89 NY Inf.		454	Middletown
Nichols, Frederick E.	Pvt. C	8 OH Inf.	09-17-1862	1355	Antietam
Nichols, George F.	Pvt. I	12 NH Inf.	10-21-1862	2819	Antietam, Died Disease Knoxville
Nicholson, Francis	Pvt. G	28 MA Inf.	09-17-1862	953	Hagerstown, Antietam
Noal, John	Pvt. B	125 PA Inf.		3734	Antietam
Noarse, Thomas A.	Corp. A	46 PA Inf.	09-17-1862	3785	Antietam, KIA
Noble, Geary L.	Pvt. E	8 MD Inf.	01-19-1863	2577	Weverton, Antietam
Noble, Harvey	Pvt. E	104 NY Inf.	10-30-1862	250	Antietam, WIA
Noble, John					See Nobles, John
Noble, John	Pvt. F	11 OH Inf.	09-27-1862	1261	Frederick, Antietam
Noble, William	Pvt. D	30 OH Inf.	10-11-1862	1403	Middletown, WIA S. Mt.
Nobles, John	Pvt. D	30 OH Inf.	10-05-1862	1499	Frederick, WIA S. Mt.
Noch, W. H. H.	Pvt. D	72 PA Inf.	09-17-1862	3766	Antietam, KIA
Nokes, Martin	Pvt. K	16 NY Inf.	10-24-1862	563	Bakersville, Antietam
Noon, Thomas	Pvt. G	1 WV Inf.	05-11-1862	2871	Oakland
Norfolk, William	Pvt. A	15 WV Inf.	12-29-1862	2765	Cumberland
Noricond, Isreal M.	Pvt. G	3 WI Inf.	12-16-1861	3277	Fred., Disease, Age 52
Noricong, Israel W.					See Noricond, Isreal M.
Northrop	Pvt. A	NY	10-16-1864	335	Weverton

Name	Rank/Co.	Reg./State	Death	Grave No.	Removed from/ Comments
Northrop, A. Delos	Pvt. I	1 PA Res.	09-17-1862	3899	South Mountain, WIA
Northrup, Horace		WI		3217	Antietam
Norton, David	Pvt. M	PA Cav.		3955	Hagerstown
Nugen, Jasper	Pvt. C	27 IN Inf.	02-17-1863	3424	Frederick
Nulty, John	Pvt. C	28 MA Inf.	01-20-1863	1034	Frederick, WIA Antietam
Nuss, Jacob	Pvt. E	28 PA Inf.	09-17-1862	3748	Antietam, WIA
O'Brien, James	Sgt. F	42 NY Inf.	02-17-1862	190	Frederick
O'Brien, John A.	Sgt. C	42 NY Inf.		836	Antietam
O'Brien, Patrick	Pvt. D	2 NY Inf.	10-10-1862	256	Hagerstown, Antietam
O'Brien, Thomas	Pvt. D	69 NY Inf.	10-04-1862	147	Frederick, Antietam
O'Bryen, Frank	Pvt.	14 IN Inf.		3439	Antietam
O'Connell, John	Pvt. H	9 NY Inf.	09-02-1862	770	Antietam
O'Conner, Dennis	Pvt. K	NY Cav.	08-02-1864	325	Weverton, Monocacy, Age 27
O'Conner, N.	Pvt.	OH Inf.	07-03-1862	1503	Frederick
O'Dowd, James		4 US Cav.		3524	Antietam
O'Hara	Pvt. G	29 OH Inf.		1408	South Mountain, Likely 23 OH
O'Hara, James	Pvt. D	194 NY Inf.	09-17-1862	534	Antietam, KIA
O'Neal, Patrick	Pvt. C	88 NY Inf.	09-30-1862	146	Frederick, Antietam
O'Neal, Samuel	Pvt. D	17 MI Inf.		2511	South Mountain
O'Neale, Daniel	Pvt. K	32 NY Inf.	02-11-1863	193	Frederick
O'Neale, John	Corp. I	69 NY Inf.	10-04-1862	148	Frederick, Antietam
O'Neil, John	Pvt. G	7 MI Inf.	10-07-1862	2517	Antietam, WIA, From Lapeer
O'Reilly, Patrick	Pvt. E	42 NY Inf.	10-07-1862	168	Frederick, Antietam
Oakes, Charles	Pvt. C	16 ME Inf.	11-07-1862	3182	Smoketown
Odenbaugh, H. C.	Pvt. A	100 PA Inf.		3886	South Mountain
Olcott, Harrison	Pvt. E	7 US Inf.	07-14-1863	3557	Frederick, Age 29
Olds, Orrin W.	Pvt. C	121 NY Inf.	11-08-1862	233	Hagerstown, Antietam
Oleson, John	Pvt. F	3 WI Inf.	09-17-1862	3325	Antietam, KIA
Olin, Uriel P.	Corp. B	2 WI Inf.	09-17-1862	3314	Antietam, KIA
Oliver, Henry	Pvt. F	36 OH Inf.	09-01-1864	1312	Frederick, Monocacy
Oliver, John H.	Corp. K	5 US Cav.	07- -1863	3535	Funkstown
Orcott, Alvin	Pvt. E	34 NY Inf.	09-17-1862	825	Antietam
Orcutt, George	Pvt. F	1 MI Cav.	01-30-1862	2414	Frederick, From Lapeer
Ordinary, Elijah	Pvt. A	17 MI Inf.	11-12-1863	2485	Weverton, Typhoid Fever
Ordway, Benjamin P.	Pvt. D	7 WI Inf.	10-03-1862	3274	Frederick, WIA Antietam
Orskins, Thomas	Pvt. A	1 DE Inf.	09-17-1862	3046	Antietam, KIA
Osborn	Pvt.			3252	Unknown
Osborn, Charles D.	Pvt. G	5 WI Inf.	10-24-1862	3260	Hagerstown, Died Disease
Osmundson, Ole	Pvt. K	3 WI Inf.	10-17-1861	3287	Frederick, Died Disease
Otis, James	Pvt. H	PA Art.	02-16-1863	3902	Middletown, Antietam
Otten, Henry	Pvt. A	3 PA Res.	10-12-1862	3813	Smoketown, WIA Antietam
Oty, Henry	Pvt. C	194 OH Inf.	04-14-1865	1201	Clarysville
Outwater, John W.	Pvt. I	1 NJ Inf.	09-16-1862	2793	Weverton
Overdorff, David C.	Pvt. H	12 PA Res.	09-17-1862	3780	Antietam, KIA
Pabst, J. P.	Pvt. F	80 NY Inf.		652	Antietam
Pack, Newton R.	Pvt. F	5 WV Inf.	09-16-1864	2623	Frederick, Monocacy
Page, Alvah G.	Pvt. F	3 VT Inf.	07-22-1863	2649	Frederick, Age 21
Page, Hiram T.	Pvt. K	15 VT Inf.	07-23-1863	2650	Frederick, Age 23
Page, Ira E.	Pvt. A	12 NH Inf.	07-03-1863	2892	Frederick
Page, W. H. H.	Pvt. M	8 NY Cav.	11-01-1862	249	Frederick, Antietam
Pagefall, Max	Pvt. E	15 NY Cav.	11-03-1864	25	Clarysville
Paige, James L.	Pvt. H	66 NY Inf.	10-11-1862	261	Frederick, Antietam
Paiste, William H.	Pvt. K	124 PA Inf.	09-30-1862	4214	Frederick, WIA Antietam
Palmatier, Almeron	Pvt. D	17 MI Inf.	09-14-1862	2512	S. Mt., KIA, From Johnstown
Palmer, George	Pvt. B	7 MI Inf.	09-25-1862	2524	Antietam, WIA,

Name	Rank/Co.	Reg./State	Death	Grave No.	Removed from/ Comments
					From Ingham Co.
Palmer, John L.	Pvt. B	7 MI Cav.	06-05-1865	2423	Clarysville
Palmer, Thomas	Corp. B	2 MA Inf.	03-25-1865	1053	Frederick
Palmerton, William S.	Pvt. F	8 OH Inf.	09-17-1862	1336	Antietam
Pardee, Marcus	Pvt. A	2 WI Inf.	09-17-1862	3306	Antietam, KIA
Pardoe, Robert J.	Sgt. A	139 PA Inf.	11-07-1864	3952	Frederick, Age 36
Parish, William C.	Pvt. G	39 IL Inf.	11-29-1861	3034	Cumberland, Age 34
Parker, Charles	Pvt. A	14 NJ Inf.	11-08-1863	2915	Frederick
Parker, Isaac N.	Pvt. H	126 OH Inf.	07-18-1864	1285	FRederick, Monocacy
Parker, John A.	Pvt. F	28 PA Inf.	09-17-1862	3638	Antietam, KIA
Parker, Thomas H.	Pvt. C	19 IN Inf.	10-20-1862	3472	Antietam
Parmatier, John H.	Pvt. E	23 NY Inf.	10-02-1862	538	Antietam, WIA
Parson, Lander C.	Pvt. B	3 DE Inf.	09-05-1862	3110	Frederick
Parsons, Edwin	Pvt. A	1 VT Art.	08-11-1864	2644	Frederick, Monocacy, Age 19
Parsons, Henry	Pvt. H	23 OH Inf.	09-14-1862	1498	Frederick, S. Mt.
Parsons, Henry	Pvt. H	1 US Cav.		3513	Weverton
Parsons, Thomas	Pvt. C	45 PA Inf.	09-14-1862	3874	South Mountain, KIA
Partenheimer, William	Pvt. H	34 MA Inf.	08-14-1864	1045	Frederick, Monocacy
Partridge, George M.	Pvt. D	6 VT Inf.	07-10-1863	2694	Funkstown, Age 22
Patterson, Andrew	Pvt. I	Engineers	06-11-1865	2403	Frederick
Patterson, Charles	Pvt. K	14 NJ Inf.	11-23-1863	2901	Frederick
Patterson, John	Pvt. I	67 NY Inf.	11-04-1862	363	Hagerstown, Antietam
Patterson, William	Corp.	9 NY Inf.		751	Antietam
Pattison, T. M.	Pvt. K	14 PA Cav.	07-07-1864	4096	Frederick
Pattong, John	Pvt. I	3 MA Cav.	06-08-1865	1071	Clarysville
Paulus, Samuel	Pvt. F	110 PA Inf.		4179	Cumberland
Pazzant, Lewis	Pvt. C	2 MA Inf.	03-06-1865	1052	Frederick
Pearson, William	Sgt. I	152 OH N.G.	08-02-1864	1250	Cumberland
Penn, George	Corp. L	28 PA Inf.	09-17-1862	3642	Antietam, KIA
Pennock, Jacob	Pvt. F	196 OH Inf.	04-26-1864	1143	Clarysville
Pepper, Nathaniel	Pvt. C	15 NY Cav.	05-21-1864	15	Clarysville
Percefield, John	Pvt. H	91 OH Inf.	07-24-1864	1204	Cumberland
Perkins, Orrin W. B.	Pvt. D	30 ME Inf.	09-08-1864	3124	Frederick, Monocacy
Pero, William	Pvt. G	122 OH Inf.	11-14-1864	1306	Frederick
Perry, Charles	Pvt. F	15 MA Inf.	09-17-1862	896	Antietam
Perry, Timothy	Pvt. C	87 PA Inf.	01-05-1865	4123	Frederick, Age 36
Perry, William H.	Pvt. C	39 IL Inf.	02-25-1862	3106	Cumberland
Perrys, L.	Pvt. K	11 IN Inf.	09-13-1864	3417	Frederick, Monocacy
Peters, John	Pvt. H	14 IN Inf.	11-16-1862	3432	Frederick, Antietam
Peters, John	Pvt. H	8 PA Res.	10-03-1862	4212	Frederick, Antietam
Peters, John R.	Pvt. C	27 IN Inf.		3464	Antietam
Peyton, Andrew J.	Pvt. B	126 OH Inf.	07-18-1864	1296	Frederick, Monocacy
Pfeiffer, Augustus	Pvt. K	8 NY		20	Clarysville
Phillips, Edgar A.	Pvt. K	161 OH Inf.		1398	Middletown, From Eaton, Age 16
Phillips, Jonathan K.	Corp. B	6 ME Inf.	07-19-1863	3128	Frederick, Age 20
Phillips, Samuel	Pvt. A	118 PA Inf.	09-20-1862	359	0rick, Antietam
Pickard, John E.	Pvt. E	1 ME Cav.	11-14-1862	3134	Frederick, Antietam
Pickering, Joseph J.	Pvt.	90 PA Inf.	09-17-1862	3647	Antietam, KIA
Pickett, James D.	Pvt. H	11 WV Inf.	09-27-1864	2869	Clarysville
Pickett, Thomas	Pvt. I	29 MA Inf.	03-20-1863	1037	Frederick
Pierce, Erwin	Pvt. H	3 WI Inf.	10-30-1861	3279	Frederick
Pierce, Hiram	Pvt. A	7 WI Inf.	10-07-1862	3246	Middletown, WIA Antietam
Pierce, James	Pvt. H	2 MA Inf.	12-26-1861	1062	Frederick
Pierce, Sylvester	Pvt. K	29 OH Inf.	10-20-1862	1478	Frederick, Antietam
Pierson, Henry	Pvt. D	5 MI Cav.	02-1864	2416	Clarysville, Disease, From Wayne Co.
Pike, George W.	Pvt. I	37 MA Inf.	11-19-1862	1029	Frederick, Antietam

Name	Rank/Co.	Reg./State	Death	Grave No.	Removed from/ Comments
Piles, Isaac	Pvt. A	1 WV Art.	10-03-1864	2722	Weverton, Monocacy
Pinkins, Charles	Pvt.	10 ME Inf.		3206	Antietam
Pinner, Samuel	Pvt. H	64 NY Inf.	12-26-1862	200	Frederick, Antietam
Piper, Frederick	Pvt. F	7 MI Inf.	01-28-1863	2553	Frederick, Disease, From Houghton
Pittinger, Smith	Pvt. F	5 NY Art.	08-26-1864	292	Weverton, Monocacy
Ploss, Peter P.	Pvt.	20 NY Inf.		646	Antietam
Ploss, Wheeler	Pvt. D	111 PA Inf.	09-17-1862	3670	Antietam, KIA
Pohl, John	Pvt. C	14 PA Cav.	05-02-1865	4159	Clarysville
Pole, Gabriel	Pvt. D	123 OH Inf.	04-16-1864	1467	Weverton
Pollack, W. J.	Corp. A	80 NY Inf.		653	Antietam
Pollay, Samuel B.	Pvt. G	108 NY Inf.	09-17-1862	812	Antietam
Pollman, William	Pvt. H	1 MD Cav.	03-25-1864	2599	Frederick, Died Disease
Pool, E. G.	Pvt. G	12 MA Inf.	10-14-1862	975	Smoketown
Poor, George	Pvt.	26 NY Inf.		684	Antietam
Popple, Orville	Pvt.	NY Art.	10-12-1864	113	Frederick
Porter, James M.	Pvt. A	4 CT Inf.	09-06-1861	1134	Hagerstown
Porter, John	Pvt. H	1 DE Inf.	10-16-1862	3055	Frederick, Antietam
Powell, Abraham	Pvt. B	3 MD	06-26-1864	2466	Frederick
Powers, Earl	Pvt. F	152 IN Inf.	04-01-1865	3365	Clarysville
Powers, Nathan F.	Pvt. D	17 MI Inf.	10-24-1862	2547	Big Spring, Disease, From Johnstown
Pratt, David S.	Pvt. C	17 MI Inf.	12-12-1862	2376	Weverton, Disease, From Ovid
Pratt, Oliver P.	Pvt. L	1 ME Cav.	11-18-1862	3138	Frederick, Antietam
Pressey, Charles M.	Pvt. G	10 ME Inf.	09-17-1862	3168	Antietam
Price, Abraham	Pvt. E	6 PA Res.	09-14-1862	3849	South Mountain, KIA
Price, Chauncey	Pvt. K	49 NY Inf.	11-18-1862	364	Hagerstown, Antietam
Price, Edward					See Price, James
Price, F. H.	Pvt. D	49 PA Inf.	10-07-1862	3992	Weverton
Price, James	Pvt. D	4 NY Inf.		805	Antietam
Price, John	Pvt. B	62 OH Inf.	02-26-1862	1240	Cumberland
Price, Thomas P.	Pvt.	20 NY Inf.		647	Antietam
Priester, Solomon	Lt.	7 WV Cav.		881	Berlin(Brunswick)
Pritehard, C. B.	Pvt.	59 NY Inf.		708	Antietam
Proctor, George F.	Pvt. L	12 PA Cav.	11-11-1864	4008	Weverton, Sandy Hook
Propson, Charles	Pvt.	20 NY Inf.		719	Antietam
Provo, George	Pvt. D	13 WV Inf.	08-11-1864	2732	Weverton, Monocacy, Age 19
Putnam, William	Pvt. I	116 NY Inf.	11-28-1864	122	Frederick
Queen, Joseph	Pvt. C	14 IN Inf.		3372	Cumberland
Quigley, Edward	Pvt. A	2 DE Inf.	09-17-1862	3051	Antietam, KIA
Quigley, John			10-08-1862	1697	Frederick
Quigley, Patrick	Pvt.	51 NY Inf.		784	Antietam
Quinn, Charles A.	Pvt. F	5 NH Inf.	09-17-1862	2807	Antietam, WIA
Quinn, James	Pvt. A	3 IN Cav.	09-30-1862	3401	Frederick, Antietam
Quinn, James F.	Pvt. K	2 PA Res.	10-17-1862	3710	Smoketown
Quinn, Michael	Pvt. D	28 MA Inf.	09-17-1862	952	Hagerstown, Antietam
Quinn, Patrick	Pvt. A	28 PA Inf.	09-17-1862	3632	Antietam, KIA
R., John J.	Pvt.	PA Cav.		3994	Weverton
Racey, Giles	Pvt. C	5 VT	11-26-1862	2667	Hagerstown, Age 21
Radcliffe, James H.	Pvt. G	30 ME	09-06-1864	3195	Weverton, Monocacy
Rafford, James C.	Pvt. C	16 ME	10-27-1862	3188	Smoketown
Rager, David C.	Pvt. D	115 PA	06-29-1863	4074	Frederick
Raines, Reuben	Teamster		02-16-1865	1714	Frederick
Rainey, John W.	Pvt. C	195 OH	04-13-1865	1277	Cumberland
Rancy	Sgt.	134 PA Inf.		3607	Antietam
Randall, James H.	Pvt. K	12 PA Cav.		4013	Brownsville
Randall, Norton S.	Pvt. H	9 NY	07-12-1864	68	Fred., WIA Monocacy, Age 28

Name	Rank/Co.	Reg./State	Death	Grave No.	Removed from/ Comments
Ranerd, C. H.	Pvt.	5 NY Art.		411	Burkettsville
Ransom, J. H.	Pvt.	12 US Inf.		3532	Antietam
Rasiga, Eugene	Pvt. B	9 NY	09-17-1862	771	Antietam
Rath, Charles	Pvt. A	5 WI	11-08-1862	3257	Hagerstown, Died Disease
Rawley, James	Pvt. M	4 NY	09-19-1864	315	Weverton
Ray, Charles	Pvt. K	51 NY	10-23-1862	340	Weverton, Antietam
Ray, Madison	Pvt.	PA		3915	Middletown
Raybur, H.	Pvt. H	12 NY Inf.		773	Antietam
Raymond, Henry	Pvt. C	3 WI	10-16-1861	3286	Fred., KIA Harpers Ferry
Reader, John	Pvt. K	5 WV	04-17-1865	2865	Clarysville
Recer, Jacob	Pvt. E	34 OH	11-19-1864	1259	Clarysville
Redington, J. P.	Pvt. K	9 NH	10-20-1862	2805	Antietam, Died Disease
Reed, Alexander N.	1st Lt. I	3 WI	09-17-1862	851	Antietam, KIA
Reed, Asa	Pvt. K	10 ME	09-17-1862	3158	Antietam
Reed, C. B.	Pvt. B	17 US	08-28-1863	3562	Frederick, Age 26
Reed, Francis C.	Pvt. G	7 MD Inf.		4231	Hagerstown
Reed, Israel S.	Pvt. I	2 MA	03-16-1863	1038	Frederick
Reed, James	Pvt. K	1 NY	03-30-1864	56	Frederick
Reed, James C.	Pvt. G	134 PA	12-07-1862	4054	Frederick, Age 18
Reed, Jonathan	Pvt. C	3 NJ Cav.		2939	Clarysville
Reed, Silas L.	Pvt. D	35 MA	10-12-1862	985	Antietam, Age 25
Reedy, Michael	Corp. C	69 PA	09-17-1862	3788	Antietam, KIA
Reese, John	Pvt. K	2 NY	11-30-1864	333	Sandy Hook, Age 22
Rehier, Joseph	Pvt. B	20 NY Inf.		651	Antietam
Rehill, Phillip	Pvt.	2 US Art.		493	Antietam
Reibe, Ferdinand	Pvt. B	2 WI	09-17-1862	3305	Antietam, KIA
Reichman, Jacob	Pvt. H	12 OH	09-19-1862	1362	Antietam
Reiff, Jacob	Pvt. I	9 PA Res.	09-17-1862	3760	Antietam, KIA
Reilley, Eugene	Pvt. K	131 NY Inf.	110-18-1864	120	Frederick
Reilley, Thomas	Pvt. C	131 NY	11-11-1864	115	Frederick
Reinninger, Frederick M.	Pvt. A	84 PA	03-04-1862	4184	Cumberland
Remich, Prescott	Pvt. G	2 MA	10-27-1862	978	Smoketown
Remington, George R.	Pvt. B	14 VT	07-19-1863	2664	Middletown, Age 19
Remington, Thomas F.	Pvt. K	11 CT	09-26-1862	1114	Antietam, WIA
Remmele, John	Pvt. K	3 WI	09-24-1861	3276	Frederick
Renchler, John A.	Pvt. F	77 NY Inf.		733	Antietam
Resch, Victor	Pvt. A	40 NY	07-09-1863	182	Frederick
Resling, J. C.	Pvt. M	3 WV	05-12-1865	2775	Clarysville
Rever, Jacob	Pvt. I	72 PA	09-17-1862	3678	Antietam, KIA
Rexroad, Loftus	Pvt. F	3 WV	03-07-1865	2705	Frederick
Reynear, Theodore F.	Pvt. F	14 NJ	12-28-1862	2895	Frederick, Antietam
Reynolds, Emmor	Sgt. C	28 PA	09-17-1862	3630	Antietam, KIA
Reynolds, Hugh H.	Pvt. F	1 MI	10-01-1864	2479	Fred., Monocacy, From Detroit
Reynolds, J. K.	Sgt.			1358	Unknown
Reynolds, Leander	Pvt.	51 NY Inf.		781	Antietam
Reynolds, Stoel F.	Corp. F	51 NY Inf.		582	Antietam
Rhoades, Chester S.	Pvt. H	34 NY	09-17-1862	828	Antietam, KIA
Rhoads, Peter M.	Pvt. B	13 WV	05-26-1865	2878	Clarysville
Rhoda, Frederick	Pvt. M	5 NY Art.		410	Maryland Heights
Rhodes, Charles	Pvt. C	2 MA	10-29-1864	1049	Frederick
Rice, Charles H.	Sgt. D	21 NY Inf.		293	Weverton
Rice, Edward W.	Pvt.	41 US Res.		3573	Clarysville
Rice, Jacob	Pvt. E	106 PA	10-14-1862	3701	Smoketown, WIA Antietam
Rice, William	Pvt. K	36 OH	09-15-1862	1448	South Mountain
Rich, Henry	Pvt. H	19 IN	09-17-1862	3445	Antietam
Richard, John	Pvt. E	14 IN	09-17-1862	3442	Antietam
Richards, Thomas	Pvt. C	3 NY	11-21-1862	281	Hagerstown, Antietam
Richardson, Daniel J.	Pvt. H	23 OH	09-27-1862	1407	South Mountain

Name	Rank/Co.	Reg./State	Death	Grave No.	Removed from/ Comments
Richardson, George C.	Pvt. H	6 VT	12-08-1862	2653	Frederick, Age 19
Richardson, Orson F.	Pvt. E	6 ME	10-16-1862	3184	Smoketown
Richardson, William	Pvt. A	27 NY	11-08-1862	386	Hagerstown, Antietam
Richardson, William P.	Pvt. A	8 OH	09-17-1862	1339	Antietam
Richerson, J. W.	Lt.	39 IL Inf.		863	Williamsport
Richey, William C.	Pvt. G	28 PA	09-17-1862	3728	Antietam, KIA
Rickabaugh, John H.	Pvt. K	91 OH	11-07-1864	1303	Frederick
Riddle, James F.	Pvt. G	10 WV	01-15-1864	2771	Cumberland
Rifenberger, H. H.	Pvt.	146 PA Inf.		3974	Hagerstown
Riggle, Thomas	Pvt. G	122 OH	08-14-1863	1491	Frederick, Age 21
Riley, John	Pvt. K	20 MA	09-17-1862	902	Antietam
Riley, T. O.	Corp. I	3 MA	10-11-1864	1048	Frederick
Rimple, George W.	Corp.	103 NY Inf.		764	Antietam
Rinehart, Abraham	Pvt. B	152 IN	04-02-1865	3361	Clarysville
Ring, Charles H.	Pvt. C	16 ME	11-30-1862	3186	Smoketown
Ring, Johnathan	Pvt.	8 OH Inf.		1262	Antietam
Ringgold, Mathias	Pvt. I	42 NY Inf.		577	Antietam
Riordon, William	Pvt.	2 NY Inf.		665	Antietam
Ripley, Levi D.	Pvt. E	10 WV	10-18-1864	2735	Weverton, Age 29
Risdorph, John	Corp. F	102 NY	07-05-1862	49	Frederick
Rising, Henry	Pvt. D	11 CT	09-17-1862	1177	Antietam
Ritter, Charles	Pvt.	20 NY Inf.		721	Antietam
Ritter, George J.	Pvt. D	28 PA	09-17-1862	3629	Antietam, KIA
Ritter, William L.	Pvt. K	126 OH	11-26-1862	1236	Cumberland
Rivers, Israel	Pvt. F	106 NY	07-22-1864	90	Frederick, Monocacy
Robatham, Thomas	Pvt.	8 NY Cav.		392	Hagerstown
Robbins, C. H.	Pvt. H	35 MA	09-17-1862	989	Antietam, WIA, Age 23
Robbins, H. P.	Corp.	53 IL Inf.		3035	Weverton
Robbins, Sanford	Pvt. A	32 NY	11-03-1862	362	Hagerstown, Antietam
Roberts, Johnsey	Sgt. A	9 WV	08-24-1864	2954	Clarysville
Roberts, Peter	Pvt.	PA		3910	Middletown
Roberts, William	Pvt. G	10 WV	08-24-1864	2714	Weverton, Monocacy
Robinson, Edward S.	Pvt. E	12 WV	12-03-1862	2760	Cumberland
Robinson, George	Pvt. A	63 NY	10-22-1862	246	Antietam, WIA
Robinson, James	Pvt. M	7 MI	03-04-1865	2474	Clarysville
Robinson, Joseph	Pvt. E	2 CT	09-17-1864	1193	Frederick, Monocacy
Robinson, M. E.	Pvt. E	13 WV	02-20-1865	2743	Cumberland
Robinson, Nelson A.	Pvt. G	107 NY	11-16-1862	584	Smoketown
Robinson, Robert I.	Musician	6 US	09-17-1862	3530	Antietam
Robinson, Rufus	Corp. I	122 NY	11-06-1862	602	Smoketown, Typhoid Fever
Roby, John	Pvt. A	10 WV	12-24-1862	2756	Cumberland
Rockwell, Daniel	Pvt. K	44 NY	11-14-1862	382	Hagerstown, Antietam
Rockwell, P.	Pvt. B	12 US Inf.		3517	South Mountain
Roddenon, William	Corp. K	16 NY	09-16-1862	443	South Mountain, WIA
Rodenbaugh, William	Pvt. A	138 PA	07-20-1864	4111	Fred., Monocacy, Age 21
Rodgers, Jacob			09-20-1862	1708	Frederick
Rodgers, Samuel C.	Pvt. H	11 CT	09-17-1862	1176	Antietam
Roe, John	Pvt. B	42 NY	10-30-1862	252	Frederick, Antietam
Rogers, Amos S.	Sgt. F	107 NY Inf.		417	Burkettsville
Rogers, Remus	Pvt. F	6 MI Cav.		2391	Hagerstown
Rogers, W. H.	Pvt. C	25 NY	09-21-1864	110	Frederick, Monocacy
Rogers, William W.	Corp. E	105 NY	10-11-1862	592	Smoketown
Rohn, Job	Pvt. D	11 PA	11-19-1862	3712	Smoketown, WIA Antietam
Rollins, Sylvester	Pvt. B	14 IN	10-17-1862	3491	Frederick, Antietam
Rollins, Sylvester	Corp. B	14 IN	10-24-1862	3496	Frederick, Antietam
Romig, Franklin S.	Pvt. K	54 PA	08-08-1863	4150	Clarysville
Rooks, G. B.	Pvt. E	122 OH	07-16-1864	1297	Frederick, Monocacy
Rooney, Michael	Pvt. F	MD	09-1862	2567	Smoketown
Rose, Samuel B.	Wagoner	14 NJ	02-08-1863	2894	Frederick, Antietam
Rose, William M.	Pvt. E	2 MD	05-25-1863	2428	Cumberland

Name	Rank/Co.	Reg./State	Death	Grave No.	Removed from/ Comments
Rosegie, S.	Pvt.	59 NY Inf.		700	Antietam
Rosel, William	Pvt. K	7 OH	06-01-1862	1509	Frederick
Ross, Jacob	Corp. E	22 NY	10-14-1862	597	Smoketown
Ross, John	Pvt. F	91 OH	08-16-1864	1254	Cumberland
Ross, John C.	Pvt. E	19 MA	09-17-1862	935	Antietam
Ross, R.	Corp. H	8 IL	07-09-1864	3070	Frederick, Monocacy
Rourk, John	Pvt. G	4 US	09-21-1862	3521	Antietam
Rowland, William	Pvt.	3 PA	-1861	3947	Hagerstown
Rowley, Charles	Drummer	39 IL	02-20-1862	3077	Cumberland
Rowley, Simeon E.	Pvt. H	77 NY	11-08-1862	378	Hagerstown, Antietam
Rubbins, William	Pvt. G	34 NY	09-17-1862	829	Antietam, KIA
Rubinet, James A.	Pvt. H	8 NY Cav.		308	Weverton
Rudesill, Musser J.	Pvt. A	134 PA	10-10-1862	3623	Sharpsburg, Antietam
Rudy, Joseph P.	Pvt. D	129 PA	11-14-1862	4051	Frederick
Rulapaugh, Nicholas	Sgt. C	89 NY	09-17-1862	767	Antietam, KIA
Rumple, Jacob	Pvt. C	53 IN	03-21-1865	3367	Clarysville
Rush, George	Pvt. E	150 IN	04-04-1865	3404	Frederick
Russ, John M.	Pvt.	122 NY	10-26-1862	573	Antietam, Downsville, Age 38
Russell, Benjamin S.	Corp. I	2 DE	01-03-1863	3062	Frederick, Antietam
Russell, Nathaniel J.	Pvt. C	49 NY	11-19-1862	367	Hagerstown, Antietam
Rust, Andrew J.	Pvt. C	150 IN	04-10-1865	3416	Frederick
Ryan, James	Pvt. K	33 NY	11-09-1862	342	Hagerstown, Antietam
Ryon, Martin	Pvt. A	2 NY	11-1864	332	Sandy Hook
S., D. W.	Pvt.	19 IN Inf.		3446	Antietam
S., T.	Pvt.	20 OH Inf.		1424	South Mountain, 30 OH ?
S., V.	Pvt.	11 PA Res.		3846	Weverton
Salisbury, Norman	Pvt. H	29 OH	04-03-1862	1508	Frederick
Salisbury, William A.	Pvt. C	34 NY	09-17-1862	827	Remains Not His
Salmon, S.	Pvt.	NY Vol.		631	Antietam
Salsbury, Reuben E.	Pvt. G	13 NY	09-17-1862	629	Antietam
Sandford	Pvt.	PA		3729	Antietam
Sanford, O. W.	2nd Lt. I	2 WI	10-13-1862	853	Antietam, WIA
Saol, Louis	Pvt. E	1 NY	04-04-1865	24	Clarysville
Sargeant, Gustavus	Corp. E	7 WI	09-17-1862	3331	Antietam, KIA
Sarver, Labanah	Pvt. G	11 PA Res.	09-14-1862	3848	Weverton, KIA S. Mt.
Sauber, John D.	Pvt. C	69 PA	09-19-1862	523	Antietam, WIA
Saur, Andrew	Pvt. K	1 NY	06-27-1864	66	Frederick
Savoy, William P.	Pvt. D	2 DE	09-17-1862	3050	Antietam, KIA
Sawhill, Andrew J.	Pvt. B	122 OH	07-15-1864	1289	Frederick, Monocacy
Sawyer, J. D.	Pvt. A	7 WI	09-17-1862	3337	Antietam, KIA
Saxton, Charles A.	Pvt.	9 PA Res.		3836	Burkettsville
Schalk, John	Pvt. C	18 CT	08-16-1863	1132	Hagerstown
Schardein	Sgt. D	27 IN	06-18-1862	3490	Williamsport
Schellhorn, John	Pvt. K	74 PA	04-30-1865	4152	Clarysville, Age 40
Schenek, Mabury	Pvt. K	5 US	12-09-1862	3544	Frederick, Antietam
Scherlott, John	Pvt. G	30 OH	10-20-1862	1367	Antietam
Schernitzanner, Florane	Pvt. F	50 PA	09-17-1862	3726	Locust Spring, Antietam
Schlaich, John	Pvt. G	46 NY Inf.		290	Weverton
Schlictor, Jacob	Pvt.	5 US	08-01-1864	3509	Weverton, Monocacy
Schlosser, John	Pvt. K	11 OH	09-17-1862	1415	South Mountain
Schmidt, Charles	Pvt. C	11 PA Res.	09-14-1862	3834	South Mountain, KIA
Schmit, Frederick	Pvt. D	118 PA	09-20-1862	3604	Ant., KIA Shepherdstown, WV
Schmitt, Julius	Pvt. L	5 US Art.	11-01-1862	3543	Frederick, Anthietam
Schneider, Jacob	Pvt. C	20 MA	09- -1862	897	Antietam
Schnell, Conrad	Pvt. H	1 NJ	11-08-1861	2917	Hagerstown
Scholfield, Henry M.	Pvt. H	11 CT	09-28-1862	1109	Antietam, WIA
Schrecengost, Simon	Pvt. K	155 PA	12-07-1862	4053	Frederick, Age 32
Schrey, Christian	Pvt. F	103 NY	09-17-1862	762	Antietam, KIA

Name	Rank/Co.	Reg./State	Death	Grave No.	Removed from/ Comments
Schurman, Heinrichs	1st Sgt. G	103 NY	09-17-1862	760	Antietam, KIA
Schutts, John	Pvt. D	105 NY	10-26-1862	508	Smoketown
Schwarneeberger, John	Pvt. K	20 MA	03-06-1863	1036	Frederick
Schwartz, Frederick	Pvt. A	6 MD	02-28-1863	2566	Smoketown, WIA Antietam
Schweitzer, Samuel Jr.	Pvt. A	161 OH	07-29-1864	1299	Frederick, Monocacy
Schwerin, Herman	Pvt. G	103 NY	10-16-1862	580	Antietam
Sciffoucher, Theodore	Pvt. M	5 NY	05-30-1865	135	Frederick
Scott, George	Pvt. B	6 VT	11-04-1862	2670	Hagerstown, Ant., Age 21
Scott, George M.	Pvt. B	65 IL	09-05-1862	3072	Frederick
Scott, Henry	Pvt. D	14 IN	09-17-1862	3437	Antietam
Scott, Joseph	Pvt. I	12 WV	07-30-1864	2733	Weverton, Monocacy
Scott, Mark	Pvt. D	4 OH	11-27-1862	1484	Frederick, Antietam
Scribner, Elmore	Pvt. G	152 IN	04-21-1865	3352	Clarysville
Scullen, Patrick	Pvt. A	106 PA	09-17-1862	3658	Antietam, KIA
Scully, Thomas	Pvt. G	17 MI	12-17-1862	2548	Ant., WIA, From Jackson
Searburg, Zachariah	Pvt. K	2 OH	09-07-1864	1321	Frederick, Monocacy
Sears, Eli	Pvt. K	17 MI	09-14-1862	2492	South Mountain, KIA
Sears, James	Pvt. M	6 MI	04-19-1865	2390	Boonsboro
Sears, Urbane	Pvt. H	37 MA	11-12-1862	1018	Hagerstown, Died Disease
Seeley, T. B.	Pvt. B	7 MI	09-17-1862	2525	Ant., KIA, From Jackson
Seeley, W. S.	Pvt. F	1 MI	02-13-1862	2413	Frederick
Seemen, Jacob B.	Sgt. E	156 IN	06-07-1865	3375	Clarysville
Seever, S. W.	Pvt. E	3 IN Cav.		3484	Middletown
Seibert, Jacob L.	Pvt. I	149 PA	08-08-1863	4086	Frederick, Age 27
Seibert, Josephus	Pvt.	NY Inf.		469	South Mountain
Seigfried, Charles P.	Pvt. A	33 NY	09-17-1862	723	Antietam, KIA
Seipe, William	Pvt. A	14 US	10-23-1862	3537	Frederick, Antietam
Selby, Meredith	Pvt. G	3 WV	01-18-1865	2717	Weverton
Sell, William H.	Pvt. K	14 PA	08-17-1864	4174	Clarysville
Sellers, Samuel	Pvt. B	50 PA	09-17-1862	3624	Antietam, KIA
Sendner, Philips	Pvt. B	5 US	07-30-1864	3575	Clarysville
Sergeant, William D.	Corp. E	9 WV	08-18-1864	2945	Clarysville
Seuft, Rudolph	Pvt.	30 NY	07-27-1863	830	Antietam, Age 57
Severance, Gersham	Pvt. C	60 NY	09-23-1862	599	Smoketown
Seville, William	Pvt. G	1 DE	01-11-1863	3061	Frederick, Antietam
Seward, W. M.	Corp.	9 NY Inf.		746	Antietam
Seybold, David	Pvt. M	17 PA	07-18-1863	4091	Frederick, Age 29
Seyfert, John	Pvt. C	109 PA	08-22-1862	4137	Frederick
Seymour, George B.	Pvt. K	122 NY	10-29-1862	371	Hagerstown, Ant., Age 24
Shackelford, James	Pvt. A	WV	03-29-1864	2730	Mean's Loudoun Rangers
Shae, Michael	Sgt. B	61 NY	11-25-1862	213	Frederick, Antietam
Shafer, Charles	Pvt. I	107 PA	10-02-1862	4213	Frederick, Antietam
Shaffer W.	Pvt.	2 NY Inf.		680	Antietam
Shaffer, Eli	Pvt.	2 NH	12-03-1862	2808	Smoketown
Shaffer, John	Pvt.	9 NY Inf.		756	Antietam
Shanefelt, James	Pvt. C	11 PA	09-18-1862	3790	Antietam, KIA
Shannon, Anderson	Corp. C	134 PA	11-05-1862	4057	Frederick, Age 21
Shannon, James	Pvt. A	123 OH	12-29-1862	1223	Cumberland
Sharat, Daniel	Pvt. C	54 NY Inf.		27	Clarysville
Sharp, Jeremiah F.	Pvt. E	5 WV	07-24-1864	2737	Clarysville
Shaughnassey, John	Corp. G	8 US	10-14-1862	3536	Frederick, Antietam
Shaw, William B.	Pvt. C	1 ME	11-13-1862	3136	Frederick, Antietam
Shed, S.	Pvt.	36 OH Inf.		1446	South Mountain
Shedrone, Peter	Pvt. H	22 PA	07-11-1864	4102	Frederick
Shelby, Joseph	Pvt. E	93 PA	09-28-1862	3966	Hagerstown, Age 21
Shell, David	Pvt. B	6 PA Res.	09-14-1862	3907	Weverton, South Mountain
Shell, John S.	Pvt. I	7 WV	11-04-1862	2605	Smoketown
Shemp, John	Pvt.	NY	09-26-1862	133	Frederick
Shepard, John	Pvt. G	7 MD	11-26-1862	2589	Clearspring, Accidentally Shot

Name	Rank/Co.	Reg./State	Death	Grave No.	Removed from/ Comments
Shephard, L. W.	Pvt. F	104 PA	11-08-1862	569	Smoketown
Shepherd, Hezekiah	Pvt. D	7 WV	09-17-1862	2608	Antietam
Sheppard, Elie	Pvt. A	1 DE	09-17-1862	3047	Antietam, KIA
Sherman, Aaron	Pvt. F	22 NY	10-10-1862	258	Frederick, Antietam
Sherman, Ira	Pvt.	14 PA Cav.		3990	Hagerstown
Sherman, Moses	Pvt. G	28 PA	10-05-1862	3702	Smoketown, WIA Antietam
Sherrick, George O.	Pvt. B	7 OH	09-17-1862	1353	Antietam
Sherron, Laban	Pvt. I	12 OH Inf.		1363	Antietam
Shessler, Philip	Pvt. C	20 NY Inf.		727	Antietam
Shiffer, John F.	Corp. F	2 MA	09-18-1864	1044	Frederick, Monocacy
Shilling, John	Pvt. B	20 MA	09-20-1862	979	Smoketown
Shlaffly, Christian	Pvt. F	1 ME Rifles	10-20-1862	3146	Frederick, Antietam
Shoemaker, William	Pvt.	72 PA Inf.		3679	Antietam
Sholes, William L.	Pvt. D	15 MA	09-17-1862	3173	Antietam
Shook, George L.	Corp. C	37 MA	10-18-1864	962	Weverton, Died Wounds
Shores, William A. N.	Pvt. D	14 NJ	07-09-1864	2935	Frederick, Monocacy
Short, James H.	Pvt. C	10 WV	-1862	2858	Cumberland
Short, Peter	Pvt. B	9 WV Inf.		2751	Cumberland
Showalter, Martin	Pvt. F	195 PA	08-27-1864	4114	Fred., Monocacy, Age 19
Shran, George S.	Corp. E	36 MA Inf.		970	Middletown
Shreve, William	Pvt. F	145 PA	12-19-1862	4060	Frederick
Shriney, Michael	Pvt. C	49 NY Inf.	10-	300	Weverton, Age 19
Shronk, Joseph	Pvt. B	2 DE	09-17-1862	3043	Antietam, KIA
Shultz, Charles W.	Corp. E	87 PA	10-12-1864	4122	Frederick, WIA Monocacy
Shultz, Henry	Pvt. F	51 PA	09-17-1862	3582	Antietam, KIA
Shuman, Emile	Pvt. L	3 NJ	05-15-1865	2941	Clarysville
Shumate, C.	Pvt.	1 WV Cav.		2750	Cumberland
Shupe William J.	Pvt. D	14 IN	12-04-1862	3429	Frederick, Antietam
Shuster, Nicholas	Pvt. C	175 NY	01-02-1865	121	Frederick
Sickles, Silas	Pvt. K	95 NY Inf.		459	Middletown
Sim, Edmund A.	Pvt. D	23 OH	09-14-1862	1433	South Mountain
Simmons, L. B.	Pvt. K	36 OH	09-14-1862	1445	South Mountain
Simon, Jacob	Pvt. I	5 US	03-15-1865	3569	Frederick
Simons, John A.	Sgt. F	3 MD	08-16-1864	2598	Frederick, Monocacy
Simpson, George A.	Sgt. C	125 PA	09-17-1862	3953	Hagerstown, KIA Ant., Age 22
Simpson, James	Pvt. H	2 NY Inf.		671	Antietam
Simpson, William H.	Pvt. K	2 PA Res.	09-14-1862	3860	Weverton, KIA S. Mt.
Sims, Beverly	Pvt. K	144 IN	04-13-1865	3405	Frederick, Age 20
Six, Isaac	Pvt. K	14 WV	08-14-1864	2740	Clarysville
Slack, Charles D.	Pvt. G	8 VT	03-16-1865	2681	Frederick, Age 33
Slack, William	Pvt. C	104 NY	11-08-1862	604	Sharpsburg, Antietam
Slade, Frederick	Pvt. L	2 CT	09-21-1864	1194	Fred., Monocacy, From Bridgeport
Slater, J.	Pvt.	8 IL	09-29-1862	3032	Frederick
Slater, O.	Pvt. D	106 OH	07-12-1864	1288	Frederick, Monocacy
Slattery, Patrick	Pvt. C	10 NY	01-15-1863	188	Frederick, Ant., Age 30
Slider, Wesley	Pvt. D	27 IN	04-03-1863	3419	Frederick, Age 20
Sloan, Joseph V.	Corp. E	35 MA	10-06-1862	968	Middletown, Antietam
Slough, Abraham	Pvt. I	19 IN	02-19-1863	3421	Frederick
Smidt, Charles	Pvt.	NY Inf.		838	Antietam
Smith, Adellert	Pvt. D	14 US	11-04-1862	3547	Frederick, Antietam
Smith, Alexander	Pvt. I	1 VT	10-22-1864	2639	Frederick, Age 37
Smith, Andrew W.	Pvt.	14 PA Cav.		3987	Hagerstown
Smith, Benjamin F.	Pvt. F	23 OH	09-22-1862	1265	Frederick, Antietam
Smith, Charles L.	Pvt. B	2 US	09-11-1864	3511	Weverton, Monocacy
Smith, Charles R.	Pvt. G	19 ME	10-15-1862	2397	Frederick, Antietam
Smith, Franklin	Pvt. E	27 IN Inf.		3457	Antietam
Smith, Granville H.	Corp. B	12 MA	10-20-1862	974	Smoketown
Smith, Henry	Sgt. K	2 WI	10-16-1862	3262	Antietam

Name	Rank/Co.	Reg./State	Death	Grave No.	Removed from/ Comments
Smith, Hezekiah	Corp. I	76 NY	11-02-1862	617	Smoketown
Smith, J.	Pvt.	34 NY Inf.		843	Antietam
Smith, J. A.	Pvt.	9 NY Inf.		743	Antietam
Smith, James A.	Pvt. K	131 PA	11-19-1862	3922	Frederick
Smith, John	Pvt.	4 NY Art.		467	South Mountain
Smith, John H.	Pvt. B	132 PA	09-17-1862	3597	Antietam, KIA
Smith, John W.	Pvt. K	20 MI	11-10-1862	2380	Weverton, Disease, From Sylvan
Smith, Joshua	Sgt.	4 NY Inf.		806	Antietam
Smith, Merton L.	Sgt. F	13 NJ	10-25-1862	2790	Weverton, Antietam
Smith, Michael	Pvt. G	16 CT	09-17-1862	1086	Antietam, KIA
Smith, Philips	Pvt. B	145 PA	10-23-1862	3931	Frederick
Smith, Robert R.	Pvt. I	28 PA	10-01-1862	4209	Frederick, Antietam
Smith, Robert R.		PA	09-21-1862	1709	Frederick
Smith, Royal	Pvt. G	4 VT	11-24-1862	2683	Hagerstown, Ant., Age 21
Smith, Simpson	Pvt. L	1 OH	04-14-1864	1144	Clarysville
Smith, Stephen B.	Pvt.	49 NY Inf.	10-	320	Weverton
Smith, Thomas	Pvt. C	2 NY Inf.		589	Smoketown
Smith, Valentine	Pvt. A	8 PA Res.	09-14-1862	4072	South Mountain, KIA
Smith, W. H.	Pvt. D	27 IN	09-17-1862	3456	Antietam
Smith, Wilbur F.	Pvt. D	17 MI	09-14-1862	2515	S. Mt., KIA, From Cooper
Smith, William	Pvt.	PA		3963	Hagerstown
Smith, William E.	Corp. F	8 IL	07-09-1863	3033	Frederick, KIA
Smith, William M.	Pvt. G	1 MI	01-25-1862	2411	Frederick
Snodgrass, James L.	Pvt. F	155 PA	11-16-1862	3798	Antietam
Snow, Alfred J.	Pvt. G	13 MA	10-15-1862	1024	Frederick, Antietam
Snow, John	Pvt. I	5 NY	09-06-1864	104	Frederick, Monocacy
Snow, John S.	Pvt. D	137 PA	10-19-1862	3983	Hagerstown
Snow, Samuel C.	Pvt. L	14 PA	01-04-1865	4121	Frederick
Snyder, David	Pvt. H	15 WV	07-18-1864	2739	Clarysville
Snyder, Edwin R.	Pvt. D	3 WI	09-27-1862	3315	Antietam, WIA
Snyder, William	Pvt. D	97 NY	10-07-1862	622	Smoketown
Sokolosky, Leonard	Pvt. B	20 NY Inf.		840	Antietam
Soule, John W.	Corp. D	6 MI	09-08-1863	2558	Boonsboro, KIA, From Cohoctah
Sours, William	Pvt. C	9 NY	07-14-1864	72	Fred., WIA Monocacy, Age 32
Sowards, William W.	Pvt. G	13 WV	09-18-1864	2731	Weverton, Monocacy
Spahr, David	Pvt. A	7 PA Res.	09-17-1862	3744	Antietam, KIA
Spahr, George	Pvt. D	9 NY	08-12-1864	106	Fred., WIA Monocacy, Age 23
Spain, David R.	Corp. F	23 OH	09-17-1862	1330	Antietam
Spear, William F.	Pvt. F	20 ME	10-23-1862	3154	Antietam
Speel, Henry	Pvt. H	98 PA	01-07-1865	4125	Frederick
Spellman, William	Pvt. E	5 OH	09-17-1862	1347	Antietam
Spencer, Cyrus J.	Pvt, C	12 PA Res.	09-17-1862	3774	Antietam, KIA
Speneer, Harrison	Pvt. H	12 ME	09-12-1864	3198	Weverton, Monocacy
Spicer, Oscar A.	Pvt. B	121 NY	11-30-1862	385	Hagerstown, Antietam
Spicer, Philip R.	Sgt. G	1 DE	09-20-1862	3044	Antietam, KIA
Spiers, Myron A.	Sgt. K	26 NY	10-13-1862	265	Frederick, Antietam
Spiker, J.	Pvt.	120 NY	07-12-1864	67	Frederick, Monocacy
Spink, J. M.	Pvt. F	122 NY	11-14-1862	381	Hagerstown, Antietam
Spitter, Isaiah	Pvt. K	91 OH Inf.		1237	Cumberland
Spix, Bernard	Pvt. H	12 US	11-29-1862	3550	Frederick, Antietam
Spoor, Joseph	Pvt. G				See Spiers, Myron
Spoth, Andrew	Pvt. F	7 MI	02-10-1863	2519	Antietam, WIA, From Haughton
Spotts, Philip B.	Pvt. D	45 PA	10-03-1862	3725	Antietam, WIA
Sprague, George	Pvt. K	5 VT	11-13-1862	2678	Hagerstown, Ant., Age 20
Spriggle, Benjamin	Pvt. I	17 PA	08-12-1863	4088	Frederick, Age 19

Name	Rank/Co.	Reg./State	Death	Grave No.	Removed from/ Comments
Spring, John A.	Teamster		02-22-1862	2682	Frederick
Springer, C.	Pvt.	23 NY Inf.		649	Antietam
Squires, Jacob	Pvt. G	45 PA	09-14-1862	3876	Weverton, KIA S. Mt.
Stacey, John S.	Corp. K	1 ME	11-09-1862	3139	Frederick, Antietam
Stacey, Michael E.	Pvt. C	4 RI	09-17-1862	2826	Antietam, KIA
Stafford, Solomon	Pvt. E	7 WV	10-04-1862	2607	Antietam
Stall, William	Pvt. E	20 PA	05-13-1864	4009	Weverton
Stamp, Charles E.	Pvt. A	76 NY	09-14-1862	474	South Mountain, KIA
Standiford, Stewart					See Standford, Richard
Stanford, Richard	Corp. D	42 NY Inf.		710	Antietam
Stanley, George	Pvt. G	10 ME	09-17-1862	3167	Antietam
Stannard, Ezra D.	Pvt. G	14 CT	12-21-1862	1142	Hagerstown, Age 21
Stansbury, William	Pvt. I	3 WI	09-17-1862	3320	Antietam, KIA
Stant, J. B.	Pvt. I	6 MI	02-23-1865	2475	Frederick
Stanton, Chancey W.	Pvt.	7 MI	06-06-1865	2418	Clarysville
Stearns, Sebastian	Corp. C	105 NY	10-31-1862	619	Smoketown
Steel, John H.	Pvt. I	194 OH	04-19-1865	1278	Frederick
Steers, Isaac N.	Pvt. E	160 OH N.G.	07-31-1864	1320	Frederick, Monocacy
Steigman, John	Corp. B	3 WI	10-28-1861	3280	Frederick, Died Disease
Steinback, Michael	Pvt. M	NY	10-09-1864	323	
Steiner, Reinhardt	Corp. I	108 NY Inf.		552	Antietam
Steinmetz, William H.	Pvt. A	71 PA	08-03-1863	4080	Frederick, Age 23
Stephany, Hiram	Pvt.	32 NY	04-03-1865	136	Frederick
Stettwell, Clark	Pvt. K	57 NY	10-11-1862	259	Frederick, WIA Antietam
Stevens, Alfred	Pvt. G	2 MA	03-30-1862	1064	Frederick
Stevens, George E.	Pvt. D	144 NY	07-20-1862	170	Frederick, Age 22
Stevens, Henry	Pvt. E	4 CT	08-17-1861	1189	Frederick, From Chesline
Stevens, Henry S.	Pvt. F	12 CT	09-24-1864	1186	Fred., Monocacy, From Madison
Stevens, Jacob	Pvt. K	11 PA	09-27-1862	4206	Frederick, Antietam
Stevens, Peter C.	Pvt. H	5 NY	12-03-1862	216	Frederick, WIA Antietam
Stevens, William H.	Pvt. C	124 PA	09-17-1862	3692	Antietam
Stevenson, James J.	Pvt. A	84 NY	09-24-1864	47	Frederick, Monocacy
Stevenson, R. S.	Pvt. C	2 WI	09-17-1862	3302	Antietam, KIA
Stevenson, W. R.	Pvt.	9 NY Inf.		757	Antietam
Steward, David	Pvt. H	27 IN	12-05-1862	3478	Smoketown
Stewart, Charles	Pvt. H	122 OH	01-24-1863	1221	Cumberland
Stewart, Ephraim	Pvt. B	13 WV	08-05-1864	2601	Weverton, Monocacy
Stewart, Frank M.	Pvt. K	67 OH	03-06-1862	1253	Cumberland
Stewart, Gerard	Pvt.	1 WV Cav.		2766	Cumberland
Stewart, Harry H.	1st Sgt. A	2 MD	09-17-1862	2457	Antietam, KIA
Stewart, Samuel T.	1st Sgt. G	11 PA Res.	09-14-1862	3833	Burkettsville, KIA S. Mt.
Stickler, Gilbert C.	Pvt. F	107 NY	10-12-1862	416	Burkettsville
Stickney, William C.	Pvt. C	7 ME	09-17-1862	3172	Antietam
Stiles, George	Pvt. I	106 NY	04-04-1862	41	Cumberland
Stiles, George W.	Pvt. C	12 PA Cav.		3819	Antietam
Stodden, P. E.	Pvt.	PA		3912	Weverton
Stoll, Frederick	Pvt.	3 OH Cav.		1215	Cumberland
Stoll, Samuel				1647	Cumberland
Stone, Edward	Pvt. A	1 RI	09-17-1862	2833	Antietam, KIA
Stoneking, James A.	Pvt. H	116 OH	11-30-1862	1231	Cumberland
Storm, Henry	Pvt. H	2 WI	09-17-1862	3225	Antietam, KIA
Storms, William J.	Pvt. C	18 NY	09-14-1862	430	Crampton Pass, KIA
Stout, Peter	Pvt. E	18 PA	08-12-1865	4180	Clarysville
Stoyes, William	Pvt. C	6 WV	05-21-1864	2843	Cumberland
Strickland, Henry E.	Sgt. C	8 CT	10-17-1862	1115	Antietam, WIA
Stringer, Michael	Pvt. C	5 NY	12-23-1864	21	Clarysville
Stropper, Sebastian	Pvt. M	30 MA	12-04-1864	1074	Clarysville
Strout, Elias	Pvt. C	17 ME	06-19-1863	3127	Frederick
Strout, Luke	Pvt. K	14 NJ	03-31-1863	2921	Frederick

Name	Rank/Co.	Reg./State	Death	Grave No.	Removed from/ Comments
Struble, Henry	Pvt. C	8 PA Res.	09-14-1862	3829	S. Mt., Remains Not His
Strump, Charles	Pvt. C	2 PA Res.	09-14-1862	3864	Weverton, KIA S. Mt.
Stuber, Adam	Pvt. C	13 WV	07-04-1863	2632	Frederick
Stuchell, Henry	Pvt. B	11 PA Res.	09-14-1862	3835	Burkettsville, KIA S. Mt.
Sturdivant, Charles	Pvt. K	49 NY	09-30-1862	564	Ant. Disease, Bakersville
Sturns, J.J.	Pvt.	9 NY Inf.		761	Antietam
Suffolk, Owen	Pvt. K	66 NY	11-12-1962	232	Frederick, Antietam
Suhager, Robert	Pvt.	4 RI	09-17-1862	2830	Antietam, KIA
Sullivan, Jeremiah	Pvt.	PA		4185	Elk County PA
Sullivan, John	Pvt. B	61 NY Inf.		820	Antietam
Sullivan, John	Pvt. A	1 MD Inf.		2460	Antietam
Sullivan, Simon	Pvt. H	15 MA	10-21-1862	1026	Frederick, Antietam
Sullivan, William	Pvt. G	110 PA Inf.		4176	Cumberland
Sumner, A. P.	Pvt. C	12 US	10-20-1862	3533	Antietam
Sumner, Lewis S.	Pvt. B	17 US	10-31-1862	3541	Frederick, Antietam
Sumner, Samuel W.	Sgt. G	8 VT	08-05-1864	2642	Fred., Monocacy, Age 40
Supplee, Robert	Corp. A	51 PA	10-27-1862	4004	Weverton, Antietam
Surenkamp, Henry	Pvt. C	28 OH	02-02-1865	1145	Clarysville
Sutliff, David L.	Pvt. I	84 PA	08-14-1863	3964	Hagerstown
Sutter, Nicholas	Pvt. B	6 WI	09-17-1862	3332	Antietam, KIA
Swan, James O.	Pvt. M	25 NY	05-19-1865	9	Cumberland
Swank, Daniel	Pvt. A	28 PA	10-16-1861	3977	Hagerstown
Swartzlander, Adam	Pvt. C	9 PA Res.	09-17-1862	3759	Antietam, KIA
Swearinger, George W.	Pvt. A	60 OH	07-10-1862	1501	Frederick
Sweet, Charles H.	Pvt. E	1 PA Res.	09-14-1862	3854	Weverton, KIA S. Mt.
Sweetman, Henry	Pvt. E	9 NY Inf.		578	Antietam
Swift, Edward B	Pvt. E	9 NY	08-18-1864	103	Fred., Monocacy, Age 21
Swisher, James W.	Pvt. E	1 WV	07-23-1863	2749	Hancock
Switzer, John	Pvt. C	74 PA	07-12-1862	4191	Frederick
T., J.		NY		444	Middletown
Taafe, Edward	Pvt.	42 NY	10-07-1862	615	Smoketown
Tail, Henry H.	Pvt. G	3 WI	09-30-1862	3318	Antietam
Talbott, W. H.	Pvt.	2 WI	09-30-1862	3322	Antietam, WIA
Tallman, Henry S.	Pvt. C	8 MI	09-17-1862	2520	Ant., WIA, From Aliedon
Tapley, George S.	Corp. B	11 OH	09-14-1862	1419	South Mountain
Taplin, Osman B.	Pvt. E	2 WI	09-24-1862	3226	Antietam, WIA
Tapper, George	Pvt. E	2 DE	09-17-1862	3048	Antietam
Tapping, John	Pvt. I	7 WI	09-17-1862	3338	Antietam, KIA
Tarbox, Brainerd D.	Lt. B	108 NY	09-17-1862	850	Boonsboro, Antietam
Tarbox, George W.	Pvt. E	18 CT	08-10-1864	1179	Clarysville, From Columbia
Tatlock, Robert M.	Pvt. F	27 IN	01-15-1862	3389	Frederick
Taylor	Pvt.	MI		2388	Sandy Hook
Taylor, Charles D.	Pvt. A	5 US	11-02-1864	3577	Clarysville
Taylor, Charles W.					See Terry, G. W.
Taylor, Clayton	Pvt. C	14 IN	01-02-1862	3395	Frederick
Taylor, David	Corp. I	30 OH	09-17-1862	1361	Antietam
Taylor, Eldridge F.	Pvt. L	21 NY	10-04-1864	23	Clarysville, Died Cumberland
Taylor, Henry H.	Pvt. I	6 NY	09-30-1862	739	Antietam
Taylor, Isaac S.	Sgt. D	11 PA	09-17-1862	3635	Antietam, KIA
Taylor, James	Pvt. H	8 PA	08-13-1863	4085	Frederick, Age 45
Taylor, Jarvis	Pvt.	CT	10-23-1862	1178	Hancock
Taylor, John	Pvt. H	91 OH	08-10-1864	1159	Clarysville
Taylor, John T.	Pvt. I	147 IN	06-01-1865	3358	Clarysville
Taylor, Robert B.	Corp. D	11 PA	09-17-1862	3675	Antietam, KIA
Taylor, W. C.	Pvt. B	28 PA	07-19-1862	4134	Frederick
Taylor, Washington L.	Pvt. I	43 NY Inf.		343	Hagerstown
Taylor, Watson	Pvt. F	153 OH N.G.		1202	Cumberland
Teats, Jahn A.	Pvt. B	125 PA	11-30-1862	4043	Fred., Ant. WIA, Age 26
Teller, Pierre	Pvt. K	88 NY	11-08-1862	234	Frederick, Antietam

Name	Rank/Co.	Reg./State	Death	Grave No.	Removed from/ Comments
Telling, George	Corp. D	6 MI	07-15-1863	4237	Boonsboro, Removed 03-10-1898
Temple, J. L.	Pvt. D	3 WI	09-17-1862	3326	Antietam, KIA
Temrisson, James	Pvt.	7 MI Cav.		2526	Antietam
Teneyck, John H.	Sgt. B	132 PA	09-17-1862	3595	Antietam, KIA
Tennis, James	Pvt. G	156 OH N.G.	08-18-1864	1165	Cumberland
Terry, G. W.	Pvt. C	59 NY Inf.		705	Antietam
Thayer, Horace P.	Pvt. D	3 US	01-12-1863	3553	Frederick, Antietam
Thesang, H. T.	Pvt. C	3 US	10-29-1862	3539	Frederick, Antietam
Thomas, George C.	Pvt. E	11 VT	08-25-1864	2654	Weverton, Monocacy
Thomas, Horace	Pvt.	59 NY Inf.		703	Antietam
Thomas, James	Pvt. G	29 IN Inf.		3379	Cumberland
Thomas, John	Pvt. K	1 MD	08-05-1864	2454	Keedysville, KIA
Thompson, Asa L.	Pvt.	4 ME	12-27-1862	3130	Frederick, Antietam
Thompson, John	Pvt. B	51 NY Inf.		785	Antietam
Thompson, William	Pvt. I	123 PA	11-11-1862	3923	Frederick, Age 21
Thompson, William	Pvt. G	96 PA	12-18-1862	4061	Frederick
Thompson, William F.	Pvt. L	22 PA	07-12-1864	4100	Frederick
Thompson, William H.	Corp. H	122 OH	08-05-1862	1346	Antietam (?)
Thorn, Henry C.	Pvt. I	14 WV	08-12-1864	2882	Clarysville
Thorn, Isaac W.	Pvt. D	194 OH N.G.	04-04-1865	1281	Frederick
Thornton, James	Pvt. B	126 OH N.G.	10-28-1864	1310	Frederick
Thurlow, Isaac	Pvt. C	3 WI	09-17-1862	3330	Antietam, KIA
Tice, Charles W.	Pvt. F	23 NY	10-05-1862	596	Smoketown
Tice, Jonathan	Pvt. F	14 NJ	04-21-1863	2923	Frederick
Ticknor, William	Pvt. D	90 PA	11-15-1862	3708	Smoketown
Tierney, David	Pvt. G	21 NY	07-23-1864	91	Frederick, Monocacy
Tilley, James E.	Pvt. K	194 OH N.G.	03-31-1865	1275	Frederick
Tillotson, Charles A.	Pvt. G	108 NY Inf.		560	Antietam
Timbers, Charles	Pvt. E	1 PA	07-30-1863	3958	Hagerstown
Timmerson, Oscar	Pvt. C	9 NY	11-11-1864	112	Frederick, Age 18
Tinder, Nathan	Pvt. D	27 IN	03-05-1862	3396	Frederick
Towle, Ezra	Pvt. G	10 ME	09-17-1862	3176	Antietam
Townsend, G. W.	Pvt.	PA		3818	Antietam
Townsend, Thomas	Pvt.	20 ME	07-12-1863	3208	Smoketown
Tracy, Michael		9 NY Inf.		451	Smoketowm
Trail, Noah	Pvt. H	126 OH N.G.	07-15-1864	1284	Frederick, Monocacy
Trainor, Patrick	Pvt. C	42 NY	11-05-1862	219	Frederick, Antietam
Trask, Augustus A.	Sgt. D	1 PA Res.	09-14-1862	3868	South Mountain, KIA
Treadwell, Nathaniel C.	Pvt. I	35 MA	10-25-1862	1027	Fred., Disease, Age 19
Treen, John S.	Pvt. E	2 MA	09-17-1862	937	Antietam, KIA
Tremain, James R.	Pvt. H	45 PA	09-14-1862	3894	South Mountain
Treon, Franklin	Pvt. G	96 PA	09-17-1862	3652	Antietam, KIA
Tripp, Charles W.	Pvt. F	146 NY	07-08-1863	179	Frederick, Age 26
Tripp, William B.	Pvt. D	15 NY	09-02-1864	8	Clarysville
Trochler, George	Pvt. H	149 OH	08-06-1864	1389	Middletown
Trott, George	Drummer	6 MD	06-30-1864	2433	MD Heights, KIA, From Baltimore
Troup, Simon	Pvt. B	6 PA Res.	10-01-1862	3850	South Mountain
Troup, Simon				1977	South Mountain
Trow, Charles P.	Corp. G	6 NH	11-19-1862	2815	Knoxville, Died Disease
Trow, Josiah	Pvt. G	6 NH	10-25-1862	2814	Weverton, Died Disease
Trowbridge, John	Pvt. B	10 ME	09-17-1862	3160	Antietam
Trube, Franklin	Pvt. E	8 OH	09-17-1862	1337	Antietam
Truman, Robert T.	Pvt. B	12 WV	12-14-1862	2753	Clarysville
Truman, Samuel	Pvt. I	1 WV	02-14-1865	2862	Clarysville
Truslow, James	Pvt. I	13 WV	04-06-1865	2885	Clarysville
Tryon, William B.	Pvt. C	1 NY	03-03-1865	127	Frederick
Tschudy, David	Pvt. F	3 MD Inf.		4234	Hagerstown
Tucker, A. W.	Pvt.	US		3523	Antietam

Name	Rank/Co.	Reg./State	Death	Grave No.	Removed from/ Comments
Tucker, Frank (Francis)	Corp. F	14 NY	10-13-1863	260	Frederick, Age 26
Tucker, Samuel	Pvt. A	2 MD	10-31-1863	2576	Weverton
Turner, Alexander	Pvt. B	8 MD	06-30-1863	2571	Boonsboro, KIA
Turner, Burton C.	Pvt. D	2 VT	11-05-1864	2662	Weverton, Age 18
Turner, D.	Pvt. L	7 MI	12-22-1864	2477	Frederick
Turner, J. H.		NY Inf.		453	Middletown
Turner, J. W.	Pvt. D	126 OH N.G.		1208	Cumberland
Turner, Marcus B.	Pvt. F	152 IN	04-13-1862	3356	Clarysville
Turner, P. H.	Pvt. D	2 NY	10-08-1862	54	Frederick, Antietam
Turner, R. H.	Pvt. E	1 MD	09-03-1862	2463	Frederick
Turner, W. H.	Pvt. A	27 IN	01-14-1862	3426	Frederick
Turney, Enoch B.	Pvt. I	7 ME	10-24-1862	3143	Frederick, Antietam
Turry, Benjamin F.			10-09-1862	1696	Frederick
Tuttle, Lorenzo F.	Pvt. A	3 WI	10-16-1861	3282	Frederick, KIA Harpers Ferry WV
Twiss, Jason E.	Pvt. I	16 CT	09-17-1862	1083	Antietam, KIA
Tyler, Edwin	Pvt. E	4 RI	10-13-1862	2837	Antietam
Tyler, John	Pvt. F	12 PA Res.	09-17-1862	3687	Antietam, KIA
Tyneson, Daniel F.	Pvt. I	21 NY	08-08-1864	282	Weverton, Monocacy
Tyson, Jesse	Pvt. I	88 PA	09-17-1862	3656	Antietam, KIA
Ulrich, John	Pvt. E	45 PA	10-19-1862	3914	Middletown, WIA S. Mt.
Ulrick, W. F.	Pvt.	1 MD Inf.		2564	Antietam
Unger, Peter	Pvt. G	150 IN	04-20-1865	3414	Frederick
Unknown				1966	S. Mt., Drummer Boy
Van Antwerp, A. J.	Corp. C	89 NY	09-17-1862	737	Antietam, KIA
Van Arnum, M. U.	Pvt. D	16 NY	09-14-1862	428	Crampton's Pass, KIA S. Mt.
Van Brunt, Benjamin	Pvt. G	14 NJ	12-05-1862	2906	Frederick, Antietam
Van Brunt, Jacob	Pvt. E	14 NJ	01-03-1863	2898	Frederick, Antietam
Van Cott, David	Pvt. A	9 NY Inf.		847	Antietam
Van Sickles, Seymour	Pvt. K	78 NY	09-10-1862	132	Frederick
Van Tassel, Isaac	Corp. A	6 NY Inf.		407	Burkettsville
Vananken, Frank	Pvt. G	5 CT	02-01-1862	1180	Hancock
Vanderberg, Delas W.	Pvt. H	17 MI	09-14-1862	2500	S. Mt., KIA, From Olive
Vanderberg, Jacob	Pvt. A	33 NY	11-16-1862	380	Hagerstown, Antietam
Vandereve, William B.	Pvt. E	9 NY Inf.		522	Antietam
Vandergriff, Samuel	Pvt. H	OH	02-19-1865	1276	Frederick
Vanoredall, William		27 IN Inf.		3461	Antietam
Vanscoit, William H.	Pvt. B	29 OH	04-05-1862	1505	Frederick
Vantesson, Robert	Pvt. E	12 PA	03-04-1864	4149	Clarysville
Vater, Charles	Pvt. A	7 NY	09-30-1862	143	Frederick, Antietam
Vaughan, Beverly K.	Pvt. E	69 PA	09-17-1862	3680	Antietam, KIA
Vaughn, Richard	Pvt. F	146 IN	07-18-1865	3360	Clarysville
Veith, Bernard	Pvt. F	10 WV	11-25-1864	2613	Frederick
Venable, Charles	Pvt.	90 PA	09-17-1862	3650	Antietam, KIA
Vermillion, Helfrey	Pvt. E	10 PA Res.		4181	Hancock
Vermillion, J. K.	Pvt. B	1 WV	08-21-1864	2627	Frederick, Monocacy
Vetter, Frederick	Pvt. B	149 NY	02-23-1863	181	Frederick
Vining, James L.	Pvt. A	9 WV	08-27-1864	2729	Weverton, Monocacy
Vinson, Richard C.	Sgt. K	8 IL	07-06-1863	3039	Boonsboro
Vinton, Everill C.	Pvt. F	108 NY	12-09-1862	209	Frederick, Antietam
Von Bachelle, Wernir	Capt. L	6 WI	09-17-1862	858	Antietam, KIA
Von Send, Andrew W.	Pvt. B	9 PA Res.		3727	Antietam
Voodry, Charles	Pvt. C	94 NY Inf.		484	South Mountain
Wade, William	2nd Lt. I	10 ME Inf.	09-17-1862	865	Antietam
Wagner, Daniel	Pvt. G	20 NY Inf.		725	Antietam
Wagner, Franklin	Pvt. B	45 PA Inf.	09-14-1862	3875	South Mountain, KIA
Wagner, John	Pvt. B	49 NY Inf.	02-15-1862	610	Smoketown
Wagner, Joseph	Pvt. K	23 OH Inf.	09-17-1862	1325	Antietam
Wait, Warran B.	Pvt. K	106 NY Inf.	07-30-1862	98	Frederick, WIA Monocacy

Name	Rank/Co.	Reg./State	Death	Grave No.	Removed from/ Comments
Walby, Howard	Pvt.	4 NY Inf.		718	Antietam
Waldin, L. F.	Corp. H	1 US Art.	07-09-1863	3501	Frederick, Age 30
Walduck, John	Pvt. E	4 OH Inf.	11-26-1862	1485	Frederick, Antietam
Waler	Pvt.	59 NY Inf.		685	Antietam
Walker, Alexander	Pvt. E	20 NY Inf.		643	Antietam
Walker, E. K.	Pvt. D	2 US Art.		3499	Hagerstown, Capt. Frank's Co.
Walker, Moses	Pvt. B	110 OH Inf.	12-31-1862	1216	Cumberland
Walker, Peter	Corp. B	103 NY Inf.	09-17-1862	765	Antietam, KIA
Walker, Stephen B.	Pvt. D	8 MI Inf.	11-02-1862	2488	Middletown, From Holland
Walker, William A.	Pvt. I	3 VT Inf.	08-04-1864	2659	Frederick, Monocacy
Wall, Clarence	Pvt. B	149 OH N.G.	07-07-1864	1302	Frederick, Monocacy
Wallace, J. A.	Pvt. B	2 MA Inf.	04-09-1862	1065	Frederick
Waltemeyer, H. J.	Pvt. C	89 PA Inf.	09-10-1864	4110	Frederick
Walter, Alex				2063	Weverton
Walters, Jonathan	Pvt. I	144 OH N.G.	07-19-1864	1295	Frederick, Monocacy
Walther, Jacob	Pvt. E	2 MA Cav.	10-17-1864	1051	Frederick
Walton, Amos	Pvt. B	45 PA Inf.	09-14-1862	3870	South Mountain, KIA
Wands, Charles	Pvt.	59 NY Inf.		692	Antietam
Ward, Benjamin	Pvt. D	17 MI Inf.	09-14-1862	2514	S. Mt., KIA, From Pipestone
Ward, Benjamin	Pvt. F	147 IN Inf.	04-08-1865	3354	Cumberland
Ward, David D.	Pvt. K	121 NY Inf.	10-28-1862	370	Burkettsville
Ward, Frederick C.	Pvt. K	125 PA Inf.	09-19-1862	3749	Antietam, WIA
Ward, John	Pvt. E	91 OH Inf.	09-10-1864	1319	Frederick, Monocacy
Ward, John	Pvt. H	2 NY Inf.	07-31-1863	177	Frederick, Age 50
Ward, Maurice	Pvt. H	63 NY Inf.	10-19-1862	274	Frederick, Antietam
Wardwell, Emerson	Pvt. D	16 CT Inf.	10-17-1862	1136	Frederick, Antietam
Warner, C. M.	Pvt. K	21 NY Cav.	07-16-1864	75	Frederick, Monocacy
Warner, Daniel	Pvt. B	170 OH N.G.	08-24-1862	1451	Middletown
Warner, George W.	Sgt. B	132 PA Inf.	09-17-1862	3596	Antietam, KIA
Warner, John F.	Pvt. A	10 WV Inf.	12-23-1862	2884	Cumberland
Warner, William D.	Pvt. A	10 WV Inf.	12-31-1862	2845	Cumberland
Warnich, Andrew L.	Pvt.	3 MD		2426	Cumberland
Warren, George G.	Pvt. G	123 OH Inf.	01-04-1864	1146	Clarysville
Washburn, Daniel M.	Pvt. A	19 ME Inf.	10-17-1862	3209	Frederick
Washburn, Martin B.	Pvt. C	20 ME Inf.	10-27-1862	3178	Antietam
Wasson, Samuel	Pvt. A	89 NY Inf.	09-17-1862	579	Antietam, KIA
Waterhouse, M. J.		WI		3290	Unknown
Waters, Alexander	Pvt. B	90 PA Inf.	09-17-1862	3646	Antietam, KIA
Waters, G. H.		WV		2718	Weverton
Waters, George	Pvt.	20 PA Cav.		4017	Brownsville
Waters, H. S.	Pvt. F	196 OH Inf.		1249	Cumberland
Waters, Sylvanus C.	Pvt. F	6 NH Inf.	09-17-1862	2806	Antietam, KIA
Watkins, Richard	Pvt. M	5 MI Cav.	09-08-1864	2480	Fred., Disease, From Leonidas
Watson, Colbert R.	Pvt.	17 MI Inf.		2549	Antietam
Watson, J. H.	Pvt.	9 NY Inf.		747	Antietam
Watson, James	Sgt. K	1 MD Cav.	08-05-1864	2560	Keedysville, KIA
Watson, James	Pvt. H	144 IN Inf.	04-02-1865	3357	Clarysville
Watson, Robert J.	Pvt. A	1 MD Art.	12-02-1862	2453	Antietam
Watson, Samuel	Pvt. C	118 PA Inf.	10-15-1862	3587	Ant., WIA Shepherdstown
Watts, Wesley	Pvt. E	1 VT Cav.	07-06-1863	2684	Hagerstown, Age 18
Wayne, Walter G.	Pvt. F	66 NY Inf.	11-05-1862	220	Frederick, Antietam
Weaklam, William	Pvt. I	96 PA Inf.	09-14-1862	4022	Burkettsville, Crampton's Gap
Weaver, Benoni	Pvt. K	4 RI Inf.	09-17-1862	2825	Antietam, KIA
Weaver, J. B.	Pvt. O	28 PA Inf.	02-25-1862	4199	Frederick
Weaver, Joseph	Pvt. B	68 PA Inf.	09-14-1862	4175	Cumberland
Weaver, Joshua				1976	South Mountain

Name	Rank/Co.	Reg./State	Death	Grave No.	Removed from/ Comments
Webb, Charles W.	Pvt. C	5 ME Inf.	10-30-1862	3144	Frederick, Antietam
Webb, Joseph	Pvt. I	14 IN Inf.		3353	Cumberland
Weber, George	Pvt. E	3 WI Inf.	10-10-1862	3232	Smoketown, WIA Antietam
Weber, Lewis	Pvt. I	1 NY Cav.	04-05-1864	57	Frederick
Weber, Peter	Pvt. H	6 WI Inf.	10-23-1862	3265	Frederick, WIA Antietam
Webster, John R.	Corp. K	14 CT Inf.	10-06-1862	1135	Frederick, Antietam
Weed, Raymond	Pvt. B	17 CT Inf.	07-07-1862	1197	Frederick, Age 20
Weeks, Charles L.	Pvt. I	17 MI Inf.	09-28-1862	2487	South Mountain, WIA
Weiser, Andrew	Pvt. E	2 US Cav.	10-20-1862	3514	Brownsville, Age 31
Welch, Daniel	Pvt. B	59 NY Inf.	10-08-1862	55	Frederick, Antietam
Welch, William J.	Pvt. C	88 NY Inf.	10-18-1862	275	Frederick, Antietam
Welden, Charles L.	Pvt. F	35 NY Inf.	09-17-1862	654	Antietam, KIA
Wellchance, Layfayette	Pvt. K	4 OH Inf.	11-16-1862	1487	Frederick, Antietam
Wellens, H. C.	Pvt. G	27 IN Inf.	12-27-1862	3422	Frederick, Antietam
Wells, Charles B.	Pvt. H	72 PA Inf.	09-17-1862	3614	Antietam, KIA
Wells, Peter	Sgt. K	5 PA Res.	09-22-1862	3916	Middletown, WIA S. Mt.
Welsh, Patrick	Pvt. E	110 OH Inf.	12-18-1864	1305	Frederick
Welsh, Thomas S.	Farrier	3 WV Cav.	05-05-1865	2888	Clarysville
Welton, Harry S.	Pvt. C	27 CT Inf.	07-14-1862	1131	Hagerstown, Age 19
Wengert, Frederick	Pvt. E	1 MD Cav.	07-26-1864	2565	Falling Waters, KIA
Went, Lewis	Pvt. C	12 OH Inf.	09-21-1862	1365	Antietam
Wentworth, Charles H.	Pvt. H	10 ME Inf.	09-17-1862	3163	Antietam
Werner, John	Pvt. K	11 OH Inf.	09-17-1862	1329	Antietam
Wescott, Charles	Pvt. I	3 WI Inf.	09-21-1862	3321	Antietam, WIA
Wescott, Randall	Pvt. H	106 NY Cav.	07-19-1864	84	Frederick, Monocacy
Wessner, Charles	Pvt. K	96 PA Inf.	03-05-1863	3703	Antietam
West, Albert D.	Sgt. H	8 OH Inf.	09-17-1862	1335	Antietam
West, Hamilton	Pvt. G	5 WV Inf.	10-13-1864	2616	Frederick
Westerman, George	Pvt. F	5 OH Inf.	11-27-1862	1370	Smoketown
Westgate, Joseph	Pvt. F	29 MA Inf.	10-09-1862	1059	Frederick, Antietam
Weston, J. L.	Pvt. A	1 NY Cav.	04-15-1864	58	Frederick
Westworth, J.	Sgt. E	1 PA Cav.	07-17-1863	4087	Frederick
Wetherholt, George	Pvt. C	22 PA Cav.	09-29-1864	4162	Clarysville
Whale, James	Pvt.	2 NY Inf.		662	Antietam
Whalen, John	Pvt. G	66 NY Inf.	09-28-1862	149	Frederick, Antietam
Whalen, William	Pvt.	68 NY Inf.	10-06-1862	167	Frederick, Antietam
Whaler, John	Pvt.	2 NY Inf.		660	Antietam
Whales, William H.	Pvt. G	4 NY Art.	12-22-1862	208	Frederick, Antietam
Wheaton, Frank	Pvt. G	107 NY Inf.	10-10-1862	419	Burkettsville, Harpers Ferry
Wheeler, Alonzo	Pvt. G	1 MI Cav.	10-17-1864	2478	Frederick
Wheeler, Edwin	Pvt. B	7 WI Inf.	09-17-1862	3249	Antietam, KIA
Wheeler, Nathan S.	Pvt. E	5 CT Inf.	08-28-1861	1185	Frederick
Whip, Joseph				2116	Middletown
Whisler, Daniel	Pvt. G	23 OH Inf.	09-14-1862	1435	South Mountain, KIA
Whitacker, John N.	Pvt. B	2 MD Art.		2434	Cumberland
White	Pvt.	PA		4147	Methodist Graveyard
White, A. Jackson	Pvt. D	53 PA Inf.	09-17-1862	3591	Antietam
White, Abraham	Pvt. C	143 NY Inf.		466	South Mountain
White, Edward		1 US Art.		3512	Weverton
White, Harrison	Pvt. B	28 PA Inf.	09-17-1862	3751	Antietam, KIA
White, Harvey G.	Pvt. D	150 IN Inf.	04-02-1865	3415	Frederick
White, Henry	Pvt. G	1 ME Cav.	10-21-1862	3142	Frederick, Antietam
White, Isaac M.	Corp. I	160 OH N.G.	07-07-1864	1287	Frederick
White, John J.	Pvt. A	16 CT Inf.	02-13-1863	1124	Chronic Diarrhea
White, Laertes	Pvt. B	123 PA Inf.	10-19-1862	3800	Antietam
White, Madison I.	Pvt. F	91 OH N.G.	08-16-1864	1293	Frederick, Monocacy
White, Thomas A.	Pvt. I	3 WI Inf.	09-17-1862	3323	Antietam, KIA
Whitington, John	Pvt.	8 US Inf.		3501	Hagerstown, Capt. Frank's Co.

Name	Rank/Co.	Reg./State	Death	Grave No.	Removed from/ Comments
Whitney, Isaac	Pvt. C	104 NY Inf.	09-17-1862	632	Antietam, KIA
Whitney, Isaac N.	Corp. H	23 OH Inf.	09-14-1862	1438	South Mountain
Whitney, John	Pvt. D	103 NY Inf.	09-17-1862	507	Antietam, KIA
Whitney, Seldon L.	Pvt. H	22 NY Inf.	09-14-1862	491	South Mountain, KIA
Wilber, Winfield S.	Pvt. E	2 MA Cav.	09-18-1864	963	Weverton, Monocacy
Wilcox, Daniel	Pvt. G	7 WI Inf.	10-28-1862	3268	Middletown, WIA Antietam
Wilcox, George A.	Sgt. A	16 PA Cav.		3654	Antietam
Wilcox, Hiram	Pvt. G	45 PA Inf.	09-16-1862	3901	South Mountain, WIA
Wilcox, William	Pvt. H	3 WI Inf.	09-17-1862	3328	Antietam, KIA
Wilcox, Williard	Corp. B	4 RI Inf.	09-17-1862	2821	Antietam, KIA
Wildman, Henry	Pvt. A	3 WV Cav.	05-19-1865	2949	Clarysville
Wiles, Jacob F.	Pvt.	1 MD Inf.		2574	Weverton
Wilhelm, Jacob	Pvt. C	175 NY Inf.	10-12-1864	119	Frederick
Wilkins, James	Pvt. K	5 NY Art.		317	Weverton
Will, John	Pvt. B	57 NY Inf.	10-11-1862	257	Frederick, Antietam
Willers, John A.	Pvt. K	83 NY Inf.		351	Antietam
Willey, James A.	Pvt. H	1 WV Inf.	02-22-1862	2847	Cumberland
William, Evan	Pvt. B	1 MD Art.	03-06-1865	2435	Clarysville
Williams, Clark	Pvt.	US S.C.	11-15-1864	3578	Clarysville, Signal Corps
Williams, Elijah	Pvt. A	161 OH N.G.	07-05-1864	1147	Clarysville
Williams, George	Pvt. E	9 NY Art.	08-04-1864	97	Frederick, WIA Monocacy
Williams, George A. F.	Pvt. C	1 OH Cav.		1226	Cumberland
Williams, Isaac	Pvt. K	73 OH Inf.	07-18-1863	1492	Frederick, Age 21
Williams, John	Pvt. L	1 NY Cav.	07-11-1864	59	Frederick, Monocacy
Williams, John W.	Pvt. F	13 WV Inf.	09-12-1864	2727	Weverton, Monocacy
Williams, Richard E.	Pvt. E	97 NY Inf.	11-03-1862	608	Smoketown
Williams, S.	2nd Lt.	Cav.		884	Cavetown
Williams, William	Sgt.	11 WV Inf.	09-21-1864	1195	Frederick, Monocacy
Williamson, Charles	Pvt. K	2 NJ Inf.	11-16-1862	2799	Hagerstown, Antietam
Willis, Francis M.	Pvt. A	3 WV Cav.	06-15-1865	2876	Clarysville
Willis, George W.	Pvt. E	5 WV Inf.	03-21-1865	2872	Clarysville
Willis, Ozre	Pvt. H	108 NY Inf.		546	Antietam
Willman, Jehiel	Pvt.	7 IN Inf.		3481	Antietam
Wilsey, Julius	Pvt. H	16 CT Inf.	09-17-1862	1089	Antietam, KIA
Wilson, Charles	Pvt. I	PA		4168	Oldtown
Wilson, Enos P.	Pvt. K	14 WV Inf.	08-02-1864	2713	Weverton, Monocacy
Wilson, Frederick	Pvt. D	8 CT Inf.		1103	Antietam, KIA
Wilson, James	Pvt. D	42 NY Inf.		715	Antietam
Wilson, James	Pvt. B	122 NY Inf.	11-07-1862	611	Smoketown
Wilson, James G.	Corp. A	118 PA Inf.	09-20-1862	3606	Ant., KIA Shepherdstown, WV
Wilson, Joseph G.	Pvt. B	12 WV Inf.	12-26-1862	2855	Cumberland
Wilson, Orvil M.	Pvt. G	16 CT Inf.	11-02-1862	1108	Weverton, WIA Antietam
Wilson, Richard	Pvt. G	3 PA Res.	09-17-1862	3777	Antietam, KIA
Wilson, William	Pvt.	1 WV		2759	Cumberland
Wilson, William	Pvt. K	15 NJ Inf.	09-14-1861	2794	Weverton
Wilson, William	2nd Lt. B	71 PA Inf.	09-21-1862	872	Keedysville, Antietam
Wilt, Joseph	Pvt. F	22 PA Cav.	09-14-1864	4000	Weverton, WIA Sandy Hook
Wiltinger, A.	Pvt. A	87 PA Inf.	07-13-1864	4101	Frederick, Monocacy
Wimer, John	Pvt. M	3 WV Cav.	10-09-1864	2875	Clarysville
Wimpfheimer, Max	2nd Lt. G	2 PA Res.	09-17-1862	874	Antietam, KIA
Winder, Joseph	Pvt. C	107 PA Inf.	10-19-1862	3816	Smoketown
Windom, Uriah B.	Pvt. I	36 OH Inf.	04-19-1865	1279	Frederick
Windsor, Frank M.	Pvt. A	34 OH Inf.		1463	Weverton
Windsor, William W.	Pvt. F	3 MI Cav.		2559	Clarysville
Winkle, Martin	Pvt. H	69 OH Inf.		1256	Cumberland
Winland, John H.	Pvt. D	116 OH Inf.	12-06-1864	1173	Clarysville
Winship, E. H.	Pvt. F	9 NH Inf.	11-14-1862	2803	Antietam, WIA
Winterhalls, John				2171	Antietam

Name	Rank/Co.	Reg./State	Death	Grave No.	Removed from/ Comments
Wintfield, George				1642	Cumberland
Wintzer, Armond	Pvt. I	42 NY Inf.	10-14-1862	1057	Frederick, Antietam
Wirt, Edward H.	Corp. I	125 PA Inf.	09-17-1862	3972	Antietam
Wise, Demas C.	Pvt. I	4 OH Inf.	12-12-1862	1486	Frederick, Antietam
Wise, William	Pvt. F	51 PA Inf.	11-1862	4010	Weverton, Antietam
Wiseman, H. W.	Pvt. B	3 IN Inf.	10-15-1862	3493	Frederick, Antietam
Wisnall, James H.	Pvt. H	8 OH Inf.	11-22-1862	1331	Antietam
Witham, James A.	Pvt. A	16 ME Inf.	09-30-1862	3157	Antietam
Witt, Louis	Pvt. C	33 NY Inf.	09-17-1862	724	Antietam
Wixon, Daniel B.	Pvt. I	59 NY Inf.	12-16-1862	207	Frederick
Wogler, Samuel	Pvt. G	102 NY Inf.	10-29-1862	247	Frederick, Antietam
Wolf, Henry	Corp. C	4 NY Inf.		807	Antietam
Wolf, Solomon	Pvt. L	1 MI Cav.		2417	Cumberland
Wolfe, Henry F.	Sgt. A	30 OH Inf.	09-21-1862	1359	Antietam
Wolff, Anthony	Pvt. H	87 PA Inf.	07-11-1864	4098	Frederick, WIA Monocacy
Womer, Andrew	Corp. A	125 PA Inf.	09-17-1862	3669	Antietam, KIA
Wonderly, Charles H.	Pvt. C	28 PA Inf.	09-17-1862	3633	Antietam, KIA
Wood, Edwin H.	Pvt. D	33 NY Inf.	11-21-1862	393	Hagerstown, Antietam
Wood, Emony M.	Pvt. C	104 NY Inf.	10-03-1862	549	Pry's Mill, Died Disease
Wood, George	Pvt. F	2 RI Inf.	10-22-1862	2841	Frederick, Antietam
Wood, George	Pvt. F	51 NY Inf.		583	Antietam
Wood, Nelson	Pvt. M	NY Cav.	05-11-1864	401	Downsville
Woodcock, Selvey H.	Pvt. C	12 US Inf.		3534	Antietam
Woodford, Byron D.	Pvt. C	152 IN Inf.	03-25-1865	3363	Clarysville
Woods, Alfred H.	Pvt. B	9 NH Inf.	11-03-1862	2813	Weverton, Antietam
Woods, Charles P.	Pvt. G	13 WV Inf.	09-16-1864	2624	Frederick, Monocacy
Woodward, John	Pvt. D	8 PA Res.	09-17-1862	3781	Antietam, KIA
Woodworth, Adolphus	Pvt. F	193 NY Inf.	08-16-1865	31	Cumberland
Wools, D. E.	Pvt. E	95 NY Inf.		457	Middletown
Wooster, W. S.	Pvt. K	1 US Art.	07-08-1863	3558	Frederick, Age 24
Wordley, Joseph	Pvt. K	151 NY Cav.	07-18-1864	83	Frederick, Monocacy
Workmeister, George W.	Pvt. D	90 PA Inf.	10-18-1862	3939	Frederick, Antietam
Worster, Charles W.	Corp. H	12 IN Inf.	12-07-1861	3444	Antietam, Age 21
Wray, Orrin	Pvt. B	1 MI Cav.	09-02-1864	2543	Died Wounds, From Niles
Wright, George W.	Pvt.	11 OH Inf.		1422	South Mountain
Wright, Greenbery	Pvt. D	144 IN Inf.	07-02-1865	3359	Clarysville
Wright, Rufus C.	Pvt. E	16 NY Inf.	11-07-1862	368	Hagerstown
Yarger, Perry L.	Pvt. C	3 WI Inf.	11-26-1861	3219	Frederick
Yarnell, Reuben	Pvt. A	45 PA Inf.	09-21-1862	4139	Frederick, WIA S. Mt.
Yates, Alexander	Pvt. A	18 PA Cav.	07-25-1863	4082	Frederick, Age 20
Yates, John	Pvt. F	2 WI Inf.	09-17-1862	3304	Antietam, KIA
Yates, William R.	Pvt. B	5 NH Inf.	09-27-1862	2802	Antietam, WIA
Yemmons, Joseph	Pvt. E	8 CT Inf.	11-10-1862	1122	Weverton, Died Disease
Yocum, Malon	Pvt.	20 MI Cav.	07-31-1863	2378	Weverton
Yongker, David	Pvt. A	8 OH Inf.	09-17-1862	1338	Antietam
York, William H.	Pvt. B	7 ME Inf.	11-15-1862	3135	Frederick, Antietam
Yost, John R.	Pvt. C	7 WV Inf.		2748	Cumberland
Young, Andrew	Pvt. C	21 NY Inf.		545	Antietam
Young, David Jr.	Pvt. A	106 NY Inf.	07-22-1864	82	Frederick, Monocacy
Young, David Z.	Corp. B	6 WI Inf.	09-17-1862	3342	Antietam, KIA
Young, Harvey	Pvt. B	77 NY Inf.	12-27-1862	196	Frederick, Antietam
Young, James S.	Pvt. G	150 IN Inf.	04-02-1865	3407	Frederick
Young, Nelson	Pvt.	2 ME Art.	11-01-1862	3145	Frederick, Antietam
Young, Nicholas	Pvt. B	108 NY Inf.	01-11-1863	186	Frederick, Antietam
Young, Sampson	Pvt. F	144 IN Inf.	03-27-1865	3413	Frederick
Young, William	Pvt. D	19 MA Inf.	07-06-1863	1039	Frederick
Youngblud, Jacob	Pvt. A	36 OH Inf.	09-04-1864	1459	Weverton, Monocacy
Zimmerman, Martin B.	Pvt. C	21 NY Cav.	08-20-1864	395	Weverton, Monocacy
Zimmerman, P. J.	Pvt. K	46 PA Inf.	12-26-1861	4204	Frederick, Age 19

Index